ITALIAN

PHRASE BOOK
& DICTIONARY

Avalon Travel
a member of the
Perseus Books Group
1700 Fourth Street
Berkeley, CA 94710, USA

Printed in the United States of America by Worzalla.
Sixth edition. Fourth printing July 2010.

For the latest on Rick's lectures, guidebooks, tours, and public television
series, contact Europe Through the Back Door, P.O. Box 2009, Edmonds,
WA 98020, tel. 425/771-8303, fax 425/771-0833, www.ricksteves.com,
rick@ricksteves.com.

ISBN-10: 1-59880-188-0
ISBN-13: 978-1-59880-188-0

Europe Through the Back Door Managing Editor: Risa Laib
Europe Through the Back Door Editors:
  Cameron Hewitt, Jill Hodges, Gretchen Strauch
Avalon Travel Editor: Jamie Andrade
Translation: Giulia Fiorini, Manfredo Guerzoni,
  Simona Bondavalli, Heidi Sewell
Phonetics: Risa Laib, Cameron Hewitt
Production: Darren Alessi
Cover Design: Kimberly Glyder Design
Maps & Graphics: David C. Hoerlein, Zoey Platt
Photography: Rick Steves, Dominic Bonuccelli,
  Julie Coen, Andrea Johnson
Front Cover Photo: © 2004 Chuck Pefley/DRR.net

Distributed to the book trade by
Publishers Group West, Berkeley, California

Rick Steves' Guidebook Series

Country Guides

Rick Steves' Best of Europe
Rick Steves' Croatia & Slovenia
Rick Steves' Eastern Europe
Rick Steves' England
Rick Steves' France
Rick Steves' Germany
Rick Steves' Great Britain
Rick Steves' Ireland
Rick Steves' Italy
Rick Steves' Portugal
Rick Steves' Scandinavia
Rick Steves' Spain
Rick Steves' Switzerland

City and Regional Guides

Rick Steves' Amsterdam, Bruges & Brussels
Rick Steves' Athens & the Peloponnese (new in 2009)
Rick Steves' Budapest (new in 2009)
Rick Steves' Florence & Tuscany
Rick Steves' Istanbul
Rick Steves' London
Rick Steves' Paris
Rick Steves' Prague & the Czech Republic
Rick Steves' Provence & the French Riviera
Rick Steves' Rome
Rick Steves' Venice
Rick Steves' Vienna, Salzburg & Tirol (new in 2009)

Rick Steves' Phrase Books

French
French/Italian/German
German
Italian
Portuguese
Spanish

Other Books

Rick Steves' Europe Through the Back Door
Rick Steves' Europe 101: History and Art for the Traveler
Rick Steves' European Christmas
Rick Steves' Postcards from Europe

(Avalon Travel)

CONTENTS

TABLE OF CONTENTS

TABLE OF CONTENTS

Hi, I'm Rick Steves.

I'm the only monolingual speaker I know who's had the nerve to design a series of European phrase books. But that's one of the things that makes them better. You see, after 30 summers of travel through Europe, I've learned first-hand (1) what's essential for communication in another country, and (2) what's not. I've assembled these important words and phrases in a logical, no-frills format, and I've worked with native Europeans and seasoned travelers to give you the simplest, clearest translations possible.

But this book is more than just a pocket translator. The words and phrases have been carefully selected to help you have a smarter, smoother trip in my favorite country without going broke. Italy used to be cheap and chaotic. These days it's neither. It's better organized than ever—and often more expensive than France or Germany. The key to getting more out of every travel dollar is to get closer to the local people, and to rely less on entertainment, restaurants, and hotels that cater only to foreign tourists. This book will not only help you order a meal at a locals-only Venetian restaurant—it'll help you talk to the family that runs the place . . . about their kids, social issues, travel dreams, and favorite flavors of *gelati.* Long after your memories of museums have faded, you'll still treasure the personal encounters you had with your new Italian friends.

A good phrase book should help you enjoy your Italian experience—not just survive it—so I've added a healthy dose of humor. A few phrases are just for fun and aren't meant to be used at all. Most of the phrases are for real and should be used with "please" (*per favore*). I know you can tell the difference.

To get the most out of this book, take the time to internalize and put into practice my Italian pronunciation tips. Remember that Italians, more than their European neighbors, are forgiving of your linguistic fumbling. Don't worry too much about memorizing grammatical rules, like which gender a particular noun is—the important thing is to rise above sex . . . and communicate!

This book has a dictionary and a nifty menu decoder. You'll also find Italian telephone tips and a handy tear-out cheat sheet.

Tear it out and keep it in your pocket so you can easily use it to memorize key phrases during idle moments. As you prepare for your trip, you may want to read this year's edition of my guidebooks on Italy, Rome, Venice, and Florence & Tuscany.

Italy can be the most intense, difficult, and rewarding destination in Europe. Travelers either love it—or they quickly see the big sights and flee to Switzerland. To me, someone's love of Italy is a sign of a good traveler—thoughtful, confident, and extroverted. If this phrase book helps make that happen, or if you have suggestions for making it better, I'd love to hear from you. I personally read and value all feedback. My address is Europe Through the Back Door, P.O. Box 2009, Edmonds, WA 98020, tel. 425/771-8303, fax 425/771-0833, rick@ricksteves.com.

Happy travels, and *buona fortuna* (good luck) as you hurdle the language barrier!

GETTING STARTED

User-friendly Italian

...is easy to get the hang of. Some Italian words are so familiar, you'd think they were English. If you can say *pizza, lasagna,* and *spaghetti,* you can speak Italian.

Italian pronunciation differs from English in some key ways:

C usually sounds like C in cat.
  But C followed by E or I sounds like CH in chance.
CH sounds like C in cat.
E often sounds like AY in play.
G usually sounds like G in get.
  But G followed by E or I sounds like G in gentle.
GH sounds like G in spaghetti.
GLI sounds like LI in million. The G is silent.
GN sounds like GN in lasagna.
H is never pronounced.
I sounds like EE in seed.
R is rolled as in brrravo!
SC usually sounds like SK in skip.
  But SC followed by E or I sounds like SH in shape.
Z usually sounds like TS in hits, and sometimes like the
  sound of DZ in kids.

Have you ever noticed that most Italian words end in a vowel? It's *o* if the word is masculine and *a* if it's feminine. So a **bambino** gets blue and a **bambina** gets pink. A man is **generoso** (generous), a woman is **generosa**. A man will say, "**Sono sposato**" (I am married). A woman will say, "**Sono sposata**." In this book, we show gender-bender words like this: **generoso[a].** If you are speaking of a woman (which includes women speaking about themselves), use the *a* ending. It's always pronounced "ah." If a noun or adjective ends in *e*, such as **cantante** (singer) or **gentile** (kind), the same word applies to either sex.

Adjective endings agree with the noun. It's **cara amica** (a dear female friend) and **caro amico** (a dear male friend). Sometimes the adjective comes after the noun, as in **vino rosso** (red wine).

Plurals are formed by changing the final letter of the noun: *a* becomes *e,* and *o* becomes *i.* So it's one **pizza** and two **pizze,** and one cup of **cappuccino** and two cups of **cappuccini**. If you're describing any group of people that includes at least one male, the adjective should end with *i.* But if the group is female, the adjective ends with *e.* A handsome man is **bello** and an attractive group of men (or men and women) is **belli**. A beautiful woman is **bella** and a bevy of beauties is **belle.** In this book, you'll see plural adjective endings depicted like this: **belli[e].**

Italians usually pronounce every letter in a word, so **due** (two) is **doo**-ay. Sometimes two vowels share one syllable. **Piano** sounds like peeah-noh. The "peeah" is one syllable. When one vowel in a pair should be emphasized, it will appear in bold letters: **Italiano** is ee-tah-lee**ah**-noh.

The key to Italian inflection is to remember this simple rule: most Italian words have their accent on the second-to-last syllable. To override this rule, Italians sometimes insert an accent: **città** (city) is pronounced chee-**tah**.

Italians are animated. You may think two Italians are arguing when in reality they're agreeing enthusiastically. Be confident and have fun communicating in Italian. The Italians really do want to understand you, and are forgiving of a yankee-fied version of their language.

Here's a quick guide to the phonetics used in this book:

ah   like A in father.
ay   like AY in play.
eh   like E in let.
ee   like EE in seed.
ehr sounds like "air."
g   like G in go.
oh   like O in note.
oo   like OO in too.
or   like OR in core.
ow   like OW in now.
s   like S in sun.
ts   like TS in hits. It's a small explosive sound.
         Think of pizza (**pee**-tsah).

ITALIAN BASICS

In 800, Charlemagne traveled to Rome and became the Holy Roman Emperor using only these phrases.

Meeting and Greeting

Good day.	Buon giorno.	bwohn **jor**-noh
Good morning.	Buon giorno.	bwohn **jor**-noh
Good evening.	Buona sera.	**bwoh**-nah **say**-rah
Good night.	Buona notte.	**bwoh**-nah **noh**-tay
Hi / Bye. (informal)	Ciao.	chow
Welcome.	Benvenuto. /	behn-vay-**noo**-toh /
(said to male /	Benvenuta. /	behn-vay-**noo**-tah /
female / group)	Benvenuti.	behn-vay-**noo**-tee
Mr. / Mrs.	Signore / Signora	seen-**yoh**-ray / seen-**yoh**-rah
Miss	Signorina	seen-yoh-**ree**-nah
How are you?	Come sta?	**koh**-may stah
Very well.	Molto bene.	**mohl**-toh **behn**-ay
Thank you.	Grazie.	**graht**-seeay
And you?	E lei?	ay **leh**ee
My name is ___.	Mi chiamo ___.	mee kee**ah**-moh
What's your name?	Come si chiama?	**koh**-may see kee**ah**-mah
Pleased to meet you.	Piacere.	peeah-**chay**-ray
Where are you from?	Di dove è?	dee **doh**-vay eh
I am / We are / Are you...?	Sono / Siamo / È...?	**soh**-noh / see**ah**-moh / eh

4

...on vacation	*...in vacanza*	een vah-**kahnt**-sah
...on business	*...qui per lavoro*	kwee pehr lah-**voh**-roh
See you later.	*A più tardi.*	ah pew **tar**-dee
Goodbye.	*Arrivederci.*	ah-ree-vay-**dehr**-chee
Good luck!	*Buona fortuna!*	**bwoh**-nah for-**too**-nah
Have a good trip!	*Buon viaggio!*	bwohn vee**ah**-joh

ITALIAN BASICS

The greeting *"Buon giorno"* (Good day) turns to *"Buona sera"* (Good evening) in the late afternoon.

Essentials

Hello.	*Buon giorno.*	bwohn **jor**-noh
Do you speak English?	*Parla inglese?*	**par**-lah een-**glay**-zay
Yes. / No.	*Sì. / No.*	see / noh
I don't speak Italian.	*Non parlo l'italiano.*	nohn **par**-loh lee-tah-lee**ah**-noh
I'm sorry.	*Mi dispiace.*	mee dee-spee**ah**-chay
Please.	*Per favore.*	pehr fah-**voh**-ray
Thank you.	*Grazie.*	**graht**-seeay
Thank you very much.	*Grazie mille.*	**graht**-seeay **mee**-lay
It's (not) a problem.	*(Non) c'è una problema.*	(nohn) cheh **oo**-nah proh-**blay**-mah
Good. / Great. / Excellent.	*Bene. / Benissimo. / Perfetto.*	**behn**-ay / behn-**ee**-see-moh / pehr-**feht**-toh
It's good.	*Va bene.*	vah **behn**-ay
You are very kind.	*Lei è molto gentile.*	**leh**ee eh **mohl**-toh jehn-**tee**-lay
Excuse me. (to get attention)	*Mi scusi.*	mee **skoo**-zee
Excuse me. (to pass)	*Permesso.*	pehr-**may**-soh
It doesn't matter.	*Non importa.*	nohn eem-**por**-tah
You're welcome.	*Prego.*	**pray**-goh

ITALIAN BASICS

Sure.	*Certo.*	**chehr**-toh
O.K.	*Va bene.*	vah **behn**-ay
Let's go.	*Andiamo.*	ahn-dee**ah**-moh
Goodbye!	*Arrivederci!*	ah-ree-vay-**dehr**-chee

Where?

Where is...?	*Dov'è...?*	doh-**veh**
...the tourist	*...l'ufficio*	loo-**fee**-choh
information office	*informazioni*	een-for-maht-see**oh**-nee
...a cash machine	*...un bancomat*	oon **bahnk**-oh-maht
...the train station	*...la stazione*	lah staht-see**oh**-nay
...the bus station	*...la stazione*	lah staht-see**oh**-nay
	degli autobus	**dayl**-yee **ow**-toh-boos
...the toilet	*...la toilette*	lah twah-**leht**-tay
men	*uomini,*	**woh**-mee-nee,
	signori	seen-**yoh**-ree
women	*donne, signore*	**doh**-nay, seen-**yoh**-ray

You'll find some Italian words are similar to English if you're looking for a *banca, farmacia, hotel, ristorante, or supermercato.*

How Much?

How much is it?	*Quanto costa?*	**kwahn**-toh **koh**-stah
Write it?	*Me lo scrive?*	may loh **skree**-vay
Is it free?	*È gratis?*	eh **grah**-tees
Is it included?	*È incluso?*	eh een-**kloo**-zoh
Do you have...?	*Ha...?*	ah
Where can	*Dove posso*	**doh**-vay **poh**-soh
I buy...?	*comprare...?*	kohm-**prah**-ray
I would like...	*Vorrei....*	vor-**reh**ee
We would like...	*Vorremmo...*	vor-**ray**-moh
...this.	*...questo.*	**kweh**-stoh
...just a little.	*...un pochino.*	oon poh-**kee**-noh
...more.	*...di più.*	dee pew
...a ticket.	*...un biglietto.*	oon beel-**yay**-toh
...a room.	*...una camera.*	**oo**-nah **kah**-may-rah
...the bill.	*...il conto.*	eel **kohn**-toh

How Many?

one	*uno*	**oo**-noh
two	*due*	**doo**-ay
three	*tre*	tray
four	*quattro*	**kwah**-troh
five	*cinque*	**cheeng**-kway
six	*sei*	**seh**ee
seven	*sette*	**seht**-tay
eight	*otto*	**oh**-toh
nine	*nove*	**noh**-vay
ten	*dieci*	dee**ay**-chee

You'll find more to count on in the "Numbers" section (page 14).

When?

At what time?	*A che ora?*	ah kay **oh**-rah
open / closed	*aperto /*	ah-**pehr**-toh /
	chiuso	kee**oo**-zoh
Just a moment.	*Un momento.*	oon moh-**mayn**-toh
Now.	*Adesso.*	ah-**dehs**-soh
Soon.	*Presto.*	**prehs**-toh
Later.	*Più tardi.*	pew **tar**-dee
Today.	*Oggi.*	**oh**-jee
Tomorrow.	*Domani.*	doh-**mah**-nee

Be creative! You can combine these phrases to say: "Two, please," or "No, thank you," or "Open tomorrow?" or "Please, where can I buy a ticket?" Please is a magic word in any language. If you want something and you don't know the word for it, just point and say *"Per favore"* (Please). If you know the word for what you want, such as the bill, simply say, *"Il conto, per favore"* (The bill, please).

Struggling with Italian

Do you speak English?	*Parla inglese?*	**par**-lah een-**glay**-zay

ITALIAN BASICS

English	Italian	Pronunciation
A teeny weeny bit?	Nemmeno un pochino?	nehm-**may**-noh oon poh-**kee**-noh
Please speak English.	Parli inglese, per favore.	**par**-lee een-**glay**-zay pehr fah-**voh**-ray
You speak English well.	Lei parla bene l'inglese.	**leh**ee **par**-lah **behn**-ay leen-**glay**-zay
I don't speak Italian.	Non parlo l'italiano.	nohn **par**-loh lee-tah-lee**ah**-noh
We don't speak Italian.	Non parliamo l'italiano.	nohn par-lee**ah**-moh lee-tah-lee**ah**-noh
I speak a little Italian.	Parlo un po' d'italiano.	**par**-loh oon poh dee-tah-lee**ah**-noh
Sorry, I speak only English.	Mi dispiace, parlo solo inglese.	mee dee-spee**ah**-chay **par**-loh **soh**-loh een-**glay**-zay
Sorry, we speak only English.	Mi dispiace, parliamo solo inglese.	mee dee-spee**ah**-chay par-lee**ah**-moh **soh**-loh een-**glay**-zay
Does somebody nearby speak English?	C'è qualcuno qui che parla inglese?	cheh kwal-**koo**-noh kwee kay **par**-lah een-**glay**-zay
Who speaks English?	Chi parla inglese?	kee **par**-lah een-**glay**-zay
What does this mean?	Cosa significa?	**koh**-zah seen-**yee**-fee-kah
What is this in Italian / English?	Come si dice questo in italiano / inglese?	**koh**-may see **dee**-chay **kweh**-stoh een ee-tah-lee**ah**-noh / een-**glay**-zay
Repeat?	Ripeta?	ree-**pay**-tah
Speak slowly.	Parli lentamente.	**par**-lee layn-tah-**mayn**-tay
Slower.	Più lentamente.	pew layn-tah-**mayn**-tay
I understand.	Capisco.	kah-**pees**-koh
I don't understand.	Non capisco.	nohn kah-**pees**-koh
Do you understand?	Capisce?	kah-**pee**-shay
Write it?	Me lo scrive?	may loh **skree**-vay

Handy Questions

How much?	*Quanto?*	**kwahn**-toh
How many?	*Quanti?*	**kwahn**-tee
How long is the trip?	*Quanto tempo dura il viaggio?*	**kwahn**-toh **tehm**-poh **doo**-rah eel veea**ih**-joh
How many minutes?	*Quanti minuti?*	**kwahn**-tee mee-**noo**-tee
How many hours?	*Quante ore?*	**kwahn**-tay **oh**-ray
How far?	*Quanto dista?*	**kwahn**-toh **dee**-stah
How?	*Come?*	**koh**-may
Can you help me?	*Può aiutarmi?*	pwoh ah-yoo-**tar**-mee
Can you help us?	*Può aiutarci?*	pwoh ah-yoo-**tar**-chee
Can I / Can we...?	*Posso / Possiamo...?*	**poh**-soh / poh-seeah-moh
...have one	*...averne uno*	ah-**vehr**-nay **oo**-noh
...go in for free	*...andare senza pagare*	ahn-**dah**-ray **sehnt**-sah pah-**gah**-ray
...borrow that for a moment / an hour	*...prenderlo in prestito per un momento / un'ora*	prehn-**dehr**-loh een preh-**stee**-toh pehr oon moh-**mehn**-toh / oon-**oh**-rah
...use the toilet	*...usare la toilette*	oo-**zah**-ray lah twah-**leht**-tay
What? (didn't hear)	*Che cosa?*	kay **koh**-zah
What is this / that?	*Che cos'è questo / quello?*	kay koh-**zeh kweh**-stoh / **kway**-loh
What is better?	*Quale è meglio?*	**kwah**-lay eh **mehl**-yoh
What's going on?	*Cosa succede?*	**koh**-zah soo-**chay**-day
When?	*Quando?*	**kwahn**-doh
What time is it?	*Che ora è?*	kay **oh**-rah eh
At what time?	*A che ora?*	ah kay **oh**-rah
On time?	*Puntuale?*	poon-tooah-lay
Late?	*In ritardo?*	een ree-**tar**-doh
How long will it take?	*Quanto ci vuole?*	**kwahn**-toh chee vooo**oh**-lay
When does this open / close?	*A che ora apre / chiude?*	ah kay **oh**-rah **ah**-pray / keeoo-day
Is this open daily?	*È aperto tutti i giorni?*	eh ah-**pehr**-toh **too**-tee ee **jor**-nee

ITALIAN BASICS

ITALIAN BASICS

What day is this closed?	*Che giorno chiudete?*	kay **jor**-noh keeoo-**day**-tay
Do you have...?	*Ha...?*	ah
Where is...?	*Dov'è...?*	doh-**veh**
Where are...?	*Dove sono...?*	**doh**-vay **soh**-noh
Where can I find / buy...?	*Dove posso trovare / comprare...?*	**doh**-vay **poh**-soh troh-**vah**-ray / kohm-**prah**-ray
Where can we find / buy...?	*Dove possiamo trovare / comprare...?*	**doh**-vay poh-seeah-moh troh-**vah**-ray / kohm-**prah**-ray
Is it necessary?	*È necessario?*	eh nay-say-**chay**-reeoh
Is it possible...?	*È possibile...?*	eh poh-**see**-bee-lay
...to enter	*...entrare*	ehn-**trah**-ray
...to picnic here	*...mangiare al sacco qui*	mahn-**jah**-ray ahl **sah**-koh kwee
...to sit here	*...sedersi qui*	say-**dehr**-see kwee
...to look	*...guardare*	gwar-**dah**-ray
...to take a photo	*...fare una foto*	**fah**-ray **oo**-nah **foh**-toh
...to see this room	*...vedere questa camera*	vay-**day**-ray **kweh**-stah **kah**-may-rah
Who?	*Chi?*	kee
Why?	*Perchè?*	pehr-**keh**
Why not?	*Perchè no?*	pehr-**keh** noh
Yes or no?	*Sì o no?*	see oh noh

To prompt a simple answer, ask, "*Sì o no?*" (Yes or no?). To turn a word or sentence into a question, ask it in a questioning tone. "*Va bene*" (It's good) becomes "*Va bene?*" (Is it good?). An easy way to say, "Where is the toilet?" is to ask, "*Toilette?*"

Yin e Yang

good / bad	*buono / cattivo*	**bwoh**-noh / kah-**tee**-voh
best / worst	*il migliore / il peggiore*	eel meel-**yoh**-ray / eel pay-**joh**-ray

a little / lots	poco / tanto	**poh**-koh / **tahn**-toh
more / less	più / meno	pew / **may**-noh
cheap / expensive	economico / caro	ay-koh-**noh**-mee-koh / **kah**-roh
big / small	grande / piccolo	**grahn**-day / **pee**-koh-loh
hot / cold	caldo / freddo	**kahl**-doh / **fray**-doh
warm / cool	caldo / fresco	**kahl**-doh / **fray**-skoh
open / closed	aperto / chiuso	ah-**pehr**-toh / keeoo-zoh
entrance / exit	entrata / uscita	ehn-**trah**-tah / oo-**shee**-tah
push / pull	spingere / tirare	**speen**-jay-ray / tee-**rah**-ray
arrive / depart	arrivare / partire	ah-ree-**vah**-ray / par-**tee**-ray
early / late	presto / tardi	**prehs**-toh / **tar**-dee
soon / later	presto / più tardi	**prehs**-toh / pew **tar**-dee
fast / slow	veloce / lento	vay-**loh**-chay / **lehn**-toh
here / there	qui / lì	kwee / lee
near / far	vicino / lontano	vee-**chee**-noh / lohn-**tah**-noh
indoors / outdoors	dentro / fuori	**dehn**-troh / foo-**oh**-ree
mine / yours	mio / suo	**mee**-oh / **soo**-oh
this / that	questo / quello	**kweh**-stoh / **kweh**-loh
everybody / nobody	tutti / nessuno	**too**-tee / nehs-**soo**-noh
easy / difficult	facile / difficile	**fah**-chee-lay / dee-**fee**-chee-lay
left / right	sinistra / destra	see-**nee**-strah / **dehs**-trah
up / down	su / giú	soo / joo
above / below	sopra / sotto	**soh**-prah / **soh**-toh
young / old	giovane / anziano	joh-**vah**-nay / ahnt-seeah-noh
new / old	nuovo / vecchio	**nwoh**-voh / **vehk**-eeoh
heavy / light	pesante / leggero	pay-**zahn**-tay / lay-**jay**-roh
dark / light	scuro / chiaro	**skoo**-roh / keeah-roh

ITALIAN BASICS

happy / sad	felice / triste	fee-**lee**-chay / **tree**-stay
beautiful / ugly	bello[a] / brutto[a]	**behl**-loh / **broo**-toh
nice / mean	carino[a] / cattivo[a]	kah-**ree**-noh / kah-**tee**-voh
smart / stupid	intelligente / stupido[a]	een-tehl-ee-**jayn**-tay / **stoo**-pee-doh
vacant / occupied	libero / occupato	**lee**-bay-roh / oh-koo-**pah**-toh
with / without	con / senza	kohn / **sehnt**-sah

Italian words marked with an [a] end with "a" if used to describe a female. A handsome man is **bello**, a beautiful woman is **bella**.

Big Little Words

I	io	**ee**oh
you (formal)	Lei	**leh**ee
you (informal)	tu	too
we	noi	**noh**ee
he	lui	lwee
she	lei	**leh**ee
they	loro	**loh**-roh
and	e	ay
at	a	ah
because	perchè	pehr-**keh**
but	ma	mah
by (train, car, etc.)	in	een
for	per	pehr
from	da	dah
here	qui	kwee
if	se	say
in	in	een
it	esso	**ehs**-soh
not	non	nohn
now	adesso	ah-**dehs**-soh
only	solo	**soh**-loh
or	o	oh

that	*quello*	**kweh**-loh
this	*questo*	**kweh**-stoh
to	*a*	ah
very	*molto*	**mohl**-toh

Very Italian Expressions

Prego.	**pray**-goh	You're welcome. / Please. / All right. / Can I help you?
Pronto.	**prohn**-toh	Hello. (answering phone) / Ready. (other situations)
Ecco.	**ay**-koh	Here it is.
Dica.	**dee**-kah	Tell me.
Allora...	ah-**loh**-rah	Well...
(like our "uh" before a sentence)		
Senta.	**sayn**-tah	Listen.
Tutto va bene.	**too**-toh vah **behn**-ay	Everything's fine.
Basta.	**bah**-stah	That's enough.
È tutto.	eh **too**-toh	That's all.
la dolce vita	lah **dohl**-chay **vee**-tah	the sweet life
il dolce far niente	eel **dohl**-chay far nee**ehn**-tay	the sweetness of doing nothing
...issimo[a]	...**ee**-see-moh	very

("bravo" means good, "bravissimo" means very good)

COUNTING

NUMBERS

0	*zero*	**zay**-roh
1	*uno*	**oo**-noh
2	*due*	**doo**-ay
3	*tre*	tray
4	*quattro*	**kwah**-troh
5	*cinque*	**cheeng**-kway
6	*sei*	**seh**ee
7	*sette*	**seht**-tay
8	*otto*	**oh**-toh
9	*nove*	**noh**-vay
10	*dieci*	dee**ay**-chee
11	*undici*	**oon**-dee-chee
12	*dodici*	**doh**-dee-chee
13	*tredici*	**tray**-dee-chee
14	*quattordici*	kwah-**tor**-dee-chee
15	*quindici*	**kween**-dee-chee
16	*sedici*	**say**-dee-chee
17	*diciassette*	dee-chah-**seht**-tay
18	*diciotto*	dee-**choh**-toh
19	*diciannove*	dee-chahn-**noh**-vay
20	*venti*	**vayn**-tee
21	*ventuno*	vayn-**too**-noh
22	*ventidue*	vayn-tee-**doo**-ay
23	*ventitrè*	vayn-tee-**tray**

30	*trenta*	**trayn**-tah
31	*trentuno*	trayn-**too**-noh
40	*quaranta*	kwah-**rahn**-tah
41	*quarantuno*	kwah-rahn-**too**-noh
50	*cinquanta*	cheeng-**kwahn**-tah
60	*sessanta*	say-**sahn**-tah
70	*settanta*	say-**tahn**-tah
80	*ottanta*	oh-**tahn**-tah
90	*novanta*	noh-**vahn**-tah
100	*cento*	**chehn**-toh
101	*centouno*	chehn-toh-**oo**-noh
102	*centodue*	chehn-toh-**doo**-ay
200	*duecento*	doo-ay-**chehn**-toh
1000	*mille*	**mee**-lay
2000	*duemila*	doo-ay-**mee**-lah
2001	*duemilauno*	doo-ay-mee-lah-**oo**-noh
2002	*duemiladue*	doo-ay-mee-lah-**doo**-ay
2003	*duemilatre*	doo-ay-mee-lah-**tray**
2004	*duemila-quattro*	doo-ay-mee-lah-**kwah**-troh
2005	*duemila-cinque*	doo-ay-mee-lah-**cheeng**-kway
2006	*duemilasei*	doo-ay-mee-lah-**seh**ee
2007	*duemilasette*	doo-ay-mee-lah-**seht**-tay
2008	*duemilaotto*	doo-ay-mee-lah-**oh**-toh
2009	*duemilanove*	doo-ay-mee-lah-**noh**-vay
2010	*duemila-dieci*	doo-ay-mee-lah-dee**ay**-chee
million	*milione*	mee-lee**oh**-nay
billion	*miliardo*	meel-**yar**-doh
number one	*numero uno*	**noo**-may-roh **oo**-noh
first	*primo*	**pree**-moh
second	*secondo*	say-**kohn**-doh
third	*terzo*	**tehrt**-soh
once / twice	*una volta / due volte*	**oo**-nah **vohl**-tah / **doo**-ay **vohl**-tay
a quarter	*un quarto*	oon **kwar**-toh

COUNTING

a third	un terzo	oon **tehrt**-soh
half	mezzo	**mehd**-zoh
this much	tanto così	**tahn**-toh koh-**zee**
a dozen	una dozzina	**oo**-nah dohd-**zee**-nah
some	un po'	oon poh
enough	abbastanza	ah-bah-**stahnt**-sah
a handful	una manciata	**oo**-nah mahn-**chah**-tah
50%	cinquanta	cheeng-**kwahn**-tah
	per cento	pehr **chehn**-toh
100%	cento per	**chehn**-toh pehr
	cento	**chehn**-toh

MONEY

Where is a	Dov'è un	doh-**veh** oon
cash machine?	bancomat?	**bahnk**-oh-maht
My ATM card	La mia tessera	lah **mee**-ah teh-**say**-rah
has been...	bancomat	**bahnk**-oh-maht
	è stata...	eh **stah**-tah
...demagnetized.	...demagnetizzata.	day-man-yeht-eed-**zah**-tah
...stolen.	...rubata.	roo-**bah**-tah
...eaten by the	...trattenuta dal	trah-tay-**noo**-tah dahl
machine.	bancomat.	**bahnk**-oh-maht
Do you accept	Accettate carte	ah-chay-**tah**-tay **kar**-tay
credit cards?	di credito?	dee **kray**-dee-toh
Can you change	Può cambiare	pwoh kahm-beeah-ray
dollars?	dollari?	**dol**-lah-ree
What is your	Qual'è il	kwah-**leh** eel
exchange rate	cambio	**kahm**-beeoh
for dollars...?	del dollaro...?	dayl **dol**-lah-roh
...in traveler's	...per traveler's checks	pehr "traveler's checks"
checks		
What is the	Quant'è la	kwahn-**teh** lah
commission?	commissione?	koh-mee-seeoh-nay
Any extra fee?	C'è un	cheh oon
	sovrapprezzo?	soh-vrah-**prehd**-zoh

Key Phrases: Money

euro (€)	euro	ay-**oo**-roh
money	soldi, denaro	**sohl**-dee, day-**nah**-roh
cash	contante	kohn-**tahn**-tay
credit card	carta di credito	**kar**-tah dee **kray**-dee-toh
bank	banca	**bahn**-kah
cash machine	bancomat	**bahnk**-oh-maht
Where is a cash machine?	Dov'è un bancomat?	doh-**veh** oon **bahnk**-oh-maht
Do you accept credit cards?	Accettate carte di credito?	ah-chay-**tah**-tay **kar**-tay dee **kray**-dee-toh

Can you break this? (big bill into smaller bills)	Mi può cambiare questo?	mee pwoh kahm-beeah-ray **kweh**-stoh
I would like...	Vorrei....	vor-**reh**ee
...small bills.	...banconote di piccolo taglio.	bahn-koh-**noh**-tay dee **pee**-koh-loh **tahl**-yoh
...large bills.	...banconote di grosso taglio.	bahn-koh-**noh**-tay dee **groh**-soh **tahl**-yoh
...coins.	...monete.	moh-**nay**-tay
€50	cinquanta euro	cheeng-**kwahn**-tah ay-**oo**-roh
Is this a mistake?	Questo è un errore?	**kweh**-stoh eh oon eh-**roh**-ray
This is incorrect.	Questo non è corretto.	**kweh**-stoh nohn eh kor-**reht**-toh
Did you print these today?	Le ha stampate oggi?	lay ah stahm-**pah**-tay **oh**-jee
I'm broke.	Sono al verde.	**soh**-noh ahl **vehr**-day
I'm poor.	Sono povero[a].	**soh**-noh **poh**-vay-roh
I'm rich.	Sono ricco[a].	**soh**-noh **ree**-koh
I'm Bill Gates.	Sono Bill Gates.	**soh**-noh "Bill Gates"
Where is the nearest casino?	Dov'è il casinò più vicino?	doh-**veh** eel kah-zee-**noh** pew vee-**chee**-noh

Italy uses the euro currency. Euros (€) are divided into 100 cents. Use your common cents—cents are like pennies, and the euro has coins like nickels, dimes, and half-dollars.

Money Words

euro (€)	euro	ay-**oo**-roh
cents	centesimi	chehn-**tay**-zee-mee
money	soldi, denaro	**sohl**-dee, day-**nah**-roh
cash	contante	kohn-**tahn**-tay
cash machine	bancomat	**bahnk**-oh-maht
bank	banca	**bahn**-kah
credit card	carta di credito	**kar**-tah dee **kray**-dee-toh
change money	cambiare dei soldi	kahm-beeah-ray **deh**ee **sohl**-dee
exchange	cambio	**kahm**-beeoh
buy / sell	comprare / vendere	kohm-**prah**-ray / vehn-**day**-ray
commission	commissione	koh-mee-seeoh-nay
traveler's check	traveler's check	"traveler's check"
cash advance	prelievo	pray-leeay-voh
cashier	cassiere	kah-seeay-ray
bills	banconote	bahn-koh-**noh**-tay
coins	monete	moh-**nay**-tay
receipt	ricevuta	ree-chay-**voo**-tah

All cash machines are multilingual. On the small chance you'd need to conduct your transaction in Italian, you'd use these buttons: *esatto* (correct), *conferma* (confirm), and *annullare* (cancel). Your PIN code is a *codice segreto.*

TIME

What time is it?	Che ore sono?	kay **oh**-ray **soh**-noh
It's...	Sono...	**soh**-noh

Key Phrases: Time

minute	*minuto*	mee-**noo**-toh
hour	*ora*	**oh**-rah
day	*giorno*	**jor**-noh
week	*settimana*	say-tee-**mah**-nah
What time is it?	*Che ore sono?*	kay **oh**-ray **soh**-noh
It's...	*Sono...*	**soh**-noh
...8:00.	*...le otto.*	lay **oh**-toh
...16:00.	*...le sedici.*	lay **say**-dee-chee
When does this open / close?	*A che ora apre / chiude?*	ah kay **oh**-rah **ah**-pray / keeoo-day

COUNTING

...8:00 in the morning.	*...le otto di mattina.*	lay **oh**-toh dee mah-**tee**-nah
...16:00.	*...le sedici.*	lay **say**-dee-chee
...4:00 in the afternoon.	*...le quattro del pomeriggio.*	lay **kwah**-troh dayl poh-may-**ree**-joh
...10:30 in the evening.	*...le dieci e mezza di sera.*	lay deeay-chee ay **mehd**-zah dee **say**-rah
...a quarter past nine.	*...le nove e un quarto.*	lay **noh**-vay ay oon **kwar**-toh
...a quarter to eleven.	*...le undici meno un quarto.*	lay **oon**-dee-chee **may**-noh oon **kwar**-toh
It's...	*È...*	eh
...noon.	*...mezzogiorno.*	mehd-zoh-**jor**-noh
...midnight.	*...mezzanotte.*	mehd-zah-**noh**-tay
...early / late.	*...presto / tardi.*	**prehs**-toh / **tar**-dee
...on time.	*...puntuale.*	poon-tooah-lay
...sunrise.	*...alba.*	**ahl**-bah
...sunset.	*...tramonto.*	trah-**mohn**-toh
It's my bedtime.	*Per me è ora di andare a dormire.*	pehr may eh **oh**-rah dee ahn-**dah**-ray ah dor-**mee**-ray

Timely Expressions

COUNTING

I'll return / We'll return...	Torno / Torniamo...	**tor**-noh / tor-neeah-moh
...at 11:20.	...alle undici e venti.	**ah**-lay **oon**-dee-chee ay **vayn**-tee
I'll arrive / We'll arrive...	Arrivo / Arriviamo...	ah-**ree**-voh / ah-ree-veeah-moh
...by 18:00.	...per le diciotto.	pehr lay dee-**choh**-toh
When is checkout time?	A che ora bisogna liberare la camera?	ah kay **oh**-rah bee-**sohn**-yah lee-bay-**rah**-ray lah **kah**-may-rah
At what time...?	A che ora...?	ah kay **oh**-rah
...does this open / close	...apre / chiude	**ah**-pray / keeoo-day
...does the train / bus leave for __	...parte il treno / l'autobus per __	**par**-tay eel **tray**-noh / **low**-toh-boos pehr
...the next train / the bus leave for __	...parte il prossimo treno / autobus per __	**par**-tay eel **proh**-see-moh **tray**-noh / **ow**-toh-boos pehr
...the train / the bus arrive in __	...arriva a __ il treno / l'autobus?	ah-**ree**-vah ah __ eel **tray**-noh / **low**-toh-boos
I / We want to take the 16:30 train.	Vorrei / Vorremmo prendere il treno delle sedici e trenta.	vor-**rehee** / vor-**ray**-moh **prehn**-day-ray eel **tray**-noh **dehl**-lay **say**-dee-chee ay **trayn**-tah
Is the train / the bus...?	È... il treno / l'autobus?	eh... eel **tray**-noh / **low**-toh-boos
...early / late	...in anticipo / in ritardo	een ahn-tee-**chee**-poh / een ree-**tar**-doh
...on time	...in orario	een oh-**rah**-reeoh

In Italy, the 24-hour clock (or military time) is used by hotels, for opening/closing hours of stores, and for train, bus, and ferry schedules. Friends use the same "clock" we do. You'd meet a friend at 3:00 in the afternoon (*tre del pomeriggio*) to catch a train that leaves at 15:15. In Italy, the *pomeriggio* (afternoon) turns to *sera* (evening) generally about 5:00 P.M. (5:30 P.M. is *cinque e mezza di sera*).

More Time

minute	*minuto*	mee-**noo**-toh
hour	*ora*	**oh**-rah
in the morning	*di mattina*	dee mah-**tee**-nah
in the afternoon	*di pomeriggio*	dee poh-may-**ree**-joh
in the evening	*di sera*	dee **say**-rah
at night	*di notte*	dee **noh**-tay
at 6:00 sharp	*alle sei in punto*	**ah**-lay **seh**ee een **poon**-toh
from 8:00 to 10:00	*dalle otto alle dieci*	**dah**-lay **oh**-toh **ah**-lay dee**ay**-chee
in half an hour	*tra mezz'ora*	trah mehd-**zoh**-rah
in one hour	*tra un'ora*	trah oon-**oh**-rah
in three hours	*tra tre ore*	trah tray **oh**-ray
anytime	*a qualsiasi ora*	ah kwahl-see**ah**-zee **oh**-rah
immediately	*immedia- tamente*	ee-may-deeah- tah-**mayn**-tay
every hour	*ogni ora*	**ohn**-yee **oh**-rah
every day	*ogni giorno*	**ohn**-yee **jor**-noh
daily	*giornaliero*	jor-nahl-**yehr**-oh
last	*passato*	pah-**sah**-toh
this	*questo*	**kweh**-stoh
next	*prossimo*	**proh**-see-moh
May 15	*il quindici maggio*	eel **kween**-dee-chee **mah**-joh
high season	*alta stagione*	**ahl**-tah stah-jee**oh**-nee
low season	*bassa stagione*	**bah**-sah stah-jee**oh**-nee
in the future	*in futuro*	een foo-**too**-roh
in the past	*nel passato*	nehl pah-**sah**-toh

The Day

day	*giorno*	**jor**-noh
today	*oggi*	**oh**-jee

yesterday	*ieri*	**yay**-ree
tomorrow	*domani*	doh-**mah**-nee
tomorrow morning	*domani*	doh-**mah**-nee
	mattina	mah-**tee**-nah
day after tomorrow	*dopodomani*	doh-poh-doh-**mah**-nee

The Week

week	*settimana*	say-tee-**mah**-nah
last week	*la settimana*	lah say-tee-**mah**-nah
	scorsa	**skor**-sah
this week	*questa*	**kweh**-stah
	settimana	say-tee-**mah**-nah
next week	*la settimana*	lah say-tee-**mah**-nah
	prossima	**proh**-see-mah
Monday	*lunedì*	loo-nay-**dee**
Tuesday	*martedì*	mar-tay-**dee**
Wednesday	*mercoledì*	mehr-koh-lay-**dee**
Thursday	*giovedì*	joh-vay-**dee**
Friday	*venerdì*	vay-nehr-**dee**
Saturday	*sabato*	**sah**-bah-toh
Sunday	*domenica*	doh-**may**-nee-kah

The Month

month	*mese*	**may**-zay
January	*gennaio*	jay-**nah**-yoh
February	*febbraio*	fay-**brah**-yoh
March	*marzo*	**mart**-soh
April	*aprile*	ah-**pree**-lay
May	*maggio*	**mah**-joh
June	*giugno*	**joon**-yoh
July	*luglio*	**lool**-yoh
August	*agosto*	ah-**goh**-stoh
September	*settembre*	say-**tehm**-bray
October	*ottobre*	oh-**toh**-bray
November	*novembre*	noh-**vehm**-bray
December	*dicembre*	dee-**chehm**-bray

COUNTING

The Year

year	*anno*	**ahn**-noh
spring	*primavera*	pree-mah-**vay**-rah
summer	*estate*	ay-**stah**-tay
fall	*autunno*	ow-**too**-noh
winter	*inverno*	een-**vehr**-noh

Holidays and Happy Days

holiday	*festa*	**fehs**-tah
national holiday	*festa nazionale*	**fehs**-tah naht-seeoh-**nah**-lay
religious holiday	*festa religiosa*	**fehs**-tah ray-lee-**joh**-zah
Is today / tomorrow a holiday?	*Oggi / Domani è festa?*	**oh**-jee / doh-**mah**-nee eh **fehs**-tah
Is a holiday coming up soon? When?	*Siamo vicini a una festa? Quand'è?*	seeah-moh vee-**chee**-nee ah **oo**-nah **fehs**-tah kwahn-deh
What is the holiday?	*Che festa è?*	kay **fehs**-tah eh
Merry Christmas!	*Buon Natale!*	bwohn nah-**tah**-lay
Happy new year!	*Felice anno nuovo!*	fay-**lee**-chay **ahn**-noh **nwoh**-voh
Easter	*Pasqua*	**pahs**-kwah
Happy (wedding) anniversary!	*Buon anniversario (di matrimonio).*	bwohn ah-nee-vehr-**sah**-reeoh (dee mah-tree-**moh**-neeoh)
Happy birthday!	*Buon compleanno!*	bwohn kohm-play-**ahn**-noh

COUNTING

Italians celebrate birthdays with the same "Happy Birthday" tune that we use. The Italian words mean "Best wishes to you": "*Tanti auguri a te, tanti auguri a te, tanti auguri, caro[a] ___, tanti auguri a te!*"

Holidays which strike during tourist season are April 25 (Liberation Day), May 1 (Labor Day), June 24 (*San Giovanni,* northern Italy), August 15 (*Ferragosto,* or Assumption of Mary), and November 1 (All Saints' Day). In Italy, every saint gets a holiday—these are sprinkled throughout the year and celebrated in local communities with flair.

TRAVELING

FLIGHTS

All of Italy's airports have bilingual signage with Italian and English. Also, nearly all airport service personnel and travel agents speak English these days. Still, these words and phrases could conceivably come in handy.

Making a Reservation

I'd like to... my reservation / my ticket.	Vorrei... la mia prenotazione / il mio biglietto.	vor-**reh**ee... lah **mee**-ah pray-noh-taht-see**oh**-nay / eel **mee**-oh beel-**yay**-toh
We'd like to... our reservation / our tickets.	Vorremmo... la nostra prenotazione / i nostro biglietti.	vor-**ray**-moh... lah **noh**-strah pray-noh-taht-see**oh**-nay / ee **noh**-stroh beel-**yay**-tee
...confirm	...confermare	kohn-fehr-**mah**-ray
...change	...cambiare	kahm-bee**ah**-ray
...cancel	...cancellare	kahn-cheh-**lah**-ray
seat...	posto...	**poh**-stoh
...by the window	...vicino al finestrino	vee-**chee**-noh ahl fee-nay-**stree**-noh
...on the aisle	...vicino al corridoio	vee-**chee**-noh ahl koh-ree-**doh**-yoh

At the Airport

Which terminal?	*Quale terminal?*	kwah-lay tehr-mee-**nahl**
international flights	*voli inter- nazionali*	**voh**-lee een-tehr- naht-seeoh-**nah**-lee
domestic flights	*voli interni*	**voh**-lee een-**tehr**-nee
arrival	*arrivo*	ah-**ree**-voh
departure	*partenza*	par-**tehn**-zah
baggage check	*check-in bagagli*	"check-in" bah-**gahl**-yee
baggage claim	*ritiro bagagli*	ree-**tee**-roh bah-**gahl**-yee
Nothing to declare.	*Niente da dichiarare.*	nee-**ehn**-tay dah dee-keeah-**rah**-ray
I have only carry-on luggage.	*Ho solo bagaglio a mano.*	oh **soh**-loh bah-**gahl**-yoh ah **mah**-noh
flight number	*numero del volo*	**noo**-may-roh dehl **voh**-loh
departure gate	*cancello di imbarco*	kahn-**chehl**-loh dee eem-**bar**-koh
duty free	*duty free*	"duty free"
luggage cart	*carrello per i bagagli*	kar-**ehl**-loh pehr ee bah-**gahl**-yee
jet lag	*fus'orario*	fooz-oh-**rah**-reeoh

Getting to/from the Airport

Approximately how much is a taxi ride...?	*Quanto costa più o meno un viaggio in taxi fino...?*	**kwahn**-toh **koh**-stah pew oh **may**-noh oon veeah-joh een **tahk**-see **fee**-noh
...to downtown	*...al centro*	ahl **chehn**-troh
...to the train station	*...alla stazione*	**ah**-lah staht-seeoh-nay
...to the airport	*...all'aeroporto*	ah-lah-ay-roh-**por**-toh
Does a bus (or train) run...?	*C'è un autobus (o treno) che va...?*	cheh oon **ow**-toh-boos (oh **tray**-noh) kay vah
...from the airport to downtown	*...dall'aeroporto al centro*	dah-lah-ay-roh-**por**-toh ahl **chehn**-troh

...to the airport from downtown	...dal centro all'aeroporto	dahl **chehn**-troh ah-lah-ay-roh-**por**-toh
How much is it?	Quanto costa?	**kwahn**-toh **koh**-stah
Where does it leave from...?	Da dove parte...?	dah **doh**-vay par-tay
Where does it arrive...?	Dove arriva...?	**doh**-vay ah-**ree**-vah
...at the airport	...all'aeroporto	ah-lah-ay-roh-**por**-toh
...downtown	...in centro	een **chehn**-troh
How often does it run?	Ogni quanto passa?	**ohn**-yee **kwahn**-toh **pah**-sah

TRAINS

TRAVELING

The Train Station

Where is the...?	Dov'è la...?	doh-**veh** lah
...train station	...stazione	staht-see**oh**-nay
Italian State Railways	Ferrovie dello Stato (FS)	fay-**roh**-veeay **dehl**-loh **stah**-toh
train information	informazioni sui treni	een-for-maht-see**oh**-nee **soo**ee **tray**-nee
train	treno	**tray**-noh
fast train	inter-city (IC, EC)	"inter-city"
fastest train	Eurostar (ES)	**yoo**-roh-star
fast / faster	veloce / più veloce	vay-**loh**-chay / pew vay-**loh**-chay
arrival	arrivo	ah-**ree**-voh
departure	partenza	par-**tehnt**-sah
delay	ritardo	ree-**tar**-doh
toilet	toilette	twah-**leht**-tay
waiting room	sala di attesa, sala d'aspetto	**sah**-lah dee ah-**tay**-zah, **sah**-lah dah-**spay**-toh
lockers	armadietti	ar-mah-dee**ay**-tee
baggage check room	deposito bagagli, consegna	day-**poh**-zee-toh bah-**gahl**-yee, kohn-**sayn**-yah
lost and found office	ufficio oggetti smarriti	oo-**fee**-choh oh-**jeht**-tee smah-**ree**-tee

Key Phrases: Trains

train station	*stazione*	staht-see**oh**-nay
train	*treno*	**tray**-noh
ticket	*biglietto*	beel-**yay**-toh
transfer (verb)	*cambiare*	kahm-bee**ah**-ray
supplement	*supplemento*	soo-play-**mehn**-toh
arrival	*arrivo*	ah-**ree**-voh
departure	*partenza*	par-**tehnt**-sah
platform or track	*binario*	bee-**nah**-reeoh
train car	*vagone*	vah-**goh**-nay
A ticket to ___.	*Un biglietto per ___.*	oon beel-**yay**-toh pehr
Two tickets to ___.	*Due biglietti per ___.*	doo-ay beel-**yay**-tee pehr
When is the	*Quando è il*	**kwahn**-doh eh eel
next train?	*prossimo treno?*	**proh**-see-moh **tray**-noh
Where does the	*Da dove parte*	dah **doh**-vay par-**tay**
train leave from?	*il treno?*	eel **tray**-noh
Which train to ___?	*Quale treno per ___?*	**kwah**-lay **tray**-noh pehr

tourist information	*informazioni*	een-for-maht-see**oh**-nee
	per turisti	pehr too-**ree**-stee
to the platforms	*ai binari*	**ah**ee bee-**nah**-ree
platform, track	*binario*	bee-**nah**-reeoh
to the trains	*ai treni*	**ah**ee **tray**-nee
train car	*vagone*	vah-**goh**-nay
dining car	*carrozza*	kar-**rohd**-zah
	ristorante	ree-stoh-**rahn**-tay
sleeper car	*carrozza letto*	kar-**rohd**-zah **leht**-toh
conductor	*capotreno*	kah-poh-**tray**-noh

Some Italian train stations have wonderful (and fun) schedule computers. Once you've mastered these (start by punching the "English" button), you'll save lots of time figuring out the right train connections.

TRAVELING

You'll encounter several types of trains in Italy. Along with the various local and milk-run (*locale*) trains, you'll see:
• the slow *diretto* trains
• the medium-speed *espresso* and *InterRegionale* trains
• the fast *rapido* trains such as the *IC* (*InterCity*, domestic routes) and *EC* (*EuroCity*, international routes)
• the super-fast *Cisalpino* trains (from Florence, Milan, or Venice to Switzerland and Stuttgart)
• the super-duper-fast *Eurostar Italia*, Italy's bullet train

If you have a railpass, you will need to pay a reservation fee for the *Eurostar Italia*, *Cisalpino*, and *IC Plus*, as well as for many *IC* and *EC* trains, when indicated in schedules.

Getting a Ticket

Where can I buy a ticket?	Dove posso comprare un biglietto?	**doh**-vay **poh**-soh kohm-**prah**-ray oon beel-**yay**-toh
A ticket to ___.	Un biglietto per ___.	oon beel-**yay**-toh pehr
Where can we buy tickets?	Dove possiamo comprare i biglietti?	**doh**-vay poh-seeah-moh kohm-**prah**-ray ee beel-**yay**-tee
Two tickets to ___.	Due biglietti per ___.	**doo**-ay beel-**yay**-tee pehr
Is this the line for...?	È questa la fila per...?	eh **kweh**-stah lah **fee**-lah pehr
...tickets	...biglietti	beel-**yay**-tee
...reservations	...prenotazioni	pray-noh-taht-see**oh**-nee
How much is the fare to ___?	Quant'è la tariffa per___?	kwahn-**teh** lah tah-**ree**-fah pehr
Is this ticket valid for ___?	Questo biglietto è valido per ___?	**kwehs**-toh beel-**yay**-toh eh **vah**-lee-doh pehr
How long is this ticket valid?	Per quanto tempo è valido questo biglietto?	pehr **kwahn**-toh **tehm**-poh eh **vah**-lee-doh **kwehs**-toh beel-**yay**-toh
When is the next train?	Quando è il prossimo treno?	**kwahn**-doh eh eel **proh**-see-moh **tray**-noh

TRAVELING

Do you have a schedule for all trains departing for ___ today / tomorrow?	*Ha un orario di tutti i treni in partenza per ___ oggi / domani?*	ah oon oh-**rah**-reeoh dee **too**-tee ee **tray**-nee een par-**tehnt**-sah pehr ___ **oh**-jee / doh-**mah**-nee
I'd like to leave...	*Vorrei partire...*	vor-**reh**ee par-**tee**-ray
We'd like to leave...	*Vorremmo partire...*	vor-**ray**-moh par-**tee**-ray
I'd like to arrive...	*Vorrei arrivare...*	vor-**reh**ee ah-ree-**vah**-ray
We'd like to arrive...	*Vorremmo arrivare...*	vor-**ray**-moh ah-ree-**vah**-ray
...by ___.	*...per le ___.*	pehr lay
...in the morning.	*...di mattina.*	dee mah-**tee**-nah
...in the afternoon.	*...di pomeriggio.*	dee poh-may-**ree**-joh
...in the evening.	*...di sera.*	dee **say**-rah
Is there a...?	*C'è un...?*	cheh oon
...earlier train	*...treno prima*	**tray**-noh **pree**-mah
...later train	*...treno più tardi*	**tray**-noh pew **tar**-dee
...overnight train	*...treno notturno*	**tray**-noh noh-**toor**-noh
...cheaper train	*...treno più economico*	**tray**-noh pew ay-koh-**noh**-mee-koh
...a cheaper option	*...una possibilità più economica*	**oo**-nah poh-see-bee-lee-**tah** pew ay-koh-**noh**-mee-kah
...local train	*...treno locale*	**tray**-noh loh-**kah**-lay
...express train	*...treno espresso*	**tray**-noh ehs-**pray**-soh
What track does it leave from?	*Da che binario parte?*	dah kay bee-**nah**-reeoh **par**-tay
What track?	*Quale binario?*	**kwah**-lay bee-**nah**-reeoh
On time?	*È puntuale?*	eh poon-too**ah**-lay
Late?	*In ritardo?*	een ree-**tar**-doh

Reservations, Supplements, and Discounts

Is a reservation required?	*Ci vuole la prenotazione?*	chee **vwoh**-lay lah pray-noh-taht-see**oh**-nay
I'd like to reserve...	*Vorrei prenotare...*	vor-**reh**ee pray-noh-**tah**-ray

...a seat.	...un posto.	oon **poh**-stoh
...a couchette.	...una cuccetta.	**oo**-nah koo-**chay**-tah
...a sleeper.	...un posto in vagone letto.	oon **poh**-stoh een vah-**goh**-nay **leht**-toh
...the entire train.	...tutto il treno.	**too**-toh eel **tray**-noh
We'd like to reserve...	Vorremmo prenotare...	vor-**ray**-moh pray-noh-**tah**-ray
...two seats.	...due posti.	**doo**-ay **poh**-stee
...two couchettes.	...due cuccette.	**doo**-ay koo-**chay**-tay
...a sleeper compartment with two beds.	...un vagone letto da due letti.	oon vah-**goh**-nay **leht**-toh dah doo-ay **leht**-tee
Is there a supplement?	C'è un supplemento?	cheh oon soo-play-**mehn**-toh
Does my railpass cover the supplement?	Il mio railpass include il supplemento?	eel **mee**-oh **rayl**-pahs een-**kloo**-day eel soo-play-**mehn**-toh
Is there a discount for...?	Fate sconti per...?	**fah**-tay **skohn**-tee pehr
...youth	...giovani	joh-**vah**-nee
...seniors	...anziani	ahnt-seeah-nee
...families	...famiglie	fah-**meel**-yay

Ticket Talk

ticket window	Biglietteria	beel-yeht-ay-**ree**-ah
reservations window	Prenotazioni	pray-noh-taht-see**oh**-nay
national	nazionali	naht-seeoh-**nah**-lee
international	internazio-nali	een-tehr-naht-seeoh-**nah**-lee
ticket	biglietto	beel-**yay**-toh
one way	andata	ahn-**dah**-tah
roundtrip	andata e ritorno	ahn-**dah**-tah ay ree-**tor**-noh
first class	prima classe	**pree**-mah **klah**-say
second class	seconda classe	say-**kohn**-dah **klah**-say
validate	timbrare, obliterare	teem-**brah**-ray, oh-blee-tay-**rah**-ray

schedule	orario	oh-**rah**-reeoh
departure	partenza	par-**tehnt**-sah
direct	diretto	dee-**reht**-toh
transfer (verb)	cambiare	kahm-bee**ah**-ray
connection	coincidenza	koh-een-chee-**dehnt**-sah
with supplement	con supplemento	kohn soo-play-**mehn**-toh
reservation	prenotazione	pray-noh-taht-see**oh**-nay
seat...	posto...	**poh**-stoh
...by the window	...vicino al finestrino	vee-**chee**-noh ahl fee-nay-**stree**-noh
...on the aisle	...vicino al corridoio	vee-**chee**-noh ahl koh-ree-**doh**-yoh
berth...	cuccetta...	koo-**chay**-tah
...upper	...di sopra	dee **soh**-prah
...middle	...in mezzo	een **mehd**-zoh
...lower	...di sotto	dee **soh**-toh
refund	rimborso	reem-**bor**-soh
reduced fare	tariffa ridotta	tah-**ree**-fah ree-**doh**-tah

TRAVELING

Changing Trains

Is it direct?	È diretto?	eh dee-**reht**-toh
Must I transfer?	Devo cambiare?	**day**-voh kahm-bee**ah**-ray
Must we transfer?	Dobbiamo cambiare?	doh-bee**ah**-moh kahm-bee**ah**-ray
When? Where?	Quando? Dove?	**kwahn**-doh **doh**-vay
Do I change / Do we change here for __?	Cambio / Cambiamo qui per __?	**kahm**-beeoh / kahm-bee**ah**-moh kwee pehr
Where do I change / do we change for __?	Dove cambio / cambiamo per __?	**doh**-vay **kahm**-beeoh / kahm-bee**ah**-moh pehr
At what time?	A che ora?	ah kay **oh**-rah
From what track does my / our connecting train leave?	Da che binario parte la mia / la nostra coincidenza?	dah kay bee-**nah**-reeoh **par**-tay lah **mee**-ah / lah **noh**-strah koh-een-chee-**dehnt**-sah

| How many minutes in ___ to change trains? | Quanti minuti a ___ per prendere coincidenza? | **kwahn**-tee mee-**noo**-tee ah ___ pehr **prehn**-day-ray lah koh-een-chee-**dehnt**-sah |

On the Platform

Where is...?	Dov'è...?	doh-**veh**
Is this...?	Questo è...?	**kwehs**-toh eh
...the train to ___	...il treno per ___	eel **tray**-noh pehr
Which train to___?	Quale treno per ___?	**kwah**-lay **tray**-noh pehr
Which train car for___?	Quale vagone per ___?	**kwah**-lay vah-**goh**-nay pehr
Where is first class?	Dov'è la prima classe?	doh-**veh** lah **pree**-mah **klah**-say
...front / middle / back	...in testa / in centro / in coda	een **tehs**-tah / een **chehn**-troh / een **koh**-dah
Where can I validate my ticket?	Dove posso timbrare il biglietto?	**doh**-vay **poh**-soh teem-**brah**-ray eel beel-**yay**-toh

You must validate (*timbrare*) your train ticket prior to boarding the train. Look for the yellow machines on the platform and insert your ticket—watch others and imitate.

On the Train

Is this (seat) free?	È libero?	eh **lee**-bay-roh
May I / May we...?	Posso / Possiamo...?	**poh**-soh / poh-see**ah**-moh
...sit here (me / we)	...sedermi / sederci qui	say-**dehr**-mee / say-**dehr**-chee kwee
...open the window	...aprire il finestrino	ah-**pree**-ray eel fee-nay-**stree**-noh
...eat your food	...mangiare il suo cibo	mahn-**jah**-ray eel **soo**-oh **chee**-boh
Save my place?	Mi tiene il posto?	mee tee**ay**-nay eel **poh**-stoh

Save our places?	*Ci tiene il posto?*	chee tee**ay**-nay eel **poh**-stoh
That's my seat.	*È il mio posto.*	eh eel **mee**-oh **poh**-stoh
These are our seats.	*Sono i nostri posti.*	**soh**-noh ee **noh**-stree **poh**-stee
Where are you going?	*Dove va?*	**doh**-vay vah
I'm going to ___.	*Vado a ___.*	**vah**-doh ah
We're going to ___.	*Andiamo a ___.*	ahn-dee**ah**-moh ah
Tell me when to get off?	*Mi dice quando devo scendere?*	mee **dee**-chay **kwahn**-doh **day**-voh **shehn**-day-ray
Tell us when to get off?	*Ci dice quando dobbiamo scendere?*	chee **dee**-chay **kwahn**-doh doh-bee**ah**-moh **shehn**-day-ray
Where is a (good looking) conductor?	*Dov'è un (bel) capotreno?*	doh-**veh** oon (behl) kah-poh-**tray**-noh
Does this train stop in ___?	*Questo treno si ferma a ___?*	**kwehs**-toh **tray**-noh see **fehr**-mah ah
When will it arrive in ___?	*Quando arriva a ___?*	**kwahn**-doh ah-**ree**-vah ah
When will it arrive?	*Quando arriva?*	**kwahn**-doh ah-**ree**-vah

Strikes

Is there a strike?	*C'è lo sciopero?*	cheh loh **shoh**-peh-roh
Only for today?	*È solo per oggi?*	eh **soh**-loh pehr **oh**-jee
Tomorrow, too?	*Anche domani?*	**ahn**-kay doh-**mah**-nee
Are there some trains today?	*Ci sono qualcuni treni oggi?*	chee **soh**-noh kwahl-**koo**-nee **tray**-nee **oh**-jee
I'm going to ___.	*Vado a ___.*	**vah**-doh ah

In Italy, train strikes (*scioperi*) are not unusual. They often last a day and a few trains still run, particularly the long-distance routes.

Reading Train and Bus Schedules

a	to
arrivi	arrivals
arrivo	arrival (also abbreviated "a")
binario	track
da	from
destinazione	destination
domenica	Sunday
eccetto	except
feriali	weekdays including Saturday
ferma a tutte le stazioni	stops at all the stations
festivi	Sundays and holidays
fino	until
giorni	days
giornaliero	daily
in ritardo	late
non ferma a ___	doesn't stop in ___
ogni	every
partenza	departure (also abbreviated "p")
partenze	departures
per	for
sabato	Saturday
si effettua anche ___	it also runs ___
solo	only
tutti i giorni	daily
vacanza	holiday
1-5	Monday-Friday
6, 7	Saturday, Sunday

TRAVELING

European schedules use the 24-hour clock. It's like American time until noon. After that, subtract twelve and add P.M. So 13:00 is 1 P.M., 20:00 is 8 P.M., and 24:00 is midnight. If your train is scheduled to depart at 00:01, it'll leave one minute after midnight.

Major Transportation Lines In Italy

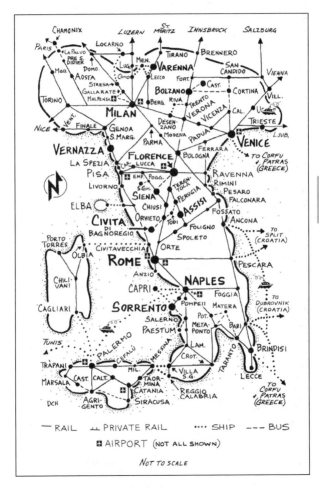

Going Places

Italy	*Italia*	ee-**tahl**-yah
Austria	*Austria*	**ow**-streeah
Belgium	*Belgio*	**behl**-joh
Czech Republic	*Repubblica Ceca*	reh-**poo**-blee-kah **cheh**-kah
England	*Inghilterra*	een-geel-**tehr**-rah
France	*Francia*	**frahn**-chah
Paris	*Parigi*	pah-**ree**-jee
Germany	*Germania*	jehr-**mahn**-yah
Munich	*Monaco di Baviera*	**moh**-nah-koh dee bah-vee**ay**-rah
Greece	*Grecia*	**gray**-chah
Ireland	*Irlanda*	eer-**lahn**-dah
Netherlands	*Paesi Bassi*	pah-**ay**-zee **bah**-see
Portugal	*Portogallo*	por-toh-**gah**-loh
Scandinavia	*Paesi Scandinavi*	pah-**ay**-zee skahn-dee-**nah**-vee
Spain	*Spagna*	**spahn**-yah
Switzerland	*Svizzera*	**sveet**-say-rah
Turkey	*Turchia*	**toor**-keeah
Europe	*Europa*	ay-oo-**roh**-pah
EU (European Union)	*UE (Unione Europeo)*	oo ay (oon-ee-**ohn**-ay ay-oo-roh-**pay**-oh)
Russia	*Russia*	**roo**-seeah
Africa	*Africa*	**ahf**-ree-kah
United States	*Stati Uniti*	**stah**-tee oo-**nee**-tee
Canada	*Canada*	kah-nah-**dah**
world	*mondo*	**mohn**-doh

Places in Italy

Bologna	*Bologna*	boh-**lohn**-yah
Cinque Terre	*Cinque Terre*	**cheeng**-kway **tehr**-ray
Civita	*Civita*	chee-**vee**-tah
Florence	*Firenze*	fee-**rehn**-tsay

TRAVELING

Italian	Riviera	reev-**yehr**-rah
Riviera	Ligure	lee-**goo**-ray
Lake Como	Lago di Como	**lah**-goh dee **koh**-moh
Milan	Milano	mee-**lah**-noh
Naples	Napoli	**nah**-poh-lee
Orvieto	Orvieto	or-vee**ay**-toh
Pisa	Pisa	**pee**-zah
Rome	Roma	**roh**-mah
San Gimignano	San Gimignano	sahn jee-meen-**yah**-noh
Sicily	Sicilia	see-**chee**-leeah
Siena	Siena	see-**ehn**-ah
Sorrento	Sorrento	sor-**rehn**-toh
Varenna	Varenna	vah-**rehn**-nah
Vatican City	Città del	cheet-**tah** dayl
	Vaticano	vah-tee-**kah**-noh
Venice	Venezia	vay-**nayt**-seeah
Vernazza	Vernazza	vehr-**naht**-tsah

BUSES AND SUBWAYS

At the Bus Station or Metro Stop

ticket	biglietto	beel-**yay**-toh
city bus	autobus	**ow**-toh-boos
long-distance bus	pullman,	**pool**-mahn,
	corriera	koh-ree-**ehr**-ah
bus stop	fermata	fehr-**mah**-tah
bus station	stazione	staht-see**oh**-nay
	degli autobus	**dayl**-yee **ow**-toh-boos
subway	metropolitana	may-troh-poh-lee-**tah**-nah
subway	stazione della	staht-see**oh**-nay **day**-lah
station	metropolitana	may-troh-poh-lee-**tah**-nah
subway map	cartina	kar-**tee**-nah
subway entrance	entrata	ayn-**trah**-tah
subway stop	fermata	fehr-**mah**-tah
subway exit	uscita	oo-**shee**-tah
direct	diretto	dee-**reht**-toh

| connection | coincidenza | koh-een-chee-**dehnt**-sah |
| pickpocket | borsaiolo | bor-sah-**yoh**-loh |

Most big cities offer deals on transportation, such as one-day tickets (*biglietto giornaliero*) and cheaper fares for youths and seniors. On a map, *voi siete qui* means "you are here." Venice has boats instead of buses. Zip around on *traghetti* (gondola ferries) and *vaporetti* (motorized ferries).

Taking Buses and Subways

How do you get to__?	Come si va a __?	**koh**-may see vah ah __
How much is a ticket?	Quanto costa un biglietto?	**kwahn**-toh **koh**-stah oon beel-**yay**-toh
Where can I buy a ticket?	Dove posso comprare un biglietto?	**doh**-vay **poh**-soh kohm-**prah**-ray oon beel-**yay**-toh
Where can we buy tickets?	Dove possiamo comprare i biglietti?	**doh**-vay poh-seeah-moh kohm-**prah**-ray ee beel-**yay**-tee
One ticket, please.	Un biglietto, per favore	oon beel-**yay**-toh pehr fah-voh-ray
Two tickets.	Due biglietti.	**doo**-ay beel-**yay**-tee
Is this ticket valid (for __)?	Questo biglietto è valido (per __)?	**kwehs**-toh beel-**yay**-toh eh **vah**-lee-doh (pehr __)
Is there a one-day pass?	C'è un biglietto giornaliero?	cheh oon beel-**yay**-toh jor-nahl-**yay**-roh
Which bus to __?	Quale autobus per __?	**kwah**-lay ow-toh-boos pehr
Does it stop at __?	Si ferma a __?	see **fehr**-mah ah
Which metro stop for __?	Qual'è la fermata per__?	kwah-**leh** lah fehr-**mah**-tah pehr
Which direction for __?	Da che parte è __?	dah kay **par**-tay eh
Must I transfer?	Devo cambiare?	**day**-voh kahm-beeah-ray
Must we transfer?	Dobbiamo cambiare?	doh-beeah-moh kahm-beeah-ray

TRAVELING

Key Phrases: Buses and Subways

bus	*autobus*	**ow**-toh-boos
subway	*metropolitana*	may-troh-poh-lee-**tah**-nah
ticket	*biglietto*	beel-**yay**-toh
How do you get to __?	*Come si va a __?*	**koh**-may see vah ah
Which stop for __?	*Qual'è la fermata per__?*	kwah-**leh** lah fehr-**mah**-tah pehr
Tell me when to get off?	*Mi dice quando devo scendere?*	mee **dee**-chay **kwahn**-doh **day**-voh **shehn**-day-ray

When does... leave?	*Quando parte...?*	**kwahn**-doh **par**-tay
...the first	*...il primo*	eel **pree**-moh
...the next	*...il prossimo*	eel **proh**-see-moh
...the last	*...l'ultimo*	**lool**-tee-moh
...bus / subway	*...autobus / metropolitana*	**ow**-toh-boos / may-troh-poh-lee-**tah**-nah
What's the frequency per hour / day?	*Quante volte passa all'ora / al giorno?*	**kwahn**-tay **vohl**-tay **pah**-sah ah-**loh**-rah / ahl **jor**-noh
Where does it leave from?	*Da dove parte?*	dah **doh**-vay **par**-tay
What time does it leave?	*A che ora parte?*	ah kay **oh**-rah **par**-tay
I'm going to __.	*Vado a __.*	**vah**-doh ah
We're going to __.	*Andiamo a __.*	ahn-dee**ah**-moh ah
Tell me when to get off?	*Mi dice quando devo scendere?*	mee **dee**-chay **kwahn**-doh **day**-voh **shehn**-day-ray
Tell us when to get off?	*Ci dice quando dobbiamo scendere?*	chee **dee**-chay **kwahn**-doh doh-bee**ah**-moh **shehn**-day-ray

TAXIS

Getting a Taxi

Taxi!	*Taxi!*	**tahk**-see
Can you call a taxi?	*Può chiamare un taxi?*	pwoh kee-ah-**mah**-ray oon **tahk**-see
Where is a taxi stand?	*Dov'è una fermata dei taxi?*	doh-veh **oo**-nah fehr-**mah**-tah **deh**ee **tahk**-see
Where can I get a taxi?	*Dov'è posso prendere un taxi?*	doh-veh **poh**-soh **prehn**-day-ray oon **tahk**-see
Where can we get a taxi?	*Dov'è possiamo prendere un taxi?*	doh-veh poh-see**ah**-moh **prehn**-day-ray oon **tahk**-see
Are you free?	*È libero?*	eh **lee**-bay-roh
Occupied.	*Occupato.*	oh-koo-**pah**-toh
To ___ , please.	*A ___ , per favore.*	ah ___ pehr fah-**voh**-ray
To this address.	*A questo indirizzo.*	ah **kwehs**-toh een-dee-**reed**-zoh
Take me to ___.	*Mi porti a ___.*	mee **por**-tee ah
Take us to ___.	*Ci porti a ___.*	chee **por**-tee ah
Approximately how much will it cost to go...?	*Quanto costa più o meno fino...?*	**kwahn**-toh **koh**-stah pew oh **may**-noh **fee**-noh
...to ___	*...a ___*	ah ___
...to the airport	*...all'aeroporto*	ah-lah-ay-roh-**por**-toh
...to the train station	*...alla stazione ferroviaria*	**ah**-lah staht-see**oh**-nay fay-roh-vee-**ah**-reeah
...to this address	*...a questo indirizzo*	ah **kweh**-stoh een-dee-**reed**-zoh
Any extra supplement?	*C'è qualche supplemento?*	cheh **kwahl**-kay soo-play-**mehn**-toh
Too much.	*Troppo.*	**troh**-poh
Can you take ___ people?	*Può portare ___ persone?*	pwoh por-tah-reh ___ pehr-**soh**-nay

Key Phrases: Taxis

Taxi!	*Taxi!*	**tahk**-see
Are you free?	*È libero?*	eh **lee**-bay-roh
To ___, please.	*A ___,per favore.*	ah ___ pehr fah-**voh**-ray
meter	*tassametro*	tah-sah-**may**-troh
Stop here.	*Si fermi qui.*	see **fehr**-mee kwee
Keep the change.	*Tenga il resto.*	**tayn**-gah eel **rehs**-toh

Any extra fee?	*C'è un sovrapprezzo?*	cheh oon soh-vrah-**prehd**-zoh
Do you have an hourly rate?	*Ha una tariffa oraria?*	ah **oo**-nah tah-**ree**-fah oh-**rah**-reeah
How much for a one-hour city tour?	*Quant'è per un giro della città di un'ora?*	kwahn-**teh** pehr oon **jee**-roh **day**-lah chee-**tah** dee oon-**oh**-rah

Cab fares are reasonable, and most drivers are honest. Expect a charge for luggage. Three or more tourists are usually better off hailing a cab than messing with city buses in Italy. If you're having a tough time hailing a taxi, ask for the nearest taxi stand (***fermata dei taxi***). The simplest way to tell a cabbie where you want to go is by stating your destination followed by "please" ("***Uffizi, per favore***"). Tipping isn't expected, but it's polite to round up.

In the Taxi

The meter, please.	*Il tassametro, per favore.*	eel tah-sah-**may**-troh pehr fah-**voh**-ray
Where is the meter?	*Dov'è il tassametro?*	doh-**veh** eel tah-sah-**may**-troh
I'm / We're in a hurry.	*Sono / Siamo di fretta.*	**soh**-noh / seeah-moh dee **fray**-tah
Slow down.	*Rallenti.*	rah-**lehn**-tee
If you don't slow down, I'll throw up.	*Se non rallenta, vomito.*	say nohn rah-**lehn**-tah **voh**-mee-toh

English	Italian	Pronunciation
Left / Right / Straight.	A sinistra / A destra / Diritto.	ah see-**nee**-strah / ah **dehs**-trah / dee-**ree**-toh
I'd like to stop here briefly.	Vorrei fermarmi un momento.	vor-**reh**ee fehr-**mar**-mee oon moh-**mehn**-toh
We'd like to stop here briefly.	Vorremmo fermarci un momento.	vor-**ray**-moh fehr-**mar**-chee oon moh-**mehn**-toh
Please stop here for ___ minutes.	Si fermi qui per ___ minuti, per favore.	see **fehr**-mee kwee pehr ___ mee-**noo**-tee pehr fah-**voh**-ray
Can you wait?	Può aspettare?	pwoh ah-spay-**tah**-ray
Crazy traffic, isn't it?	Un traffico incredibile, vero?	oon **trah**-fee-koh een-kray-**dee**-bee-lay **vay**-roh
You drive like...	Guida come...	**gwee**-dah koh-**may**
...a madman!	...un pazzo!	oon **pahd**-zoh
...Michael Schumacher.	...Michele Schumacher.	mee-**kay**-lay "Schumacher"
You drive very well.	Guida molto bene.	**gwee**-dah **mohl**-toh **behn**-ay
Where did you learn to drive?	Ma dove ha imparato a guidare?	mah **doh**-vay ah eem-pah-**rah**-toh ah gwee-**dah**-ray
Stop here.	Si fermi qui.	see **fehr**-mee kwee
Here is fine.	Va bene qui.	vah **behn**-ay kwee
At this corner.	A questo angolo.	ah **kwehs**-toh **ahn**-goh-loh
The next corner.	Al prossimo angolo.	ahl **proh**-see-moh **ahn**-goh-loh
My change, please.	Il resto, per favore.	eel **rehs**-toh pehr fah-**voh**-ray
Keep the change.	Tenga il resto.	**tayn**-gah eel **rehs**-toh
This ride is / was more fun than Disneyland.	Questo viaggio è / è stato più divertente di Disneyland.	**kwehs**-toh veeah-joh eh / eh **stah**-toh pew dee-vehr-**tehn**-tay dee "Disneyland"

DRIVING

Rental Wheels

car rental agency	*agenzia di autonoleggio*	ah-**jehnt**-seeah dee ow-toh-noh-**leh**-joh
I'd like to rent...	*Vorrei noleggiare...*	vor-**reh**ee noh-leh-**jah**-ray
We'd like to rent...	*Vorremmo noleggiare...*	vor-**ray**-moh noh-leh-**jah**-ray
...a car.	*...una macchina.*	**oo**-nah **mah**-kee-nah
...a station wagon.	*...una station wagon.*	**oo**-nah **staht**-see-ohn **wah**-gohn
...a van.	*...un monovolume.*	oon moh-noh-voh-**loo**-may
...a motorcycle.	*...una motocicletta.*	**oo**-nah moh-toh-chee-**klay**-tah
...a motor scooter.	*...un motorino.*	oon moh-toh-**ree**-noh
How much...?	*Quanto...?*	**kwahn**-toh
...per hour	*...all'ora*	ah-**loh**-rah
...per half day	*...per mezza giornata*	pehr **mehd**-zah jor-**nah**-tah
...per day	*...al giorno*	ahl **jor**-noh
...per week	*...alla settimana*	**ah**-lah say-tee-**mah**-nah
Unlimited mileage?	*Chilometraggio illimitato?*	kee-loh-may-**trah**-joh eel-lee-mee-**tah**-toh
When must I bring it back?	*Quando devo riportarla?*	**kwahn**-doh **day**-voh ree-por-**tar**-lah
Is there...?	*C'è...?*	cheh
...a helmet	*...un casco*	oon **kah**-skoh
...a discount	*...uno sconto*	**oo**-noh **skohn**-toh
...a deposit	*...una caparra*	**oo**-nah kah-**pah**-rah
...insurance	*...l'assicurazione*	lah-see-koo-raht-see**oh**-nay

At the Gas Station

gas station	*benzinaio*	baynd-zee-**nah**-yoh
The nearest gas station?	*Il benzinaio più vicino?*	eel baynd-zee-**nah**-yoh pew vee-**chee**-noh

TRAVELING

Key Phrases: Driving

car	*macchina*	**mah**-kee-nah
gas station	*benzinaio*	baynd-zee-**nah**-yoh
parking lot	*parcheggio*	par-**kay**-joh
accident	*incidente*	een-chee-**dehn**-tay
left / right	*sinistra /*	see-**nee**-strah /
	destra	**dehs**-trah
straight ahead	*sempre diritto*	**sehm**-pray dee-**ree**-toh
downtown	*centro*	**chehn**-troh
How do you get to ___?	*Come si va a ___?*	**koh**-may see vah ah
Where can I park?	*Dove posso parcheggiare?*	**doh**-vay **poh**-soh par-kay-**jah**-ray

Self-service?	*Self-service?*	"self service"
Fill the tank.	*Il pieno.*	eel pee**ay**-noh
Wash the windows.	*Pulisce le finestrine.*	poo-**lee**-shay lay fee-nay-**stree**-nay
I need...	*Ho bisogno di...*	oh bee-**zohn**-yoh dee
We need...	*Abbiamo bisogno di...*	ah-bee**ah**-moh bee-**zohn**-yoh dee
...gas.	*...benzina.*	baynd-**zee**-nah
...unleaded.	*...benzina verde.*	baynd-**zee**-nah **vehr**-day
...regular.	*...normale.*	nor-**mah**-lay
...super.	*...super.*	**soo**-pehr
...diesel.	*...gasolio.*	gah-**zoh**-leeoh
Check...	*Controlli...*	kohn-**troh**-lee
...the oil.	*...l'olio.*	**loh**-leeoh
...the air in the tires.	*...l'aria nelle gomme.*	**lah**-reeah **nay**-lay **goh**-may
...the radiator.	*...il radiatore.*	eel rah-deeah-**toh**-ray
...the battery.	*...la batteria.*	lah bah-tay-**ree**-ah
...the sparkplugs.	*...le candele.*	lay kahn-**day**-lay

...the headlights.	...gli anabbaglianti.	lyee ah-nah-bahl-yee**ahn**-tee
...the tail lights.	...le luci posteriori.	lay **loo**-chee pos-tay-ree**oh**-ree
...the directional signal.	...la freccia.	lah **freh**-chah
...the brakes.	...i freni.	ee **fray**-nee
...the transmission fluid.	...il liquido della trasmissione.	eel **lee**-kwee-doh **day**-lah trahs-mee-see**oh**-nay
...the windshield wipers.	...i tergicristalli.	ee tehr-gee-kree-**stah**-lee
...the fuses.	...i fusibili.	ee foo-**zee**-bee-lee
...the fan belt.	...la cinghia del ventilatore.	lah **cheen**-geeah dayl vehn-tee-lah-**toh**-ray
...my pulse.	...il mio battito cardiaco.	eel **mee**-oh bah-**tee**-toh kar-dee**ah**-koh
...my husband / wife.	...mio marito / mia moglie.	**mee**-oh mah-**ree**-toh / **mee**-ah **mohl**-yay

TRAVELING

Getting gas in Italy is a breeze. Regular is *normale* and super is *super*, and euros and liters replace dollars and gallons (there are about four liters in a gallon). The freeway rest stops and city *automat* gas pumps are the only places that sell gas during the afternoon siesta hours. Gas is always more expensive on the super highways.

Car Trouble

accident	incidente	een-chee-**dehn**-tay
breakdown	guasto	goo**ah**-stoh
dead battery	batteria scarica	bah-tay-**ree**-ah skah-**ree**-kah
funny noise	rumore strano	roo-**moh**-ray **strah**-noh
electrical problem	problema elettrico	proh-**blay**-mah ay-**leht**-ree-koh
flat tire	gomma a terra	**goh**-mah ah **tay**-rah
shop with parts	negozio di pezzi di ricambio	nay-**goht**-seeoh dee **pehd**-zee dee ree-**kahm**-beeoh

My car won't start.	*La mia macchina non parte.*	lah **mee**-ah **mah**-kee-nah nohn **par**-tay
My car is broken.	*La mia macchina è rotta.*	lah **mee**-ah **mah**-kee-nah eh **roh**-tah
This doesn't work.	*Non funziona.*	nohn foont-see**oh**-nah
It's overheating.	*Si sta surriscaldando.*	see stah soo-ree-skahl-**dahn**-doh
It's a lemon (a swindle).	*È una fregatura.*	eh **oo**-nah fray-gah-**too**-rah
I need...	*Ho bisogno di...*	oh bee-**zohn**-yoh dee
We need...	*Abbiamo bisogno di...*	ah-bee**ah**-moh bee-**zohn**-yoh dee
...a tow truck.	*...un carro attrezzi.*	oon **kar**-roh ah-**trayd**-zee
...a mechanic.	*...un meccanico.*	oon may-**kah**-nee-koh
...a stiff drink.	*...un whiskey.*	oon "whiskey"

For help with repair, see "Repair" in the Services chapter on page 177.

Parking

parking lot	*parcheggio*	par-**kay**-joh
parking garage	*garage*	gah-**rahj**
Where can I park?	*Dove posso parcheggiare?*	**doh**-vay **poh**-soh par-kay-**jah**-ray
Is parking nearby?	*È vicino il parcheggio?*	eh vee-**chee**-noh eel par-**kay**-joh
Can I park here?	*Posso parcheggiare qui?*	**poh**-soh par-kay-**jah**-ray kwee
Is this a safe place to park?	*È sicuro parcheggiare qui?*	eh see-**koo**-roh par-kay-**jah**-ray kwee
How long can I park here?	*Per quanto tempo posso parcheggiare qui?*	pehr **kwahn**-toh **tehm**-poh **poh**-soh par-kay-**jah**-ray kwee
Must I pay to park here?	*È a pagamento questo parcheggio?*	eh ah pah-gah-**mayn**-toh **kweh**-stoh par-**kay**-joh

| How much | *Quanto costa* | **kwahn**-toh **koh**-stah |
| per hour / day? | *all'ora / al giorno?* | ahl-**loh**-rah / ahl **jor**-noh |

Parking in Italian cities is expensive and hazardous. Plan to pay to use a parking garage in big cities. Leave nothing in your car at night. Always ask at your hotel about safe parking. Take parking restrictions seriously to avoid getting fines and having your car towed away (an interesting but costly experience).

FINDING YOUR WAY

I'm going to ___.	*Vado a ___.*	**vah**-doh ah
We're going to ___.	*Andiamo a ___.*	ahn-dee**ah**-moh ah
How do you get to ___?	*Come si va a ___?*	**koh**-may see vah ah
Do you have a...?	*Ha una...?*	ah **oo**-nah
...city map	*...cartina della città*	kar-**tee**-nah **day**-lah chee-**tah**
...road map	*...cartina stradale*	kar-**tee**-nah strah-**dah**-lay
How many minutes...?	*Quanti minuti...?*	**kwahn**-tee mee-**noo**-tee
How many hours...?	*Quante ore...?*	**kwahn**-tay **oh**-ray
...on foot	*...a piedi*	ah pee**ay**-dee
...by bicycle	*...in bicicletta*	een bee-chee-**klay**-tah
...by car	*...in macchina*	een **mah**-kee-nah
How many kilometers to___?	*Quanti chilometri per___?*	**kwahn**-tee kee-**loh**-may-tree pehr
What is the... route to Rome?	*Qual'è la strada... per andare a Roma?*	kwah-**leh** lah **strah**-dah... pehr ahn-**dah**-ray ah **roh**-mah
...most scenic	*...più panoramica*	pew pah-noh-**rah**-mee-kah
...fastest	*...più veloce*	pew vay-**loh**-chay
...most interesting	*...più interessante*	pew een-tay-ray-**sahn**-tay
Point it out?	*Me lo mostra?*	may loh **mohs**-trah
I'm lost.	*Mi sono perso[a].*	mee **soh**-noh **pehr**-soh

TRAVELING

Where am I?	Dove sono?	**doh**-vay **soh**-noh
Where is...?	Dov'è...?	doh-**veh**
The nearest...?	Il più vicino...?	eel pew vee-**chee**-noh
Where is this address?	Dov'è questo indirizzo?	doh-**veh kweh**-stoh een-dee-**reed**-zoh

Route-Finding Words

map	cartina	kar-**tee**-nah
road map	cartina stradale	kar-**tee**-nah strah-**dah**-lay
downtown	centro	**chehn**-troh
straight ahead	sempre diritto	**sehm**-pray dee-**ree**-toh
left	sinistra	see-**nee**-strah
right	destra	**dehs**-trah
first	prima	**pree**-mah
next	prossima	**proh**-see-mah
intersection	incrocio	een-**kroh**-choh
corner	angolo	**ahn**-goh-loh
block	isolato	ee-zoh-**lah**-toh
roundabout	rotonda	roh-**tohn**-dah
stoplight	semaforo	say-mah-**foh**-roh
(main) square	piazza (principale)	peeaht-sah (preen-chee-**pah**-lay)
street	strada, via	**strah**-dah, **vee**-ah
bridge	ponte	**pohn**-tay
tunnel	tunnel	**toon**-nehl
highway	autostrada	ow-toh-**strah**-dah
freeway	superstrada	soo-pehr-**strah**-dah
north	nord	nord
south	sud	sood
east	est	ayst
west	ovest	**oh**-vehst

(side tab: TRAVELING*)*

In Italy, the shortest distance between any two points is the ***autostrada***. Tolls are not cheap (about a dollar for every 10 minutes), and there aren't as many signs as we are used to, so stay alert or you may miss your exit. Italy's ***autostrada*** rest stops are among the best in Europe.

The Police

As in any country, the flashing lights of a patrol car are a sure sign that someone's in trouble. If it's you, try this handy phrase: "*Mi dispiace, sono un turista*" (Sorry, I'm a tourist). Or, for the adventurous: "*Se non le piace come guido, si tolga dal marciapiede*" (If you don't like how I drive, stay off the sidewalk).

I'm late for my tour.	*Sono in ritardo per il tour.*	**soh**-noh een ree-**tar**-doh pehr eel toor
Can I buy your hat?	*Mi vende il suo cappello?*	mee **vehn**-day eel **soo**-oh kah-**pehl**-loh
What seems to be the problem?	*Quale sarebbe il problema?*	**kwah**-lay sah-**reh**-bay eel proh-**blay**-mah

Reading Road Signs

alt / stop	stop
carabinieri	police
centro, centrocittà	to the center of town
circonvallazione	ring road
dare la precedenza	yield
deviazione	detour
entrata	entrance
lavori in corso	road work ahead
prossima uscita	next exit
rallentare	slow down
senso unico	one-way street
tutti le (altre) destinazioni	to all (other) destinations
uscita	exit
zona pedonale	pedestrian zone

Other Signs You May See

acqua non potabile	undrinkable water
affittasi, in affitto	for rent or for hire
aperto	open
aperto da__ a__	open from__ to__
attenzione	caution

TRAVELING

bagno, gabinetto, toilette, toletta, WC	toilet
cagnaccio	mean dog
camere libere	vacancy
chiuso	closed
chiuso per ferie	closed for vacation
chiuso per restauro	closed for restoration
completo	no vacancy
donne	women
entrata libera	free admission
entrata vietata	no entry
fuori servizio / guasto	out of service
non toccare	do not touch
occupato	occupied
parcheggio vietato	no parking
pericolo	danger
proibito	prohibited
saldo	sale
sciopero	on strike
signore	women
signori	men
spingere / tirare	push / pull
torno subito	I'll return soon (sign on store)
uomini	men
uscita d'emergenza	emergency exit
vendesi, in vendita	for sale
vietato	forbidden
vietato fumare	no smoking
vietato l'accesso	keep out

Standard Road Signs

 AND LEARN THESE ROAD SIGNS

Speed Limit
(km/hr)

Yield

No Passing

End of
No Passing
Zone

One Way

Intersection

Main
Road

Freeway

Danger

No Entry

No Entry
for Cars

All Vehicles
Prohibited

Parking

No Parking

Customs

Peace

TRAVELING

SLEEPING

Places to Stay

hotel	*hotel, albergo*	**oh**-tehl, ahl-**behr**-goh
small hotel	*pensione,*	payn-see**oh**-nay,
(often family-run)	*locanda*	loh-**kahn**-dah
rooms for rent	*affita camere*	ah-**fee**-tah **kah**-may-ray
youth hostel	*ostello della*	oh-**stehl**-loh **dehl**-lah
	gioventù	joh-vehn-**too**
vacancy	*camere libere*	**kah**-may-ray **lee**-bay-ray
no vacancy	*completo*	kohm-**play**-toh

Reserving a Room

I like to reserve rooms a few days in advance as I travel. But if my itinerary is set, I reserve before I leave home. To reserve from home by email or fax, use the handy form in the appendix (online at www.ricksteves.com/reservation).

Hello.	*Buon giorno.*	bwohn **jor**-noh
Do you speak English?	*Parla inglese?*	**par**-lah een-**glay**-zay
Do you have a room for...?	*Avete una camera per...?*	ah-**vay**-tay **oo**-nah **kah**-may-rah pehr
...one person	*...una persona*	**oo**-nah pehr-**soh**-nah
...two people	*...due persone*	**doo**-ay pehr-**soh**-nay
...tonight	*...stanotte*	stah-**noh**-tay

Key Phrases: Sleeping

I want to make / confirm a reservation.	*Vorrei fare / confermare una prenotazione.*	vor-**reh**ee **fah**-ray / kohn-fehr-**mah**-ray **oo**-nah pray-noh-taht-see**oh**-nay
I'd like a room (for two people), please.	*Vorrei una camera (per due persone), per favore.*	vor-**reh**ee **oo**-nah **kah**-may-rah (pehr **doo**-ay pehr-**soh**-nay) pehr fah-**voh**-ray
...with / without / and	*...con / senza / e*	kohn / **sehnt**-sah / ay
...toilet	*...toilette*	twah-**leht**-tay
...shower	*...doccia*	**doh**-chah
Can I see the room?	*Posso vedere la camera?*	**poh**-soh vay-**day**-ray lah **kah**-may-rah
How much is it?	*Quanto costa?*	**kwahn**-toh **koh**-stah
Credit card O.K.?	*Carta di credito è O.K.?*	**kar**-tah dee **kray**-dee-toh eh "O.K."

...two nights	*...due notti*	**doo**-ay **noh**-tee
...Friday	*...venerdì*	vay-nehr-**dee**
...June 21	*...il ventuno giugno*	eel vayn-**too**-noh **joon**-yoh
Yes or no?	*Sì o no?*	see oh noh
I'd like...	*Vorrei...*	vor-**reh**ee
We'd like...	*Vorremmo...*	vor-**ray**-moh
...a private bathroom.	*...un bagno completo.*	oon **bahn**-yoh kohm-**play**-toh
...your cheapest room.	*...la camera più economica.*	lah **kah**-may-rah pew ay-koh-**noh**-mee-kah
...___ bed (beds)	*...___ letto (letti)*	___ **leht**-toh (**leht**-tee)
for ___ people	*per ___ persone*	pehr ___ pehr-**soh**-nay
in ___ room (in ___rooms).	*nella ___ camera (nelle ___ camere).*	**nay**-lah ___ **kah**-may-rah (**nay**-lay ___ **kah**-may-ray)
How much is it?	*Quanto costa?*	**kwahn**-toh **koh**-stah
Anything cheaper?	*Niente di più economico?*	nee-**ehn**-tay dee pew ay-koh-**noh**-mee-koh

I'll take it.	La prendo.	lah **prehn**-doh
My name is ___.	Mi chiamo ___.	mee kee**ah**-moh
I'll stay / We'll stay...	Starò / Staremo...	stah-**roh** / stah-**ray**-moh
...for ___ night (nights).	...per ___ notte (notti).	pehr ___ **noh**-tay (**noh**-tee)
I'll come / We'll come...	Arriverò / Arriveremo...	ah-ree-vay-**roh** / ah-ree-vay-**ray**-moh
...in the morning.	...la mattina.	lah mah-**tee**-nah
...in the afternoon.	...il pomeriggio.	eel poh-may-**ree**-joh
...in the evening.	...la sera.	lah **say**-rah
...in one hour.	...tra un'ora.	trah oon-**oh**-rah
...before 16:00.	...prima delle sedici.	**pree**-mah **dehl**-lay **say**-dee-chee
...Friday before 6 P.M.	...venerdí entro le sei di sera.	vay-nehr-**dee ehn**-troh lay **seh**ee dee **say**-rah
Thank you.	Grazie.	**graht**-seeay

Using a Credit Card

If you need to secure your reservation with a credit card, here's the lingo.

Is a deposit required?	Bisogna lasciare una caparra?	bee-**sohn**-yah lah-**shah**-ray **oo**-nah kah-**pah**-rah
Credit card O.K.?	Carta di credito è O.K.?	**kar**-tah dee **kray**-dee-toh eh "O.K."
credit card	carta di credito	**kar**-tah dee **kray**-dee-toh
debit card	bancomat	**bahnk**-oh-maht
The name on the card is ___.	Il nome sulla carta è ___.	il **noh**-may **soo**-lah **kar**-tah eh
The credit card number is...	Il numero della carta di credito è...	eel **noo**-may-roh **dehl**-lah **kar**-tah dee **kray**-dee-toh eh
0	zero	**zay**-roh
1	uno	**oo**-noh
2	due	**doo**-ay
3	tre	tray
4	quattro	**kwah**-troh

5	cinque	**cheeng**-kway
6	sei	**seh**ee
7	sette	**seht**-tay
8	otto	**oh**-toh
9	nove	**noh**-vay
The expiration date is...	La data di scadenza è...	lah **dah**-tah dee shah-**dehnt**-sah eh
January	gennaio	jay-**nah**-yoh
February	febbraio	fay-**brah**-yoh
March	marzo	**mart**-soh
April	aprile	ah-**pree**-lay
May	maggio	**mah**-joh
June	giugno	**joon**-yoh
July	luglio	**lool**-yoh
August	agosto	ah-**goh**-stoh
September	settembre	say-**tehm**-bray
October	ottobre	oh-**toh**-bray
November	novembre	noh-**vehm**-bray
December	dicembre	dee-**chehm**-bray
2009	duemilanove	doo-ay-mee-lah-**noh**-vay
2010	duemila-dieci	doo-ay-mee-lah-dee**ay**-chee
2011	duemila-undici	doo-ay-mee-lah-**oon**-dee-chee
2012	duemila-dodici	doo-ay-mee-lah-**doh**-dee-chee
2013	duemila-tredici	doo-ay-mee-lah-**tray**-dee-chee
2014	duemila-quattordici	doo-ay-mee-lah-kwah-**tor**-dee-chee
2015	duemila-quindici	doo-ay-mee-lah-**kween**-dee-chee
Can I reserve with a credit card and pay in cash?	Posso prenotare con la carta di credito e pagare in contanti?	**poh**-soh pray-noh-**tah**-ray kohn lah **kar**-tah dee **kray**-dee-toh ay pah-**gah**-ray een kohn-**tahn**-tee
I have another card.	Ho un'altra carta.	oh oo-**nahl**-trah **kar**-tah

If your *carta di credito* (credit card) is not approved, you can say "*Ho un'altra carta*" (I have another card)—if you do.

L' Alfabeto

If phoning, you can use the code alphabet below to spell out your name if necessary. Unless you're giving the hotelier your name as it appears on your credit card, consider using a shorter version of your name to make things easier.

a	ah	Ancona	ahn-**koh**-nah
b	bee	Bologna	boh-**lohn**-yah
c	chee	Como	**koh**-moh
d	dee	Domodossola	doh-moh-**doh**-soh-lah
e	ay	Empoli	**ehm**-poh-lee
f	**ehf**-ay	Firenze	fee-**rehn**-tsay
g	jee	Genova	**jay**-noh-vah
h	ah-kah	Hotel, "acca"	**oh**-tehl, **ah**-kah
i	ee	Imola	**ee**-moh-lah
j	ee **loon**-gah	i lunga	ee **loon**-gah
k	**kahp**-ah	"kappa"	**kah**-pah
l	**ehl**-ay	Livorno	lee-**vor**-noh
m	**ehm**-ay	Milano	mee-**lah**-noh
n	**ehn**-ay	Napoli	**nah**-poh-lee
o	oh	Otranto	oh-**trahn**-toh
p	pee	Palermo	pah-**lehr**-moh
q	koo	quaranta (40)	kwah-**rahn**-tah
r	**ehr**-ay	Rovigo	roh-**vee**-goh
s	**ehs**-ay	Savona	sah-**voh**-nah
t	tee	Treviso	tray-**vee**-zoh
u	oo	Urbino	oor-**bee**-noh
v	vee	Venezia	vay-**nayt**-seeah
w	**dohp**-yah voo	"doppia vu"	**dohp**-yah voo
x	eeks	"ics"	eeks
y	**eep**-see-lohn	"ispilon"	**eep**-see-lohn
z	**zeht**-ah	Zara	**tsah**-rah

SLEEPING

Just the Fax, Ma'am

If you're booking a room by fax...

I want to send a fax.	Vorrei mandare un fax.	vor-**reh**ee mahn-**dah**-ray oon fahks
What is your fax number?	Qual è il suo numero di fax?	kwahl eh eel **soo**-oh **noo**-may-roh dee fahks
Your fax number is not working.	Il suo numero di fax non funziona.	eel **soo**-oh **noo**-may-roh dee fahks nohn foont-see**oh**-nah
Please turn on your fax machine.	Per favore accendere il fax.	pehr fah-**voh**-ray ah-**chehn**-day-ray eel fahks

Getting Specific

I'd like a room...	Vorrei una camera...	vor-**reh**ee **oo**-nah **kah**-may-rah
We'd like a room...	Vorremmo una camera...	vor-**ray**-moh **oo**-nah **kah**-may-rah
...with / without / and	...con / senza / e	kohn / **sehnt**-sah / ay
...toilet	...toilette	twah-**leht**-tay
...shower	...doccia	**doh**-chah
...shower down the hall	...doccia in fondo al corridoio	**doh**-chah een **fohn**-doh ahl kor-ree-**doh**-yoh
...bathtub	...vasca da bagno	**vah**-skah dah **bahn**-yoh
...double bed	...letto matrimoniale	**leht**-toh mah-tree-moh-nee**ah**-lay
...twin beds	...letti singoli	**leht**-tee **seeng**-goh-lee
...balcony	...balcone	bahl-**koh**-nay
...view	...vista	**vee**-stah
...only a sink	...solo un lavandino	**soh**-loh oon lah-vahn-**dee**-noh
...on the ground floor	...al piano terra	ahl pee**ah**-noh tay-rah
...television	...televisione	tay-lay-vee-zee**oh**-nay
...telephone	...telefono	tay-**lay**-foh-noh
...air conditioning	...aria condizionata	**ah**-reeah kohn-deet-see-oh-**nah**-tah

SLEEPING

...kitchenette	...cucina	koo-**chee**-nah
Do you have...?	Avete...?	ah-**vay**-tay
...an elevator	...l'ascensore	lah-shehn-**soh**-ray
...a swimming pool	...la piscina	lah pee-**shee**-nah
I arrive Monday,	Arrivo lunedì,	ah-**ree**-voh loo-nay-**dee**
depart Wednesday.	parto mercoledì.	**par**-toh mehr-koh-lay-**dee**
We arrive Monday,	Arriviamo	ah-ree-vee**ah**-moh
depart	lunedì,	loo-nay-**dee**
Wednesday.	partiamo	par-tee**ah**-moh
	mercoledì.	mehr-koh-lay-**dee**
I am desperate.	Sono disperato[a].	**soh**-noh dee-spay-**rah**-toh
We are	Siamo	see**ah**-moh
desperate.	disperati.	dee-spay-**rah**-tee
I will / We will	Posso / Possiamo	**poh**-soh / poh-see**ah**-moh
sleep anywhere.	dormire	dor-**mee**-ray
	ovunque.	oh-**voon**-kway
I have a sleeping	Ho un sacco	oh oon **sah**-koh
bag.	a pelo.	ah **pay**-loh
We have	Abbiamo i	ah-bee**ah**-moh ee
sleeping bags.	sacchi a pelo.	**sah**-kee ah **pay**-loh
Will you call	Chiamerebbe	kee**ah**-may-**reh**-bay
another hotel	un altro	oon **ahl**-troh
for me?	albergo per me?	ahl-**behr**-goh pehr may

Families

Do you have...?	Avete...?	ah-**vay**-tay
...a room for	...una camera	**oo**-nah **kah**-may-rah
families	grande per	**grahn**-day pehr
	una famiglia	**oo**-nah fah-**meel**-yah
...a family rate	...una tariffa	**oo**-nah tah-**ree**-fah
	per famiglie	pehr fah-**meel**-yay
...a discount	...uno sconto per	**oo**-noh **skohn**-toh pehr
for children	i bambini	ee bahm-**bee**-nee
I / We have...	Ho / Abbiamo...	oh / ah-bee**ah**-moh
...one child, age	...un bambino di	oon bahm-**bee**-noh dee
___ months / years.	___ mesi / anni.	___ **may**-zee / **ahn**-nee

SLEEPING

...two children, ages ___ and ___ years.	...due bambini, di ___ e ___ anni.	**doo**-ay bahm-**bee**-nee dee ___ ay ___ **ahn**-nee
I'd like...	Vorrei...	vor-**reh**ee
We'd like...	Vorremmo...	vor-**ray**-moh
...a crib.	...una culla.	**oo**-nah **koo**-lah
...a small extra bed.	...un letto singolo in più.	oon **leht**-toh **seeng**-goh-loh een pew
...bunk beds.	...letti a castello.	**lay**-tee ah kah-**stehl**-loh
babysitting service	servizio di baby sitter	sehr-**veet**-seeoh dee **bay**-bee **see**-tehr
Is a... nearby?	C'è.... qui vicino?	cheh... kwee vee-**chee**-noh
...park	...un parco	oon **par**-koh
...playground	...un parco giochi	oon **par**-koh **joh**-kee
...swimming pool	...una piscina	**oo**-nah pee-**shee**-nah

For fun, Italians call kids *marmocchi* (munchkins).

Mobility Issues

Stairs are... for me / us / my husband / my wife.	Le scale sono... per me / noi / mio marito / mia moglie.	lay **skah**-lay **soh**-noh... pehr may / **noh**ee / **mee**-oh mah-**ree**-toh / **mee**-ah **mohl**-yay
...impossible	...impossibili	eem-poh-**see**-bee-lee
...difficult	...difficili	dee-**fee**-chee-lee
Do you have...?	Avete...?	ah-**vay**-tay
...an elevator	...l'ascensore	lah-shehn-**soh**-ray
...a ground floor room	...una camera al piano terra	**oo**-nah **kah**-may-rah ahl peeah-noh **tay**-rah
...a wheelchair-accessible room	...una camera accessibile con la sedia a rotelle	**oo**-nah **kah**-may-rah ah-cheh-**see**-bee-lay kohn lah say-**dee**-ah ah roh-**tehl**-lay

Confirming, Changing, and Canceling Reservations

Use this template for your telephone call.

I have / We have a reservation.	Ho / Abbiamo una prenotazione.	oh / ah-bee**ah**-moh **oo**-nah pray-noh-taht-see**oh**-nay
My name is ___.	Mi chiamo ___.	mee kee**ah**-moh
I'd like to... my reservation.	Vorrei fare... una prenotazione.	vor-**reh**ee **fah**-ray...**oo**-nah pray-noh-taht-see**oh**-nay
...confirm	...confermare	kohn-fehr-**mah**-ray
...reconfirm	...riconfermare	ree-kohn-fehr-**mah**-ray
...cancel	...annullare	ah-noo-**lah**-ray
...change	...cambiare	kahm-bee**ah**-ray
The reservation is / was for...	La prenotazione è / era per...	lah pray-noh-taht-see**oh**-nay eh / **ehr**-ah pehr
...one person	...una persona	**oo**-nah pehr-**soh**-nah
...two people	...due persone	**doo**-ay pehr-**soh**-nay
...today / tomorrow	...oggi / domani	**oh**-jee / doh-**mah**-nee
...the day after tomorrow	...dopodomani	doh-poh-doh-**mah**-nee
...August 13	...il tredici agosto	eel **tray**-dee-chee ah-**goh**-stoh
...one night / two nights	...una notte / due notti	**oo**-nah **noh**-tay / **doo**-ay **noh**-tee
Can you find my / our reservation?	Può trovare la mia / nostra prenotazione?	pwoh troh-**vah**-ray lah **mee**-ah / **noh**-strah pray-noh-taht-see**oh**-nay
What is your cancellation policy?	Qual è il vostro regolamento riguardo alla cancellazione delle prenotazioni?	kwahl eh eel **voh**-stroh ray-goh-lah-**mehn**-toh ree-**gwar**-doh **ahl**-lah kahn-chehl-aht-see**oh**-nay **dehl**-lay pray-noh-taht-see**oh**-nee
Will I be billed for the first night if I can't make it?	Mi addebitate la prima notte se non ce la faccio?	mee ah-day-bee-**tah**-tay lah **pree**-mah **noh**-tay say nohn chay lah **fah**-choh

SLEEPING

I'd like to arrive instead on...	*Invece vorrei arrivare...*	een-**vay**-chay voh-**reh**ee ah-ree-**vah**-ray
We'd like to arrive instead on...	*Invece vorremmo arrivare...*	een-**vay**-chay vor-**ray**-moh ah-ree-**vah**-ray
Is everything O.K.?	*Va bene?*	vah **behn**-ay
Thank you. I'll see you then.	*Grazie. Ci vediamo al mio arrivo.*	**graht**-seeay chee vay-dee**ah**-moh ahl **mee**-oh ah-**ree**-voh
We'll see you then.	*Ci vediamo al nostro arrivo.*	chee vay-dee**ah**-moh ahl **noh**-stroh ah-**ree**-voh
I'm sorry I need to cancel.	*Mi dispiace ma devo annullare.*	mee dee-spee**ah**-chay mah **day**-voh ah-noo-**lah**-ray

Nailing Down the Price

How much is...?	*Quanto costa...?*	**kwahn**-toh **koh**-stah
...a room	*...una camera*	**oo**-nah **kah**-may-rah
for ___ people	*per ___ persone*	pehr ___ pehr-**soh**-nay
...your cheapest room	*...la camera più economica*	lah **kah**-may-rah pew ay-koh-**noh**-mee-kah
Is breakfast included?	*La colazione è inclusa?*	lah koh-laht-see**oh**-nay eh een-**kloo**-zah
Is breakfast required?	*È obbligatoria la colazione?*	eh oh-blee-gah-**toh**-reeah lah koh-laht-see**oh**-nay
How much without breakfast?	*Quant'è senza la colazione?*	kwahn-**teh sehnt**-sah lah koh-laht-see**oh**-nay
Is half-pension required?	*È obbligatoria la mezza pensione?*	eh oh-blee-gah-**toh**-reeah lah **mehd**-zah pehn-see**oh**-nay
Complete price?	*Prezzo completo?*	**prehd**-zoh kohm-**play**-toh
Is it cheaper for three-night stays?	*È più economico se mi fermo tre notti?*	eh pew ay-koh-**noh**-mee-koh say mee **fehr**-moh tray **noh**-tee
I will stay three nights.	*Mi fermo tre notti.*	mee **fehr**-moh tray **noh**-tee
We will stay three nights.	*Ci fermiamo tre notti.*	chee fehr-mee**ah**-moh tray **noh**-tee

SLEEPING

Is it cheaper if I pay in cash?	*È più economico se pago in contanti?*	eh pew ay-koh-**noh**-mee-koh say **pah**-goh een kohn-**tahn**-tee
What is the cost per week?	*Quanto costa a settimana?*	**kwahn**-toh koh-stah ah say-tee-**mah**-nah

Italian hotels almost always have larger rooms to fit three to six people. Your price per person plummets as you pack more into a room. Breakfasts are usually basic (coffee, rolls and marmalade) and expensive (about €6). They're often optional.

In resort towns, some hotels offer *mezza pensione* (half-pension), consisting of two meals per day served at the hotel: breakfast and your choice of lunch or dinner. The price for half-pension is often listed per person rather than per room. Hotels that offer half-pension often require it in summer. The meals are usually good, but if you want the freedom to forage for food, look for hotels that don't push half-pension.

Choosing a Room

Can I see the room?	*Posso vedere la camera?*	**poh**-soh vay-**day**-ray lah **kah**-may-rah
Can we see the room?	*Possiamo vedere la camera?*	poh-see**ah**-moh vay-**day**-ray lah **kah**-may-rah
Show me another room?	*Mi mostra un'altra camera?*	mee **moh**-strah oo-**nahl**-trah **kah**-may-rah
Show us another room?	*Ci mostra un'altra camera?*	chee **moh**-strah oo-**nahl**-trah **kah**-may-rah
Do you have something...?	*Avete qualcosa...?*	ah-**vay**-tay kwahl-**koh**-zah
...larger / smaller	*...più grande / più piccola*	pew **grahn**-day / pew **pee**-koh-lah
...better / cheaper	*...più bella / più economica*	pew **behl**-lah / pew ay-koh-**noh**-mee-kah
...brighter	*...più luminosa*	pew loo-mee-**noh**-zah
...in the back	*...al di dietro*	ahl dee dee**ay**-troh
...quieter	*...più tranquilla*	pew trahn-**kwee**-lah

Sorry, it's not right for me.	Mi dispiace, non mi va.	mee dee-spee**ah**-chay nohn mee vah
Sorry, it's not right for us.	Mi dispiace, non va per noi.	mee dee-spee**ah**-chay nohn vah pehr **noh**ee
I'll take it.	La prendo.	lah **prehn**-doh
We'll take it.	La prendiamo.	lah prehn-dee**ah**-moh
My key, please.	La mia chiave, per favore.	lah **mee**-ah kee**ah**-vay pehr fah-**voh**-ray
Sleep well.	Sogni d'oro.	**sohn**-yee **doh**-roh
Good night.	Buona notte.	**bwoh**-nah **noh**-tay

Breakfast

Is breakfast included?	La colazione è inclusa?	lah koh-laht-see**oh**-nay eh een-**kloo**-zah
How much is breakfast?	Quanto costa la colazione?	**kwahn**-toh **koh**-stah lah koh-laht-see**oh**-nay
When does breakfast start?	Quando comincia la colazione?	**kwahn**-doh koh-**meen**-chah lah koh-laht-see**oh**-nay
When does breakfast end?	Quando finisce la colazione?	**kwahn**-doh fee-**nee**-shay lah koh-laht-see**oh**-nay
Where is breakfast served?	Dove è servita la colazione?	**doh**-vay eh sehr-**vee**-tah lah koh-laht-see**oh**-nay

Hotel Help

I'd like...	Vorrei...	vor-**reh**ee
We'd like...	Vorremmo...	vor-**ray**-moh
...a / another...	...un / un altro...	oon / oon **ahl**-troh
...towel.	...asciugamano.	ah-shoo-gah-**mah**-noh
...a clean bath towel / clean bath towels.	...un asciugamano pulito / degli asciugamani puliti.	oon ah-shoo-gah-**mah**-noh poo-**lee**-toh / **day**-lee ah-shoo-gah-**mah**-nee poo-**lee**-tee
...pillow.	...cuscino.	koo-**shee**-noh
...clean sheets.	...lenzuola pulite.	lehnt-soo**oh**-lah poo-**lee**-tay
...blanket.	...coperta.	koh-**pehr**-tah

...glass.	...bicchiere.	bee-kee**ay**-ray
...sink stopper.	...tappo.	**tah**-poh
...soap.	...sapone.	sah-**poh**-nay
...toilet paper.	...carta igienica.	**kar**-tah ee-**jay**-nee-kah
...electrical adapter.	...adattatore elettrico.	ah-dah-tah-**toh**-ray ay-**leht**-ree-koh
...brighter light bulb.	...lampadina più potente.	lahm-pah-**dee**-nah pew poh-**tehn**-tay
...lamp.	...lampada.	lahm-**pah**-dah
...chair.	...sedia.	say-**dee**-ah
...table.	...tavolo.	**tah**-voh-loh
...Internet access.	...l'accesso a Internet.	lah-**chay**-soh ah **een**-tehr-neht
...different room.	...altra camera.	**ahl**-trah kah-**may**-rah
...silence.	...silenzio.	see-**lehnt**-seeoh
...to speak to the manager.	...parlare con il direttore.	par-**lah**-ray kohn eel dee-reht-**toh**-ray
I've fallen and I can't get up.	Sono caduto[a] e non riesco ad alzarmi.	**soh**-noh kah-**doo**-toh ay nohn reeay-skoh ahd ahlt-**sahr**-mee
How can I make the room cooler / warmer?	Come faccio a rinfrescare / riscaldare la camera?	**koh**-may **fah**-choh ah reen-frehs-**kah**-ray / rees-kahl-**dah**-ray lah **kah**-may-rah
Where can I...?	Dove posso...?	**doh**-vay **poh**-soh
...wash my laundry	...fare del bucato	**fah**-ray dayl boo-**kah**-toh
...hang my laundry	...stendere il bucato	**stehn**-day-ray eel boo-**kah**-toh
Is a full-service laundry nearby?	C'è una lavanderia qui vicino?	cheh **oo**-nah lah-vahn-deh-**ree**ah kwee vee-**chee**-noh
Is a self-service laundry nearby?	C'è una lavanderia automatica qui vicino?	cheh **oo**-nah lah-vahn-deh-**ree**ah ow-toh-**mah**-tee-kah kwee vee-**chee**-noh
I'd like to stay another night.	Vorrei fermarmi un'altra notte.	vor-**reh**ee fehr-**mar**-mee oo-**nahl**-trah **noh**-tay

We'd like to stay another night.	*Vorremmo fermarci un'altra notte.*	vor-**ray**-moh fehr-**mar**-chee oo-**nahl**-trah noh-tay
Where can I park?	*Dove posso parcheggiare?*	**doh**-vay poh-soh par-kay-**jah**-ray
When do you lock up?	*A che ora chiude?*	ah kay **oh**-rah kee**oo**-day
Please wake me at 7:00.	*Mi svegli alle sette, per favore.*	mee **zvayl**-yee **ah**-lay **seht**-tay pehr fah-**voh**-ray
Where do you go for lunch / dinner / coffee?	*Dove si va per il pranzo / la cena / il caffè?*	**doh**-vay see vah pehr eel **prahnt**-soh / lah **chay**-nah / eel kah-**fay**

Chill Out

Many hotel rooms in the Mediterranean part of Europe come with air-conditioning that you control—often with a stick (like a TV remote). Various sticks have basically the same features:

- fan icon (click to toggle through the wind power from light to gale)
- louver icon (click to choose: steady air flow or waves)
- snowflakes and sunshine icons (heat or cold, generally just one or the other is possible: cool in summer, heat in winter)
- two clock settings (to determine how many hours the air-conditioning will stay on before turning off, or stay off before turning on)
- temperature control (20 or 21 is a comfortable temperature in Celsius—see the thermometer on page 205)

Hotel Hassles

Come with me.	*Venga con me.*	**vayn**-gah kohn may
I have / We have a problem in the room.	*Ho / Abbiamo un problema con la camera.*	oh / ah-beeah-moh oon proh-**blay**-mah kohn lah **kah**-may-rah
bad odor	*cattivo odore*	kah-**tee**-voh oh-**doh**-ray

SLEEPING

SLEEPING

bugs	*insetti*	een-**seht**-tee
mice	*topi*	**toh**-pee
cockroaches	*scarafaggi*	skah-rah-**fah**-jee
prostitutes	*prostitute*	proh-stee-**too**-tay
I'm covered with bug bites.	*Sono pieno[a] di punture di insetti.*	**soh**-noh peeay-noh dee poon-**too**-ray dee een-**seht**-tee
The bed is too soft / hard.	*Il letto è troppo morbido / duro.*	eel **leht**-toh eh **troh**-poh **mor**-bee-doh / **doo**-roh
I can't sleep.	*Non riesco a dormire.*	nohn reeay-skoh ah dor-**mee**-ray
The room is too...	*La camera è troppo...*	lah **kah**-may-rah eh **troh**-poh
...hot / cold.	*...calda / fredda.*	**kahl**-dah / **fray**-dah
...noisy / dirty.	*...rumorosa / sporca.*	roo-moh-**roh**-zah / **spor**-kah
I can't open...	*Non riesco ad aprire...*	nohn reeay-skoh ahd ah-**pree**-ray
I can't shut...	*Non riesco a chiudere...*	nohn reeay-skoh ah keeoo-**day**-ray
...the door / the window.	*...la porta / la finestra.*	lah **por**-tah / lah fee-**nay**-strah
Air conditioner...	*Condiziona-tore...*	kohn-deet-see-oh-nah-**toh**-ray
Lamp...	*Lampada...*	lahm-**pah**-dah
Lightbulb...	*Lampadina...*	lahm-pah-**dee**-nah
Electrical outlet...	*Presa...*	**pray**-zah
Key...	*Chiave...*	kee**ah**-vay
Lock...	*Serratura...*	say-rah-**too**-rah
Window...	*Finestra...*	fee-**nay**-strah
Faucet...	*Rubinetto...*	roo-bee-**nay**-toh
Sink...	*Lavabo...*	**lah**-vah-boh
Toilet...	*Toilette...*	twah-**leht**-tay
Shower...	*Doccia...*	**doh**-chah
...doesn't work.	*...non funziona.*	nohn foont-see**oh**-nah
There is no hot water.	*Non c'è acqua calda.*	nohn cheh **ah**-kwah **kahl**-dah

| When is the water hot? | A che ora è calda l'acqua? | ah kay **oh**-rah eh **kahl**-dah **lah**-kwah |

Checking Out

When is check-out time?	A che ora devo lasciare la camera?	ah kay **oh**-rah **day**-voh lah-**shah**-ray lah **kah**-may-rah
I'll leave...	Parto...	**par**-toh
We'll leave...	Partiamo...	par-teeah-moh
...today / tomorrow.	...oggi / domani.	**oh**-jee / doh-**mah**-nee
...very early.	...molto presto.	**mohl**-toh **prehs**-toh
Can I pay now?	Posso pagare subito?	**poh**-soh pah-**gah**-ray **soo**-bee-toh
Can we pay now?	Possiamo pagare subito?	poh-see**ah**-moh pah-**gah**-ray **soo**-bee-toh
The bill, please.	Il conto, per favore.	eel **kohn**-toh pehr fah-**voh**-ray
Credit card O.K.?	Carta di credito è O.K.?	**kar**-tah dee **kray**-dee-toh eh "O.K."
Everything was great.	Tutto magnifico.	**too**-toh mahn-**yee**-fee-koh
I slept like a rock.	Ho dormito come un sasso.	oh dor-**mee**-toh **koh**-may oon **sah**-soh
Will you call my next hotel...?	Può chiamare il mio prossimo hotel...?	pwoh kee-**mah**-ray eel **mee**-oh **proh**-see-moh **oh**-tehl
...for tonight	...per stasera	pehr stah-**say**-rah
...to make a reservation	...per fare una prenotazione	pehr **fah**-ray **oo**-nah pray-noh-taht-see**oh**-nay
...to confirm a reservation	...per confermare una prenotazione	pehr kohn-fehr-**mah**-ray **oo**-nah pray-noh-taht-see**oh**-nay
I will pay for the call.	Pago la chiamata.	**pah**-goh lah keeah-**mah**-tah
Can I...?	Posso...?	**poh**-soh
Can we...?	Possiamo...?	poh-see**ah**-moh

| ...leave baggage here until ___ | ...lasciare il bagaglio qui fino a ___ | lah-**shah**-ray eel bah-**gahl**-yoh kwee **fee**-noh ah |

I never tip beyond the included service charges in hotels or for hotel services.

Camping

camping	campeggio	kahm-**pay**-joh
campsite	piazzuola	pee-ahd-**zwoh**-lah
tent	tenda	**tayn**-dah
The nearest campground?	Il campeggio più vicino?	eel kahm-**pay**-joh pew vee-**chee**-noh
Can I...?	Posso...?	**poh**-soh
Can we...?	Possiamo...?	poh-seeah-moh
...camp here for one night	...campeggiare qui per una notte	kahm-pay-**jah**-ray kwee pehr **oo**-nah **noh**-tay
Do showers cost extra?	Costano extra le docce?	koh-**stah**-noh **ehk**-strah lay **doh**-chay
shower token	gettone per la doccia	jeht-**toh**-nay pehr lah **doh**-chah

In some Italian campgrounds and youth hostels, you must buy a *gettone* (token) to activate a coin-operated hot shower. It has a timer inside, like a parking meter. To avoid a sudden cold rinse, buy at least two *gettoni* before getting undressed.

SLEEPING

EATING

RESTAURANTS

Types of Restaurants

Italian food is one of life's great pleasures. The Italians have an expression: "*A tavola non si invecchia*" (At the table, one does not age). Below is a guideline for restaurant types. Note that the first few names are sometimes interchangeable, and a *trattoria* can occasionally be more expensive than a *ristorante.* Always check the menu posted outside a restaurant to be sure.

Ristorante—A fine-dining establishment

Trattoria—Typically a family-owned place that serves home-cooked meals at moderate prices

Osteria—More informal, with large shared tables, good food, and wine

Pizzeria—A casual pizza joint that also offers pasta and more

Pizza Rustica—A cheap pizza shop that sells pizza by the weight or slice (often take-out only)

Rosticceria—A take-out or sit-down shop specializing in roasted meats

Tavola calda—Inexpensive hot/cold buffet-style restaurant

Bar—The neighborhood hangout that serves coffee, soft drinks, beer, liquor, snacks, and ready-made sandwiches

Enoteca—Wine shop or wine bar that also serves snacks

Freeflow—A self-serve cafeteria

Autogrill—Cafeteria and snack bar, found at freeway rest stops
   and often in city centers (Ciao is a popular chain)

Locanda—A countryside restaurant serving simple local
   specialties

Finding a Restaurant

Where's a good... restaurant nearby?	*Dov'è un buon ristorante... qui vicino?*	doh-**veh** oon bwohn ree-stoh-**rahn**-tay... kwee vee-**chee**-noh
...cheap	*...economico*	ay-koh-**noh**-mee-koh
...local-style	*...con cucina casereccia*	kohn koo-**chee**-nah kah-zay-**ray**-chah
...untouristy	*...non per turisti*	nohn pehr too-**ree**-stee
...vegetarian	*...vegetariano*	vay-jay-tah-ree**ah**-noh
...fast food (Italian-style)	*...tavola calda*	**tah**-voh-lah **kahl**-dah
...self-service buffet	*...self-service*	sehlf-**sehr**-vees
...Chinese	*...cinese*	chee-**nay**-zay
with terrace	*con terrazza*	kohn tay-**rahd**-zah
with a salad bar	*con un banco delle insalate*	kohn oon **bahn**-koh **dehl**-lay een-sah-**lah**-tay
with candles	*con candele*	kohn kahn-**day**-lay
romantic	*romantico*	roh-**mahn**-tee-koh
moderate price	*a buon mercato*	ah bwohn mer-**kah**-toh
to splurge	*fare sfoggio*	**fah**-ray **sfoh**-joh
Is it better than McDonald's?	*È migliore di McDonald's?*	eh meel-**yoh**-ray dee "McDonald's"

Getting a Table

What time does this open / close?	*A che ora apre / chiude?*	ah kay **oh**-rah **ah**-pray / kee**oo**-day
Are you open...?	*È aperto...?*	eh ah-**pehr**-toh
...today / tomorrow	*...oggi / domani*	**oh**-jee / doh-**mah**-nee
...for lunch / dinner	*...per pranzo / cena*	pehr **prahnt**-soh / **chay**-nah

Key Phrases: Restaurants

Where's a good restaurant nearby?	*Dov'è un buon ristorante qui vicino?*	doh-**veh** oon bwohn ree-stoh-**rahn**-tay kwee vee-**chee**-noh
I'd like...	*Vorrei...*	vor-**reh**ee
We'd like...	*Vorremmo...*	vor-**ray**-moh
...a table for one / two.	*...una tavola per uno / due.*	**oo**-nah **tah**-voh-lah pehr **oo**-noh / **doo**-ay
...inside / outside.	*...dentro / fuori.*	**dehn**-troh / **fwoh**-ree
...with a view.	*...con la vista.*	kohn lah **vee**-stah
Is this seat free?	*È libero questo posto?*	eh **lee**-bay-roh **kwehs**-toh **poh**-stoh
The menu (in English), please.	*Il menù (in inglese), per favore.*	eel may-**noo** (een een-**glay**-zay), pehr fah-**voh**-ray
Bill, please.	*Conto, per favore.*	**kohn**-toh pehr fah-**voh**-ray
Credit card O.K.?	*Carta di credito è O.K.?*	**kar**-tah dee **kray**-dee-toh eh "O.K."

Should I / we make reservations?	*Mi / Ci consiglia prenotare una tavola?*	mee / chee kohn-**seel**-yah pray-noh-**tah**-ray **oo**-nah **tah**-voh-lah
I'd like...	*Vorrei...*	vor-**reh**ee
We'd like...	*Vorremmo...*	vor-**ray**-moh
...a table for one / two.	*...una tavola per uno / due.*	**oo**-nah **tah**-voh-lah pehr **oo**-noh / **doo**-ay
...to reserve a table for two people...	*...prenotare un tavola per due persone...*	pray-noh-**tah**-ray oon **tah**-voh-lah pehr **doo**-ay pehr-**soh**-nay
...for today / tomorrow	*...per oggi / domani*	pehr **oh**-jee / doh-**mah**-nee
...at 8:00 P.M.	*...alle venti*	**ah**-lay **vayn**-tee
My name is ___.	*Mi chiamo ___.*	mee kee**ah**-moh

EATING

I have a reservation for ___ people.	Ho una prenotazione per ___ persone.	oh **oo**-nah pray-noh-taht-see**oh**-nay pehr ___ pehr-**soh**-nay
I'd like to sit...	Vorrei sedermi...	vor-**reh**ee say-**dehr**-mee
We'd like to sit...	Vorremmo sederci...	vor-**ray**-moh say-**dehr**-chee
...inside / outside.	...dentro / fuori.	**dehn**-troh / **fwoh**-ree
...by the window.	...vicino alla finestra.	vee-**chee**-noh **ah**-lah fee-**nay**-strah
...with a view.	...con la vista.	kohn lah **vee**-stah
...where it's quiet.	...a una tavola tranquilla.	ah oo-nah **tah**-voh-lah trahn-**kee**-lah
Is this table free?	È libero questa tavola?	eh **lee**-behr-oh **kwehs**-tah **tah**-voh-lah
Can I sit here?	Posso sedermi qui?	**poh**-soh say-**dehr**-mee kwee
Can we sit here?	Possiamo sederci qui?	poh-see**ah**-moh say-**dehr**-chee kwee

Better restaurants routinely take telephone reservations. Guidebooks include phone numbers, and the process is simple. If you want to eat at a normal European dinnertime (later than 7:30 P.M.), it's smart to call and reserve a table. Many of my favorite restaurants are filled with Americans at 7:30 P.M. and can feel like tourist traps. But if you drop in at (or reserve ahead for) 8:30 or 9:00 P.M., when the Italians are eating, they feel completely local.

The Menu

menu	menù	may-**noo**
tourist *menù* (fixed-price meal)	menù turistico	may-**noo** too-**ree**-stee-koh
menu of the day	menù del giorno	may-**noo** dayl **jor**-noh
specialty of the house	specialità della casa	spay-chah-lee-**tah** **dehl**-lah **kah**-zah
breakfast	colazione	koh-laht-see**oh**-nay
lunch	pranzo	**prahnt**-soh

dinner	cena	**chay**-nah
appetizers	antipasti	ahn-tee-**pah**-stee
sandwiches	panini	pah-**nee**-nee
bread	pane	**pah**-nay
salad	insalata	een-sah-**lah**-tah
soup	minestra, zuppa	mee-**nehs**-trah, **tsoo**-pah
first course (pasta, soup)	primo piatto	**pree**-moh pee**ah**-toh
main course (meat, fish)	secondo piatto	say-**kohn**-doh pee**ah**-toh
side dishes	contorni	kohn-**tor**-nee
meat	carni	**kar**-nee
poultry	pollame	poh-**lah**-may
fish	pesce	**peh**-shay
seafood	frutti di mare	**froo**-tee dee **mah**-ray
vegetables	legumi	lay-**goo**-mee
cheeses	formaggi	for-**mah**-jee
desserts	dolci	**dohl**-chee
munchies (tapas)	spuntini	spoon-**tee**-nee
beverages	bevande, bibite	bay-**vahn**-day, **bee**-bee-tay
beer	birra	**beer**-rah
wines	vini	**vee**-nee
cover charge	coperto	koh-**pehr**-toh
service included	servizio incluso	sehr-**veet**-seeoh een-**kloo**-zoh
service not included	servizio non incluso	sehr-**veet**-seeoh nohn een-**kloo**-zoh
hot / cold	caldo / freddo	**kahl**-doh / **fray**-doh
with / and / or / without	con / e / o / senza	kohn / ay / oh / **sehnt**-sah

EATING

Pay attention to the money-saving words in this chapter. Without them, Italy is a very expensive place to eat. Budget eaters do best in places with no or minimal service and cover charges, and by sticking to the *primo piatto* (first course dishes). A hearty minestrone and/or pasta fills the average American. Pricier restaurants are wise to this, and some don't allow you to eat without ordering the more expensive *secondo* course (note that secondo courses often consist of just the entrée listed, without any vegetables). Usually a good deal, a *menù del giorno* (menu of the day) offers you a choice of appetizer, entrée, and dessert (plus sometimes wine or mineral water) at a fixed price.

Ordering

waiter	cameriere	kah-may-ree**ay**-ray
waitress	cameriera	kah-may-ree**ay**-rah
I'm ready / We're ready to order.	Sono pronto / Siamo pronti per ordinare.	**soh**-noh **prohn**-toh / see**ah**-moh **prohn**-tee pehr or-dee-**nah**-ray
I'd like / We'd like...	Vorrei / Vorremmo...	vor-**reh**ee / vor-**ray**-moh
...just a drink.	...soltanto qualcosa da bere.	sohl-**tahn**-toh kwahl-**koh**-zah dah **bay**-ray
...a snack.	...uno spuntino.	**oon**-oh spoon-**tee**-noh
...just a salad.	...solo un'insalata.	**soh**-loh oon-een-sah-**lah**-tah
...a half portion.	...una mezza porzione.	**oo**-nah **mehd**-zah port-see**oh**-nay
...only a pasta dish.	...solo un primo piatto.	**soh**-loh oon **pree**-moh pee**ah**-toh
...a tourist *menù*. (fixed-price meal)	...un menù turistico.	oon may-**noo** too-**ree**-stee-koh
...to see the menu.	...vedere il menù.	vay-**day**-ray eel may-**noo**
...to order.	...ordinare.	or-dee-**nah**-ray
...to pay.	...pagare.	pah-**gah**-ray
...to throw up.	...vomitare.	voh-mee-**tah**-ray
Do you have...?	Avete...?	ah-**vay**-tay
...a menu in English	...un menù in inglese	oon may-**noo** een een-**glay**-zay
...a lunch special	...un piatto speciale per il pranzo	oon pee**ah**-toh spay-chee**ah**-lay pehr eel **prahnt**-soh

EATING

What do you recommend?	*Che cosa raccomanda?*	kay **koh**-zah rah-koh-**mahn**-dah
What's your favorite dish?	*Qual'è il suo piatto preferito?*	kwah-**leh** eel **soo**-oh peeah-toh preh-feh-**ree**-toh
Is it...?	*È...?*	eh
...good	*...buono*	**bwoh**-noh
...expensive	*...caro*	**kah**-roh
...light	*...leggero*	lay-**jay**-roh
...filling	*...sostanzioso*	soh-stahnt-see**oh**-zoh
What is that?	*Che cosa è quello?*	kay **koh**-zah eh **kway**-loh
What is...?	*Che cosa c'è...?*	kay **koh**-zah cheh
...local	*...di locale*	dee loh-**kah**-lay
...fresh	*...di fresco*	dee **fray**-skoh
...cheap and filling	*...di economico e sostanzioso*	dee ay-koh-**noh**-mee-koh ay soh-stahnt-see**oh**-zoh
...fast	*...di veloce*	dee vay-**loh**-chay
Can we split this and have an extra plate?	*Possiamo dividerlo e avere un altro piatto?*	poh-see**ah**-moh dee-vee-**dehr**-loh ay ah-**vay**-ray oon **ahl**-troh pee**ah**-toh
I've changed my mind.	*Ho cambiato idea.*	oh kahm-bee**ah**-toh ee-**day**-ah
Nothing with eyeballs.	*Niente con gli occhi.*	nee**ehn**-tay kohn lyee **oh**-kee
Can I substitute (something) for the ___?	*Posso sostituire (qualcosa d'altro) per il ___?*	**poh**-soh soh-stee-**twee**-ray (kwahl-**koh**-zah **dahl**-troh) pehr eel
Can I / Can we get it "to go"?	*Posso / Possiamo averlo da portar via?*	**poh**-soh / poh-see**ah**-moh ah-**vehr**-loh dah **por**-tar **vee**-ah
"To go"?	*Da portar via?* ("for the road")	dah **por**-tar **vee**-ah

To summon a waiter, ask "*Per favore?*" (Please?). The waiter brings a menu (*menù*) and asks what you'd like to drink (*Da bere?*). When ready

to take your order, the waiter will ask, *"Prego?"* He'll often expect you
to order multiple courses (he'll ask *"E dopo?"*—"And then?"), but it's
O.K. to just get one course—just say *"È tutto."* (That's all). When you're
finished, place your utensils on your plate with the handles pointing to
your right as the Italians do. This tells the waiter you're done. He'll
confirm by asking if you're finished (*Finito?*). He'll usually ask if you'd
like dessert (*Qualcosa di dolce?*) and coffee (*Un caffè?*), and if you want
anything else (*Altro?*). You ask for the bill: *"Il conto, per favore."*

Tableware and Condiments

plate	*piatto*	pee**ah**-toh
extra plate	*un altro piatto*	oon **ahl**-troh pee**ah**-toh
napkin	*tovagliolo*	toh-vahl-**yoh**-loh
silverware	*posate*	poh-**zah**-tay
knife	*coltello*	kohl-**tehl**-loh
fork	*forchetta*	for-**kay**-tah
spoon	*cucchiaio*	koo-keeah-yoh
cup	*tazza*	**tahd**-zah
glass	*bicchiere*	bee-keeay-ray
carafe	*caraffa*	kah-**rah**-fah
water	*acqua*	**ah**-kwah
bread	*pane*	**pah**-nay
breadsticks	*grissini*	gree-**see**-nee
butter	*burro*	**boo**-roh
margarine	*margarina*	mar-gah-**ree**-nah
salt / pepper	*sale / pepe*	**sah**-lay / **pay**-pay
sugar	*zucchero*	**tsoo**-kay-roh
artificial sweetener	*dolcificante*	dohl-chee-fee-**kahn**-tay
honey	*miele*	meeay-lay
mustard	*senape*	**say**-nah-pay
ketchup	*ketchup*	"ketchup"
mayonnaise	*maionese*	mah-yoh-**nay**-zay
toothpick	*stuzzicadente*	stood-see-kah-**dehn**-tay

The Food Arrives

Is this included with the meal?	*È incluso nel pasto questo?*	eh een-**kloo**-zoh nayl **pah**-stoh **kweh**-stoh

I did not order this.	*Io questo non l'ho ordinato.*	**ee**oh **kweh**-stoh nohn loh or-dee-**nah**-toh
We did not order this.	*Noi questo non l'abbiamo ordinato.*	**noh**ee **kweh**-stoh nohn lah-beeah-moh or-dee-**nah**-toh
Heat it up?	*Lo può scaldare?*	loh pwoh skahl-**dah**-ray
A little.	*Un po'.*	oon poh
More. / Another.	*Un altro po'. / Un altro.*	oon **ahl**-troh poh / oon **ahl**-troh
The same.	*Lo stesso.*	loh **stehs**-soh
Enough.	*Basta.*	**bah**-stah
Finished.	*Finito.*	fee-**nee**-toh
I'm full.	*Sono sazio.*	soh-noh **saht**-seeoh

After bringing your meal, your server might wish you a cheery *"**Buon appetito!**"* (pronounced *bwohn ah-pay-tee-toh*).

Complaints

This is...	*Questo è...*	**kweh**-stoh eh
...dirty.	*...sporco.*	**spor**-koh
...greasy.	*...grasso.*	**grah**-soh
...too salty.	*...troppo salato.*	**troh**-poh sah-**lah**-toh
...undercooked.	*...troppo crudo.*	**troh**-poh **kroo**-doh
...overcooked.	*...troppo cotto.*	**troh**-poh **koh**-toh
...inedible.	*...immangiabile.*	eem-mahn-**jah**-bee-lay
...cold.	*...freddo.*	**fray**-doh
Do any of your customers return?	*Ritornano i vostri clienti?*	ree-**tor**-nah-noh ee **voh**-stree klee-**ehn**-tee
Yuck!	*Che schifo!*	kay **skee**-foh

Compliments to the Chef

Yummy!	*Buono!*	**bwoh**-noh
Delicious!	*Delizioso!*	day-leet-see**oh**-zoh
Divinely good!	*Una vera bontà!*	**oo**-nah **vay**-rah bohn-**tah**
My compliments to the chef!	*Complimenti al cuoco!*	kohm-plee-**mayn**-tee ahl koo**oh**-koh

EATING

I love Italian food / this food.	Adoro la cucina italiana / questo piatto.	ah-**doh**-roh lah koo-**chee**-nah ee-tah-lee-**ah**-nah / **kwehs**-toh pee**ah**-toh
Better than mom's cooking.	Meglio della cucina di mia mamma.	mehl-yoh dehl-lah koo-**chee**-nah dee **mee**-ah **mah**-mah

Paying for Your Meal

The bill, please.	Il conto, per favore.	eel **kohn**-toh pehr fah-**voh**-ray
Together.	Conto unico.	**kohn**-toh oo-nee-koh
Separate.	Conto separato.	**kohn**-toh say-pah-**rah**-toh
Credit card O.K.?	Carta di credito è O.K.?	**kar**-tah dee **kray**-dee-toh eh "O.K."
Is there a cover charge?	Si paga per il coperto?	see **pah**-gah pehr eel koh-**pehr**-toh
Is service included?	È incluso il servizio?	eh een-**kloo**-zoh eel sehr-**veet**-seeoh
This is not correct.	Questo non è giusto.	**kweh**-stoh nohn eh **joo**-stoh
Explain it?	Lo può spiegare?	loh pwoh speeay-**gah**-ray
Can you explain / itemize the bill?	Può spiegare / dettagliare il conto?	pwoh speeay-**gah**-ray / day-tahl-**yah**-ray eel **kohn**-toh
What if I wash the dishes?	E se lavassi i piatti?	ay say lah-**vah**-see ee pee**ah**-tee
Is tipping expected?	Bisogna lasciare una mancia?	bee-**sohn**-yah lah-**shah**-ray **oo**-nah **mahn**-chah
What percent?	Che percentuale?	kay pehr-chehn-too**ah**-lay
tip	mancia	**mahn**-chah
Keep the change.	Tenga il resto.	**tayn**-gah eel **rehs**-toh
This is for you.	Questo è per lei.	**kweh**-stoh eh pehr **leh**ee
Could I have a receipt, please?	Posso avere una ricevuta, per favore?	**poh**-soh ah-**vay**-ray **oo**-nah ree-chay-**voo**-tah pehr fah-**voh**-ray

EATING

Most menus list the *coperto* (cover charge) and *servizio* (service) charge. There's no need to tip beyond that, but if you're happy with the service, toss in a euro per person. If there's no service charge, consider tipping 5 to 10 percent.

If you're uncertain whether to tip, ask another customer if tipping is expected (*Bisogna lasciare una mancia?*).

In Italian bars and freeway rest stops, pay first at the *cassa* (cash register), then take your receipt to the counter to get your food. There's no need to tip.

SPECIAL CONCERNS

In a Hurry

I'm / We're in a hurry.	Sono / Siamo di fretta.	**soh**-noh / seeah-moh dee **fray**-tah
I need to be served quickly. Is that a problem?	Ho bisogno di essere servito[a] rapidamente. È un problema?	oh bee-**zohn**-yoh dee eh-**say**-ray sehr-**vee**-toh rah-pee-dah-**mehn**-tay eh oon proh-**blay**-mah
We need to be served quickly. Is that a problem?	Avremmo bisogno di essere serviti rapidamente. È un problema?	ah-**vray**-moh bee-**zohn**-yoh dee eh-**say**-ray sehr-**vee**-tee rah-pee-dah-**mehn**-tay eh oon proh-**blay**-mah
I must / We must leave in a half hour / one hour.	Devo / Dobbiamo andarcene tra mezz'ora / un'ora.	**day**-voh / doh-beeah-moh ahn-dar-**chay**-nay trah med-**zoh**-rah / oo-**noh**-rah
When will the food be ready?	Tra quanto è pronto il cibo?	trah **kwahn**-toh eh **prohn**-toh eel **chee**-boh

Dietary Restrictions

I'm allergic to...	Sono allergico[a] al...	**soh**-noh ahl-**lehr**-jee-koh ahl
I cannot / He cannot / She cannot eat...	Non posso / Lui non può / Lei non può mangiare...	nohn **poh**-soh / lwee nohn pwoh / **leh**ee nohn pwoh mahn-**jah**-ray

EATING

...dairy products.	...latticini.	lah-tee-**chee**-nee
...wheat.	...frumento.	froo-**mehn**-toh
...meat / pork.	...carne / maiale.	**kar**-nay / mah-**yah**-lay
...salt / sugar.	...sale / zucchero.	**sah**-lay / **tsoo**-kay-roh
...shellfish.	...molluschi e	moh-**loos**-kee ay
	crostacei.	kroh-**stah**-chayee
...spicy foods.	...cibo piccante.	**chee**-boh pee-**kahn**-tay
...nuts.	...noci e altra	**noh**-chee ay **ahl**-trah
	frutta secca.	**froo**-tah **say**-kah
I am diabetic.	Ho il diabete.	oh eel deeah-**bay**-tay
I'd like /	Vorrei /	vor-**reh**ee /
We'd like a...	Vorremmo un...	vor-**ray**-moh oon
...light meal.	...pasto a basso	**pah**-stoh ah bah-**soh**
	contenuto	kohn-tay-**noo**-toh
	calorico.	kah-**loh**-ree-koh
...kosher meal.	...pasto kasher.	**pah**-stoh kah-shehr
No salt / sugar.	Senza sale /	**sehnt**-sah **sah**-lay /
	zucchero.	**tsoo**-kay-roh
I eat only insects.	Mangio solo	**mahn**-joh **soh**-loh
	insetti.	een-**seht**-tee
No fat.	Senza grassi.	**sehnt**-sah **grah**-see
Minimal fat.	Pochi grassi.	**poh**-kee **grah**-see
Low cholesterol.	Basso	**bah**-soh
	colesterolo.	koh-lay-stay-**roh**-loh
No caffeine.	Senza caffeina.	**sehnt**-sah kah-fay**ee**-nah
No alcohol.	Niente alcool.	nee**ehn**-tay **ahl**-kohl
Organic.	Biologico.	bee-oh-**loo**-jee-koh
I'm a...	Sono un...	**soh**-noh oon
...vegetarian.	...vegetariano[a].	vay-jay-tah-ree**ah**-noh
...strict vegetarian.	...strettamente	stray-tah-**mayn**-tay
	vegetariano[a].	vay-jay-tah-ree**ah**-noh
...carnivore.	...carnivoro[a].	kar-**nee**-voh-roh
...big eater.	...mangione.	mahn-jee**oh**-nay
Is any meat or	Contiene carne	kohn-tee**ay**-nay **kar**-nay
animal fat used	o grassi	oh **grah**-see
in this?	animali?	ah-nee-**mah**-lee

Children

Do you have...?	*Avete...?*	ah-**vay**-tay
...a children's portion	*...un platto per i bambini*	oon peeah-toh pehr ee bahm-**bee**-nee
...a half portion	*...una mezza porzione*	**oo**-nah **mehd**-zah port-see**oh**-nay
...a high chair / booster seat	*...un seggiolone / seggiolino*	oon seh-joh-**loh**-nay / seh-joh-**lee**-noh
plain noodles	*della pasta in bianco*	**dehl**-lah **pah**-stah een bee**ahn**-koh
plain rice	*del riso in bianco*	dehl **ree**-zoh een bee**ahn**-koh
with butter	*con il burro*	kohn eel **boo**-roh
no sauce	*senza sugo*	**sehnt**-sah **soo**-goh
with sauce / dressing on the side	*con il sugo / il condimento a parte*	kohn eel **soo**-goh / eel kohn-dee-**mehn**-toh ah **par**-tay
pizza	*pizza*	**peed**-zah
...cheese only	*...Margherita*	mar-gehr-**ee**-tah
...pepperoni and cheese	*...diavolo*	dee**ah**-voh-loh
cheese sandwich...	*un panino... al formaggio*	oon pah-**nee**-noh... ahl for-**mah**-joh
...toasted	*...scaldato*	skahl-**dah**-toh
hot dog	*wurstel*	**woor**-stehl
hamburger	*hamburger*	**ahm**-boor-ger
cheeseburger	*hamburger con formaggi*	**ahm**-boor-ger kohn for-**mah**-jee
French fries	*patate fritte*	pah-**tah**-tay **free**-tay
ketchup	*ketchup*	"ketchup"
crackers	*crackers*	"crackers"
Nothing spicy.	*Niente di piccante.*	nee**ehn**-tay dee pee-**kahn**-tay
Not too hot.	*Non troppo caldo.*	nohn **troh**-poh **kahl**-doh
Please keep the food separate on the plate.	*Per favore tenete separato il cibo nel piatto.*	pehr fah-**voh**-ray tay-**nay**-tay say-pah-**rah**-toh eel **chee**-boh nehl pee**ah**-toh

He / She will share our meal.	*Lui / Lei mangia parte del nostro pasto.*	lwee / **leh**ee **mahn**-jah **par**-tay dehl **noh**-stroh **pah**-stoh
They will share our meal.	*Loro mangiano parte del nostro pasto.*	**loh**-roh mahn-**jah**-noh **par**-tay dehl **noh**-stroh **pah**-stoh
Please bring the food quickly.	*Per favore ci porti da mangiare velocemente.*	pehr fah-**voh**-ray chee **por**-tee dah mahn-**jah**-ray vay-loh-chay-**mehn**-tay
Can I / Can we have an extra...?	*Potrei / Potremmo avere un altro...*	poh-**tray**ee / poh-**tray**-moh ah-**vay**-ray oon **ahl**-troh
...plate	*...piatto*	peeah-toh
...cup	*...tazza*	**tahd**-zah
...spoon / fork	*...cucchiaio / forchetta*	koo-keeah-yoh / for-**kay**-tah
Can I / Can we have two extra...?	*Potrei / Potremmo avere altri due...?*	poh-**tray**ee / poh-**tray**-moh ah-**vay**-ray **ahl**-tree **doo**-ay
...plates	*...piatti*	peeah-tee
...cups	*...tazze*	**tahd**-zay
...spoons / forks	*...cucchiai / forchette*	koo-keeah-ee / for-**kay**-tay
Small milk (in a plastic cup).	*Un po di latte (in una tazza di plastica).*	oon poh dee **lah**-tay (een **oo**-nah **tahd**-zah dee **plah**-stee-kah)
straw / straws	*cannuccia / cannucce*	kah-**noo**-chah / kah-**noo**-chay
More napkins, please.	*Degli altri tovaglioli, per favore.*	**day**-lee **ahl**-tree toh-vahl-**yoh**-lee pehr fah-**voh**-ray
Sorry for the mess.	*Scusi per il pasticcio.*	**skoo**-zee pehr eel pah-**stee**-choh

Don't expect to find peanut butter sandwiches in Italy. Italian kids would rather have a sandwich with Nutella (*un panino con la Nutella*), the popular chocolate-hazelnut spread.

WHAT'S COOKING?

Breakfast

breakfast	*colazione*	koh-laht-see**oh**-nay
bread	*pane*	**pah**-nay
roll	*brioche*	bree-**ohsh**
croissant	*cornetto*	kor-**nay**-toh
toast	*toast*	"toast"
butter	*burro*	**boo**-roh
jam	*marmellata*	mar-mehl-**lah**-tah
jelly	*gelatina*	jay-lah-**tee**-nah
milk	*latte*	**lah**-tay
coffee / tea	*caffè / tè*	kah-**feh** / teh
(see Drinking)		
Is breakfast included?	*La colazione è inclusa?*	lah koh-laht-see**oh**-nay eh een-**kloo**-zah

---

Key Phrases: What's Cooking?

food	*cibo*	**chee**-boh
breakfast	*colazione*	koh-laht-see**oh**-nay
lunch	*pranzo*	**prahnt**-soh
dinner	*cena*	**chay**-nah
bread	*pane*	**pah**-nay
cheese	*formaggio*	for-**mah**-joh
soup	*minestra, zuppa*	mee-**nehs**-trah, **tsoo**-pah
salad	*insalata*	een-sah-**lah**-tah
meat	*carni*	**kar**-nee
chicken	*pollo*	**poh**-loh
fish	*pesce*	**peh**-shay
fruit	*frutta*	**froo**-tah
vegetables	*legumi*	lay-**goo**-mee
dessert	*dolci*	**dohl**-chee
Delicious!	*Delizioso!*	day-leet-see**oh**-zoh

What's Probably Not For Breakfast

omelet	omelette, frittata	oh-may-**leht**-tay, free-**tah**-tah
eggs...	uova...	**woh**-vah
...fried	...fritte	**free**-tay
...scrambled	...strapazzate	strah-pahd-**zah**-tay
boiled egg...	uovo alla coque...	**who**-voh **ah**-lah kohk
...soft / hard	...molle / sodo	**moh**-lay / **soh**-doh
ham	prosciutto cotto	proh-**shoo**-toh **koh**-toh
cheese	formaggio	for-**mah**-joh
yogurt	yogurt	**yoh**-goort
cereal	cereali	chay-ray-**ah**-lee
pastry	pasticcini	pah-stee-**chee**-nee
fruit juice	succo di frutta	**soo**-koh dee **froo**-tah
fresh orange juice	spremuta di arancia	spray-**moo**-tah dee ah-**rahn**-chah
hot chocolate	cioccolata calda	choh-koh-**lah**-tah **kahl**-dah

Italian breakfasts, like Italian bath towels, are small: coffee and a roll with butter and marmalade. The strong coffee is often mixed about half-and-half with milk. At your hotel, refills are usually free. The delicious red orange juice is made from Sicilian blood oranges (*arancia tarocco*). Local open-air markets thrive in the morning, and a picnic breakfast followed by a *cappuccino* in a bar is a good option.

Appetizers

antipasto misto	ahn-tee-**pah**-stoh **mee**-stoh	salami and marinated vegetables
bruschetta	broo-**skay**-tah	toast brushed w/ olive oil and garlic or chopped tomatoes
carciofi alla Giudia / Romana	kar-**choh**-fee **ah**-lah **joo**-dah / roh-**mah**-nah	artichokes—deep-fried (Jewish style) or stuffed with garlic, mint, and parsley (Roman style)

EATING

carpaccio	kar-**pah**-choh	thinly sliced air-cured beef served with olive oil, lemon, and parmesan
crostini	kroh-**stee**-nee	toast topped with liver pates and other pastes
frittata con le erbe	free-**tah**-tah kohn lay **ehr**-bay	egg scrambled with fresh herbs, then pan-fried
prosciutto e melone / fichi	proh-**shoo**-toh ay may-**loh**-nay / **fee**-kee	air-cured ham wrapped around melon / fresh figs
sarde in saor	**sar**-day een **sah**or	sardines marinated with onions
salumi misti	sah-**loo**-mee **mee**-stee	assortment of sliced, cured meats
spizziccare	speed-zee-**kah**-ray	snack
vitello tonato	vee-**tehl**-loh toh-**nah**-toh	thin-sliced roasted veal w/ tuna-caper mayonnaise

Pizza and Quick Meals

For fresh, fast, and frugal pizza, *pizza rustica* shops offer the cheapest hot meal in any Italian town, selling pizza by the slice (*pezzo*) or weight (*etto*=100 grams, around a quarter pound). *Due etti* (200 grams) makes a good light lunch. You can always get it to go (*"Da portar via"*—for the road), or, if there are seats, you can eat it on the spot. For handier pizza, nearly any bar has lousy, microwavable pizza snacks. To get cold pizza warmed up, say, *"Calda, per favore"* (Hot, please). To get an extra plate, ask for *"Un altro piatto."* Here are some pizza words:

acciughe	ah-**choo**-gay	anchovies
alla diavola	**ah**-lah deeah-**voh**-lah	spicy
bianca, ciaccina	bee**ahn**-kah, chah-**chee**-nah	"white" pizza (no tomato sauce)
calzone	kahlt-**soh**-nay	folded pizza with various fillings
capricciosa	kah-pree-**choh**-zah	means "chef's choice"– usually ham, mushrooms, olives, and artichokes

EATING

carciofi	kar-**choh**-fee	artichokes
funghi	**foong**-gee	mushrooms
Margherita	mar-gehr-**ee**-tah	cheese and tomato sauce
melanzane	may-lahnt-**sah**-nay	eggplant
Napoletana	nah-poh-lay-**tah**-nah	cheese, anchovies, and tomato sauce
peperoni	pay-pehr-**oh**-nee	green or red peppers (not sausage!)
porcini	pohr-**chee**-nee	porcini mushrooms
prosciutto	proh-**shoo**-toh	ham
quattro stagioni	**kwah**-troh stah-jee**oh**-nee	four toppings on separate quarters of a pizza
ripieno	ree-peeay-noh	stuffed
salame piccante	sah-**lah**-may pee-**kahn**-tay	pepperoni
salsiccia	sahl-**see**-chah	sausage
Siciliana	see-chee-leeah-nah	capers and olives
vegetariana, ortolana	vay-jay-tah-reeah-nah or-toh-**lah**-nah	veggie

For other quick, tasty meals, drop by a *rosticceria* deli, where you'll find a cafeteria-style display of reasonably priced food. Get it "to go" or grab a seat and eat.

Say Cheese

cheese	*formaggio*	for-**mah**-joh
fresh, mild, and soft	*fresco*	**fray**-skoh
aged, sharp, and hard	*stagionato*	stah-joh-**nah**-toh
cheese plate	*piatto di formaggi misti*	peeah-toh dee for-**mah**-jee mee-stee
Can I try a taste?	*Posso avere un'assagio?*	**poh**-soh ah-**vay**-ray oo-nah-**sah**-joh

Italian Cheeses

asiago	ah-zee**ah**-goh	hard, sharp, aged cow's milk cheese
di capra	dee **kah**-prah	goat cheese
fontina	fohn-**tee**-nah	creamy, nutty, gruyere-style cheese
gorgonzola	gor-gohnt-**sohl**-lah	blue-veined cheese, either creamy (dolce) or aged and hard
mascarpone	mahs-kar-**poh**-nay	sweet, buttery dessert cheese
mozzarella	mohd-zah-**rehl**-lah	handmade cheese from water buffalo
bocconcini	boh-kohn-**chee**-nee	small balls of mozzarella
parmigiano	par-mee-**jah**-noh	Parmesan cheese
pecorino	pay-koh-**ree**-noh	sheep's milk cheese, soft and mild or aged and sharp
provolone	proh-voh-**loh**-nay	rich, firm, aged cow's milk cheese
ricotta	ree-**koht**-tah	soft, airy cheese made from whey
stracchino	strah-**kee**-noh	spreadable, soft cow's milk cheese
taleggio	tah-**lay**-joh	rich, creamy cheese

If ordering *gorgonzola* or *pecorino* cheese, specify if you'd like it *fresco* (soft and mild) or *stagionato* (hard and sharp).

Sandwiches

I'd like a sandwich.	*Vorrei un panino.*	vor-**reh**ee oon pah-**nee**-noh
We'd like two sandwiches.	*Vorremmo due panini.*	vor-**ray**-moh doo-ay pah-**nee**-nee
small sandwiches	*tramezzini*	trah-mehd-**zee**-nee
toasted ham and cheese	*toast*	"toast"

toasted	tostato	toh-**stah**-toh
cheese	formaggio	for-**mah**-joh
chicken	pollo	**poh**-loh
egg salad	insalata	een-sah-**lah**-tah
	con uova	kohn **woh**-vah
fish	pesce	**peh**-shay
ham	prosciutto	proh-**shoo**-toh
pork	porchetta	por-**kay**-tah
salami	salame	sah-**lah**-may
tuna	tonno	**toh**-noh
turkey	tacchino	tah-**kee**-noh
lettuce	lattuga	lah-**too**-gah
mayonnaise	maionese	mah-yoh-**nay**-zay
tomatoes	pomodori	poh-moh-**doh**-ree
mustard	senape	**say**-nah-pay
ketchup	ketchup	"ketchup"
onions	cipolle	chee-**poh**-lay
Does this come	Si mangia	see **mahn**-jah
cold or warm?	freddo o caldo?	**fray**-doh oh **kahl**-doh
Heated, please.	Caldo, per favore.	**kahl**-doh pehr fah-**voh**-ray

Many bars sell small, ready-made sandwiches called *tramezzini*. These crustless white bread sandwiches, displayed behind glass, come with a variety of fillings (such as shrimp) mixed with a mayonnaise dressing. Two or three make a fast, easy meal. *Panini*, made from heartier bread with meat, cheese, and veggie combinations, can be delicious toasted. Say, *"Calda, per favore"* (Heated, please). Prices are usually posted. Pay the cashier for the sandwich and your beverage, then give your receipt to the person behind the bar to get your food.

In central Italy, *porchetta* stands serve tasty rolls stuffed with slices of roasted suckling pig.

If You Knead Bread

bread	pane	**pah**-nay
whole-grain bread	pane	**pah**-nay
	integrale	een-tay-**grah**-lay

EATING

olive bread	pane di olive	**pah**-nay dee oh-**lee**-vay
rye bread	pane di segale	**pah**-nay dee say-**gah**-lay
brown bread	pane scuro	**pah**-nay **skoo**-roh
Tuscan bread (unsalted)	pane Toscano	**pah**-nay toh-**skah**-noh
breadsticks	grissini	gree-**see**-nee

Every region of Italy has its own bread, highly prized by the locals. We say "good as gold," but the Italians say, "good as bread."

Bread Specialties

focaccia	foh-**kah**-chah	thick Ligurian flatbread, baked plain or with rosemary, onion, or cheese
piadina	peeah-**dee**-nah	soft, flat bread stuffed with various vegetables, meat, and cheese
schiacciata	skah-**chah**-tah	pizza-like flatbread sprinkled w/ oil and salt

Soups and Salads

soup	minestra, zuppa	mee-**nehs**-trah, **tsoo**-pah
soup of the day	zuppa del giorno	**tsoo**-pah dayl **jor**-noh
broth...	brodo...	**broh**-doh
...chicken	...di pollo	dee **poh**-loh
...beef	...di carne	dee **kar**-nay
...vegetable	...di verdura	dee vehr-**doo**-rah
...with noodles	...con pastina	kohn pah-**stee**-nah
...with rice	...con riso	kohn **ree**-zoh
vegetable soup	minestrone	mee-nay-**stroh**-nay
salad...	insalata...	een-sah-**lah**-tah
...green	...verde	**vehr**-day
...mixed	...mista	**mee**-stah
...with ham and cheese	...con prosciutto e formaggio	kohn proh-**shoo**-toh ay for-**mah**-joh
...with egg	...con uova	kohn **woh**-vah

EATING

lettuce	lattuga	lah-**too**-gah
tomatoes	pomodori	poh-moh-**doh**-ree
onion	cipolla	chee-**poh**-lah
cucumbers	cetrioli	chay-tree**oh**-lee
oil / vinegar	olio / aceto	**oh**-leeoh / ah-**chay**-toh
tray with oil and vinegar	oliera	oh-lee**ay**-ah
What is in this salad?	Che cosa c'è in questa insalata?	kay **koh**-zah cheh een **kweh**-stah een-sah-**lah**-tah
dressing on the side	condimento a parte	kohn-dee-**mehn**-toh ah **par**-tay

Created in Tuscany, *ribollita* is a stew of white beans, veggies, and olive oil, layered with day-old bread.

In Italian restaurants, salad dressing is normally just the oil and vinegar at the table (if it's missing, ask for the *oliera*). Salad bars at fast food restaurants and *autostrada* rest stops can be a good budget bet.

Salad Specialties

insalata caprese	een-sah-**lah**-tah kah-**pray**-say	sliced tomato topped with fresh mozzarella, basil leaves, and olive oil
insalata di mare	een-sah-**lah**-tah dee **mah**-ray	chilled, cooked seafood tossed with parsley, lemon, and olive oil
insalata russa (Russian salad)	een-sah-**lah**-tah **roo**-sah	vegetable salad with mayonnaise
panzanella	pahnt-sah-**nehl**-lah	chunks of day-old bread, chopped tomatoes, onions, and basil tossed in a light vinaigrette

Pasta

Italy is the land of *pasta*, with more than 500 varieties. While there are a few differences in ingredients, the big deal is basically the shape.

EATING

Watch for *rigatoni* (little tubes), *cannelloni* (big tubes), *fettuccine* (long, flat egg noodles), *farfalle* (butterfly-shaped pasta), *gnocchi* (shell-shaped, hand-rolled noodles made from potatoes), *linguine* (thin, flat noodles), *penne* (angle-cut tubes), *rotelli* (wheel-shaped), *tagliatelle* (long, flat noodles), *tortellini* (small, C-shaped pasta filled with meat or cheese), *pici* (rough-cut thick twists), *bucatini* (hollow, thicker spaghetti), *orecchiette* (ear-shaped), *radiatore* (radiator-shaped), and surprise... *spaghetti*. Once you've decided on the pasta type, you'll need to top it with something. Here are your options:

Pasta Sauces

ai funghi	**ah**ee **foong**-gee	with porcini mushrooms
alfredo	ahl-**fray**-doh	butter, cream, and parmesan
amatriciana	ah-mah-tree-chee**ah**-nah	Roman-style with bacon, tomato, chili peppers, and onion
arrabbiata ("angry style")	ah-rah-bee**ah**-tah	spicy tomato sauce with chili peppers
Bolognese	boh-lohn-**yay**-zay	meat and tomato sauce
burro e salvia	**boo**-roh ay **sahl**-veeah	butter and sage
carbonara	kar-boh-**nah**-rah	bacon, egg, cheese, and pepper
in brodo	een **broh**-doh	in broth
marinara	mah-ree-**nah**-rah	tomato and garlic
panna	**pah**-nah	cream
seafood	pehs-kah-**toh**-rah	pescatora
pesto, Genovese	**pehs**-toh, jay-noh-**vay**-zay	olive oil, garlic, pine nuts, and basil
pomodoro	poh-moh-**doh**-roh	tomato only
puttanesca ("harlot")	poo-tah-**nays**-kah	zesty, spicy tomato sauce
quattro formaggi	**kwah**-troh for-**mah**-jee	four cheeses
ragù	rah-**goo**	meaty tomato sauce

sugo	**soo**-goh	sauce, usually tomato
vongole	**vohn**-goh-lay	with clams and spices

Seafood

seafood	*frutti di mare*	**froo**-tee dee **mah**-ray
assorted seafood	*misto di frutti di mare*	**mee**-stoh dee **froo**-tee dee **mah**-ray
fish	*pesce*	**peh**-shay
anchovies	*acciughe*	ah-**choo**-gay
barnacles	*balani*	bah-**lah**-nee
bream (fish)	*orata*	oh-**rah**-tah
clams	*vongole*	**vohn**-goh-lay
cod	*merluzzo*	mehr-**lood**-zoh
crab	*granchio*	**grahn**-keeoh
crayfish	*gambero, aragosta*	gahm-**bay**-roh, ah-rah-**goh**-stah
cuttlefish	*seppie*	**sehp**-eeay
herring	*aringa*	ah-**reeng**-gah
lobster	*aragosta*	ah-rah-**goh**-stah
mussels	*cozze*	**kohd**-zay
octopus	*polipo, polpo*	**poh**-lee-poh, **pohl**-poh
oysters	*ostriche*	**ohs**-tree-kay
prawns	*scampi, gamberi*	**skahm**-pee, gahm-**bay**-ree
salmon	*salmone*	sahl-**moh**-nay
sardines	*sardine*	sar-**dee**-nay
scad (like mackerel)	*sgombro*	**sgohm**-broh
scallops	*capesante*	kah-pay-**zahn**-tay
sea bass	*branzino*	brahnt-**see**-noh
shrimp	*gamberetti*	gahm-bay-**ray**-tee
sole	*sogliola*	sohl-**yoh**-lah
squid	*calamari*	kah-lah-**mah**-ree
swordfish	*pesce spada*	**peh**-shay **spah**-dah
tiger shrimp	*gamberoni*	gahm-bay-**roh**-nee
trout	*trota*	**troh**-tah
tuna	*tonno*	**toh**-noh

How much for a portion?	*Quanto per una porzione?*	**kwahn**-toh pehr **oo**-nah port-see**oh**-nay
What's fresh today?	*Cosa c'è di fresco oggi?*	**koh**-zah cheh dee **fray**-skoh **oh**-jee
Do you eat this part?	*Si mangia anche questa parte?*	see **mahn**-jah **ahn**-kay **kweh**-stah **par**-tay
Just the head, please.	*Solo la testa, per favore.*	**soh**-loh lah **tehs**-tah pehr fah-**voh**-ray

Italians like to stuff seafood with delicious herbs, breadcrumbs, and cheese, be it mussels, sardines, or anchovies. Most fish are served grilled and whole. Seafood is sometimes sold by the weight; if you see *100 g* or *l'etto* by the price on the menu, that's the price you'll pay per 100 grams, about a quarter pound. To find out how much a typical portion costs, ask, *"Quanto per una porzione?"*

Seafood Specialties

branzino al cartoccio	brahnt-**see**-noh ahl kar-**toh**-choh	sea bass steamed in parchment
cozze ripiene	**kohd**-zay ree-pee**ay**-nay	mussels stuffed with herbs, cheese, and bread crumbs
fritto misto	**free**-toh **mee**-stoh	deep-fried calamari, prawns, and assorted small fish
nero di seppie e polenta	**nay**-roh dee **sehp**-eeay ay poh-**lehn**-tah	cuttlefish (large squid-like creature) cooked in its own ink and served on cornmeal squares
spiedini alla griglia	speeay-**dee**-nee **ah**-lah **greel**-yah	grilled fish or shellfish on a skewer, often with vegetables
zuppa di pesce	**tsoo**-pah dee **peh**-shay	fish soup or stew

EATING

Poultry

poultry	*pollame*	poh-**lah**-may
chicken	*pollo*	**poh**-loh
duck	*anatra*	**ah**-nah-trah
turkey	*tacchino*	tah-**kee**-noh
How long has this been dead?	*Da quanto tempo è morto questo?*	dah **kwahn**-toh **tehm**-poh eh **mor**-toh **kweh**-stoh

Meat

meat	*carne*	**kar**-nay
beef	*manzo*	**mahnt**-soh
beef steak	*bistecca di manzo*	bee-**stay**-kah dee **mahnt**-soh
sirloin steak	*entrecote*	ayn-tray-**koh**-tay
ribsteak	*costata*	koh-**stah**-tah
roast beef	*roast beef*	"roast beef"
brains	*cervella*	chehr-**vehl**-lah
bunny	*coniglio*	koh-**neel**-yoh
cutlet (veal)	*cotoletta*	koh-toh-**lay**-tah
goat, baby	*capretto*	kah-**pray**-toh
ham	*prosciutto*	proh-**shoo**-toh
cooked ham	*prosciutto cotto*	proh-**shoo**-toh **koh**-toh
dried, air-cured ham	*prosciutto crudo*	proh-**shoo**-toh **kroo**-doh
lamb	*agnello*	ahn-**yehl**-loh
liver	*fegato*	**fay**-gah-toh
meat stew	*stufato di carne*	stoo-**fah**-toh dee **kar**-nay
pork	*maiale*	mah-**yah**-lay
salt-cured bacon	*pancetta*	pahn-**chay**-tah
sausage	*salsiccia*	sahl-**see**-chah
snails	*lumache*	loo-**mah**-chay
suckling pig	*porchetta*	por-**kay**-tah
sweetbreads (calf pancreas)	*animelle di vitello*	ah-nee-**mehl**-lay dee vee-**tehl**-loh
tongue	*lingua*	**leeng**-gwah
tripe	*trippa*	**tree**-pah

Avoiding Mis-Steaks		
alive	*vivo*	**vee**-voh
raw	*crudo*	**kroo**-doh
very rare	*molto al sangue*	**mohl**-toh ahl **sahn**-gway
rare	*al sangue*	ahl **sahn**-gway
medium	*cotto*	**koh**-toh
well-done	*ben cotto*	bayn **koh**-toh
very well-done	*completamente cotto*	kohm-play-tah-**mehn**-tay **koh**-toh
almost burnt	*quasi bruciato*	**kwah**-zee broo-**chah**-toh

veal	*vitello*	vee-**tehl**-loh
thin-sliced veal	*scaloppine*	skah-loh-**pee**-nay
wild boar	*cinghiale*	cheeng-**gah**-lay

On a menu, the price of steak is often listed per *etto* (100 grams, about a quarter of a pound). When ordering *bistecca* (steak) in a restaurant, it is most common to order four or five *ettos* and share it.

Main Course Specialties

abbacchio alla Romana	ah-**bah**-keeoh **ah**-lah roh-**mah**-nah	spring lamb roasted with potatoes, rosemary, and garlic (Easter)
assortito di carne arrosto	ah-sor-**tee**-toh dee **kar**-nay ah-**rohs**-toh	assortment of roasted meats, usually veal, pork, and lamb
bistecca alle Fiorentina	bee-**stay**-kah **ah**-lay feeoh-rehn-**tee**-nah	thick T-bone steak, grilled and lightly seasoned
bollito misto	boh-**lee**-toh **mee**-stoh	various meats boiled and served with a selection of sauces
fegato alla Veneziana	**fay**-gah-toh **ah**-lah vay-nayt-seeah-nah	liver and onions

involtini	een-vohl-**tee**-nee	meat or fish filets rolled around vegetables and other fillings
ossobuca alla Genovese	oh-soh-**boo**-kah **ah**-lah jay-noh-**vay**-zay	veal shank braised in broth with carrots, onions, and tomatoes
pollo alla cacciatora ("hunter's style")	**poh**-loh **ah**-lah kah-chah-**toh**-rah	chicken with olive oil, rosemary, garlic, and tomato
saltimbocca alla Romana	sahl-teem-**boh**-kah **ah**-lah roh-**mah**-nah	veal cutlet sautéed with sage, prosciutto, and white wine

Bollito misto can sometimes be quite elaborate: a cart is wheeled to your table for you to choose your meat. The side dishes and sauces often include *mostarda* (pickled vegetables), bone marrow sauce, and an herb-caper sauce.

How Food is Prepared

assorted	*assortiti*	ah-sor-**tee**-tee
baked	*al forno*	ahl **for**-noh
boiled	*bollito, lesso*	boh-**lee**-toh, **lay**-soh
braised	*brasato*	brah-**zah**-toh
broiled	*alla graticola*	**ah**-lah grah-tee-**koh**-lah
cold	*freddo*	**fray**-doh
cooked	*cotto*	**koh**-toh
deep-fried	*fritto*	**free**-toh
fillet	*filetto*	fee-**lay**-toh
fresh	*fresco*	**fray**-skoh
fried	*fritto*	**free**-toh
fried with bread crumbs	*alla Milanese*	**ah**-lah mee-lah-**nay**-zay
grilled	*alla griglia*	**ah**-lah **greel**-yah
homemade	*casalingo*	kah-zah-**leen**-goh
hot	*caldo*	**kahl**-doh
in cream sauce	*con panna*	kohn **pah**-nah

EATING

medium	medio	**may**-deeoh
microwave	forno a microonde	**for**-noh ah mee-kroh-**ohn**-day
mild	non piccante	nohn pee-**kahn**-tay
mixed	misto	**mee**-stoh
poached	affogato	ah-foh-**gah**-toh
rare	al sangue	ahl **sahn**-gway
raw	crudo	**kroo**-doh
roasted	arrosto	ah-**roh**-stoh
sautéed	saltato in padella	sahl-**tah**-toh een pah-**dehl**-lah
smoked	affumicato	ah-foo-mee-**kah**-toh
sour	agro	**ah**-groh
spicy hot	piccante	pee-**kahn**-tay
steamed	al vapore	ahl vah-**poh**-ray
steamed in parchment	al cartoccio	ahl kar-**toh**-choh
stuffed	ripieno	ree-peeay-noh
sweet	dolce	**dohl**-chay
well-done	ben cotto	bayn **koh**-toh
with cheese and breadcrumbs	alla Parmigiana	**ah**-lah par-mee-**jah**-nah
with rice	con il riso	kohn eel **ree**-zoh

Veggies

vegetables	legumi, verdure	lay-**goo**-mee, vehr-**doo**-ray
mixed vegetables	misto di verdure	**mee**-stoh dee vehr-**doo**-ray
artichoke	carciofo	kar-**choh**-foh
giant artichoke	mame	**mah**-may
asparagus	asparagi	ah-spah-**rah**-jee
beans	fagioli	fah-**joh**-lee
beets	barbabietole	bar-bah-beeay-**toh**-lay
broccoli	broccoli	**broh**-koh-lee
cabbage	verza	**vehrt**-sah
carrots	carote	kah-**roh**-tay

cauliflower	cavolfiore	kah-vohl-fee**oh**-ray
corn	granturco	grahn-**toor**-koh
cucumber	cetrioli	chay-tree**oh**-lee
eggplant	melanzana	may-lahnt-**sah**-nah
fennel	finocchio	fee-**noh**-keeoh
French fries	patate fritte	pah-**tah**-tay **free**-tay
garlic	aglio	**ahl**-yoh
green beans	fagiolini	fah-joh-**lee**-nee
lentils	lenticchie	lehn-**tee**-keeay
mushrooms	funghi	**foong**-gee
olives	olive	oh-**lee**-vay
onions	cipolle	chee-**poh**-lay
peas	piselli	pee-**zehl**-lee
peppers...	peperoni	pay-pay-**roh**-nee
...green / red	...verdi / rossi	**vehr**-dee / **roh**-see
pickles	cetriolini	chay-treeoh-**lee**-nee
potatoes	patate	pah-**tah**-tay
rice	riso	**ree**-zoh
spinach	spinaci	spee-**nah**-chee
tomatoes	pomodori	poh-moh-**doh**-ree
truffles	tartufi	tar-**too**-fee
zucchini	zucchine	tsoo-**kee**-nay

EATING

Vegetables are often ordered as a *contorno* (side dish) with a secondo course. Common side dishes include patate fritte or *patate arrosto* (potatoes fried or roasted), *spinaci* (spinach), *fagioli* (green beans), *asparagi* (asparagus) and *insalate verde* or *insalate mista* (green salad or mixed with carrots and tomato). Sometimes more elaborate choices are available, such as *fiore di zucca* (fried zucchini blossoms stuffed with mozzarella). Although the Italians are experts at cooking pasta, they tend to overcook vegetables.

Fruits

apple	mela	**may**-lah
apricot	albicocca	ahl-bee-**koh**-kah
banana	banana	bah-**nah**-nah

berries	frutti di bosco	**froo**-tee dee **bohs**-koh
cantaloupe	melone	may-**loh**-nay
cherry	ciliegia	chee-lee**ay**-jah
dates	datteri	**dah**-tay-ree
fig	fico	**fee**-koh
fruit	frutta	**froo**-tah
grapefruit	pompelmo	pohm-**pehl**-moh
grapes	uva	**oo**-vah
honeydew melon	melone verde	may-**loh**-nay **vehr**-day
lemon	limone	lee-**moh**-nay
orange	arancia	ah-**rahn**-chah
peach	pesca	**pehs**-kah
pear	pera	**pay**-rah
pineapple	ananas	**ah**-nah-nahs
plum	susina	soo-**zee**-nah
prune	prugna	**proon**-yah
raspberry	lampone	lahm-**poh**-nay
strawberry	fragola	**frah**-goh-lah
tangerine	mandarino	mahn-dah-**ree**-noh
watermelon	cocomero	koh-koh-**may**-roh

On a menu, you might see *frutta fresca di stagione* (fresh fruit of the season). Mixed berries are called *frutti di bosco* (forest fruits). If you ask for *sottobosco* (under the forest), you'll get a bowl of mixed berries with lemon and sugar.

Nuts to You

almond	mandorle	mahn-**dor**-lay
chestnut	castagne	kah-**stahn**-yay
coconut	noce di cocco	**noh**-chay dee **koh**-koh
hazelnut	nocciola	noh-**choh**-lah
peanuts	noccioline	noh-choh-**lee**-nay
pine nuts	pinoli	pee-**noh**-lee
pistachio	pistacchio	pee-**stah**-keeoh
walnut	noce	**noh**-chay

Just Desserts

dessert	dolci	**dohl**-chee
cake	torta	**tor**-tah
ice cream	gelato	jay-**lah**-toh
sherbet	sorbetto	sor-**bay**-toh
fruit cup	macedonia senza zucchero	mah-chay-**doh**-neeah **sehnt**-sah **tsoo**-kay-roh
fruit salad	macedonia	mah-chay-**doh**-neeah
fruit with ice cream	coppa di frutta	**koh**-pah dee **froo**-tah
tart	tartina	tar-**tee**-nah
pie	crostata	kroh-**stah**-tah
whipped cream	panna	**pah**-nah
chocolate mousse	mousse	moos
pudding	budino	boo-**dee**-noh
pastry	pasticceria	pah-stee-chay-**ree**-ah
strudel	strudel	"strudel"
cookies	biscotti	bee-**skoh**-tee
candies	caramelle	kah-rah-**mehl**-lay
low calorie	poche calorie	**poh**-kay kah-loh-**ree**-ay
homemade	casalingo	kah-zah-**leen**-goh
We'll split one.	Ne dividiamo uno.	nay dee-vee-deeah-moh **oo**-noh
Two forks / spoons, please.	Due forchette / cucchiai, per favore.	**doo**-ay for-**kay**-tay / koo-keeah-yee pehr fah-**voh**-ray
I shouldn't, but...	Non dovrei, ma...	nohn doh-**vreh**ee mah
Exquisite!	Squisito!	skwee-**zee**-toh
It's heavenly!	Da sogno!	dah **sohn**-yoh
I'm a glutton for chocolate.	Sono golosa per cioccolato.	**soh**-noh goh-**loh**-zah pehr choh-koh-**lah**-toh
Better than sex.	Meglio del sesso.	**mehl**-yoh dehl **say**-soh
Just looking at it fattens you.	Fa ingrassare solo a guardarlo.	fah een-grah-**sah**-ray **soh**-loh ah gwar-**dar**-loh
Sinfully good.	Un peccato di gola. ("a sin of the throat")	oon pay-**kah**-toh dee **goh**-lah
So good I even licked my moustache.	Così buono che mi sono leccato anche i baffi.	koh-**zee bwoh**-noh kay mee **soh**-noh lay-**kah**-toh **ahn**-kay ee **bah**-fee

EATING

Gelati Talk

cone / cup	*cono / coppa*	**koh**-noh / **koh**-pah
one scoop	*una pallina*	**oo**-nah pah-**lee**-nah
two scoops	*due palline*	**doo**-ay pah-**lee**-nay
with whipped cream	*con panna*	kohn **pah**-nah
A little taste?	*Un assaggio?*	oon ah-**sah**-joh
How many	*Quanti gusti*	**kwahn**-tee **goo**-stee
flavors can I get	*posso avere*	**poh**-soh ah-**vay**-ray
per scoop?	*per pallina?*	pehr pah-**lee**-nah
apricot	*albicocca*	ahl-bee-**koh**-kah
berries	*frutti di bosco*	**froo**-tee dee **bohs**-koh
blueberry	*mirtillo*	meer-**tee**-loh
cantaloupe	*melone*	may-**loh**-nay
coconut	*cocco*	**koh**-koh
chocolate	*cioccolato*	choh-koh-**lah**-toh
super chocolate	*tartufo*	tar-**too**-foh
vanilla and	*stracciatella*	strah-chah-**tehl**-lah
chocolate chips		
chocolate hazelnut	*bacio*	**bah**-choh
chocolate and mint	*After Eight*	"After Eight"
coffee	*caffè*	kah-**feh**
hazelnut	*nocciola*	noh-**choh**-lah
lemon	*limone*	lee-**moh**-nay
milk	*fior di latte*	**fee**or dee **lah**-tay
mint	*menta*	**mayn**-tah
orange	*arancia*	ah-**rahn**-chah
peach	*pesca*	**pehs**-kah
pear	*pera*	**pay**-rah
pineapple	*ananas*	**ah**-nah-nahs
raspberry	*lampone*	lahm-**poh**-nay
rice	*riso*	**ree**-zoh
strawberry	*fragola*	**frah**-goh-lah
vanilla	*crema*	**kray**-mah
yogurt	*yogurt*	**yoh**-goort

EATING

Bacio (chocolate hazelnut) also means "kiss." *Baci* (kisses) are Italy's version of Chinese fortune cookies. The poetic fortunes, wrapped around chocolate balls, are written by people whose love of romance exceeds their grasp of English.

Dessert Specialties

bignole	been-**yoh**-lay	cream puffs (Florence)
cannoli	kah-**noh**-lee	fried pastry tubes filled w/ whipped ricotta, candied fruit, and chocolate
cassata	kah-**sah**-tah	ice cream, sponge cake, ricotta cheese, fruit, and pistachios (Sicily)
granita	grah-**nee**-tah	snow cone
millefoglie ("a thousand leaves")	mee-lay-**fohl**-yay	layers of sweet, buttery pastry
panettone	pah-nay-**toh**-nay	Milanese yeast cake with raisins and candied fruit
panforte	pahn-**for**-tay	dense fruit and nut cake (Siena)
panna cotta	**pah**-nah **koh**-tah	rich, cooked cream served with berries
profiterole	proh-fee-tay-**roh**-lay	cream-filled pastry with warm chocolate sauce
sfogliatella	sfohl-yah-**tehl**-lah	crispy scallop shell shaped pastry filled w/ sweetened ricotta cheese (Naples)
tartufo	tar-**too**-foh	super-chocolate ice [or] cream (Rome)
tiramisú	tee-rah-mee-**zoo**	espresso-soaked cake with chocolate, cream, and marsala
torta di mele	**tor**-tah dee **may**-lay	apple cake
zabaglione	tsah-bahl-yee**oh**-nay	delicious egg and liquor cream
zuppa inglese	**tsoo**-pah een-**glay**-zay	trifle–rum-soaked cake layered with whipped cream and fruit

There are also hundreds of different cookies made in Italy, especially in the Veneto region. Every holiday is an excuse to celebrate with a new tasty treat. *Bussoli* are for Easter. *Frittole* (small doughnuts) are eaten during *Carnevale*. Even Romeo and Juliet have their own special sweets named for them: *baci di Giulietta* (vanilla meringues, literally "Juliet's kisses") and *sospiri di Romeo* (hazelnut and chocolate cookies, literally "Romeo's sighs").

DRINKING

Water, Milk, and Juice

mineral water...	*acqua minerale...*	**ah**-kwah mee-nay-**rah**-lay
...with / without gas	*...gassata / non gassata*	gah-**sah**-tah / nohn gah-**sah**-tah
tap water	*acqua del rubinetto*	**ah**-kwah dayl roo-bee-**nay**-toh
whole milk	*latte intero*	**lah**-tay een-**tay**-roh
skim milk	*latte magro*	**lah**-tay **mah**-groh
fresh milk	*latte fresco*	**lah**-tay **fray**-skoh
milk shake	*frappè*	frah-**peh**
hot chocolate...	*cioccolata calda...*	choh-koh-**lah**-tah **kahl**-dah
...with whipped cream	*...con panna*	kohn **pah**-nah
orange soda	*aranciata*	ah-rahn-**chah**-tah
lemon soda	*limonata*	lee-moh-**nah**-tah
juice...	*succo di...*	**soo**-koh dee
...fruit	*...frutta*	**froo**-tah
...apple	*...mela*	**may**-lah
...apricot	*...albicocca*	ahl-bee-**koh**-kah
...grapefruit	*...pompelmo*	pohm-**pehl**-moh
...orange	*...arancia*	ah-**rahn**-chah
...peach	*...pesca*	**pehs**-kah
...pear	*...pera*	**pay**-rah

freshly-squeezed orange juice	spremuta d'arancia	spray-**moo**-tah dah-**rahn**-chah
100% juice	succo al cento per cento	**soo**-koh ahl **chehn**-toh pehr **chehn**-toh
with / without...	con / senza...	kohn / **sehnt**-sah
...sugar	...zucchero	**tsoo**-kay-roh
...ice	...ghiaccio	gee**ah**-choh
glass / cup	bicchiere / tazza	bee-kee**ay**-ray / **tahd**-zah
bottle...	bottiglia...	boh-**teel**-yah
...small / large	...piccola / grande	**pee**-koh-lah / **grahn**-day
Is this water safe to drink?	È potabile quest'acqua?	eh poh-**tah**-bee-lay kweh-**stah**-kwah

I drink the tap water in Italy (Venice's is piped in from a mountain spring, and Florence's is very chlorinated), but it's good style and never expensive to order a *litro* (liter) or *mezzo litro* (half liter) of bottled water with your meal.

Coffee and Tea

coffee...	caffè...	kah-**feh**
...with milk	...latte	**lah**-tay
...with a little milk	...macchiato	mah-kee**ah**-toh
...with whipped cream	...con panna	kohn **pah**-nah
...with water	...lungo	**loon**-goh
...iced	...freddo	**fray**-doh
...instant	...solubile	soo-**loo**-bee-lay
...American-style	...Americano	ah-may-ree-**kah**-noh
coffee with foamy milk	cappuccino	kah-poo-**chee**-noh
decaffeinated	decaffeinato, Haag	day-kah-fay-**nah**-toh, hahg
black	nero	**nay**-roh
milk...	latte...	**lah**-tay
...with a little coffee	...macchiato	mah-kee**ah**-toh
sugar	zucchero	**tsoo**-kay-roh

EATING

Key Phrases: Drinking

drink	bibite	bee-**bee**-tay
(mineral) water	acqua (minerale)	**ah**-kwah (mee-nay-**rah**-lay)
tap water	acqua del rubinetto	**ah**-kwah dayl roo-bee-**nay**-toh
milk	latte	**lah**-tay
juice	succo	**soo**-koh
coffee	caffè	kah-**feh**
tea	tè	teh
wine	vino	**vee**-noh
beer	birra	**bee**-rah
Cheers!	Cin cin!	cheen cheen

---

hot water	acqua calda	**ah**-kwah **kahl**-dah
tea / lemon	tè / limone	teh / lee-**moh**-nay
herbal tea	tisana	tee-**zah**-nah
tea bag	bustina di tè	boo-**stee**-nah dee teh
fruit tea	tè alla frutta	teh **ah**-lah **froo**-tah
mint tea	tè alla menta	teh **ah**-lah **mehn**-tah
iced tea	tè freddo	teh **fray**-doh
small / large	piccola / grande	**pee**-koh-lah / **grahn**-day
Another cup.	Un'altra tazza.	oo-**nahl**-trah **tahd**-zah
Same price if I sit or stand?	Costa uguale al tavolo o al banco?	**koh**-stah oo-**gwah**-lay ahl **tah**-voh-loh oh ahl **bahn**-koh

EATING

Caffè is espresso served in a teeny tiny cup. Foamy *cappuccino* was named after the monks with their brown robes and frothy cowls. A *caffè corretto* (literally "coffee corrected") is coffee and firewater. In a bar, you'll pay at the *cassa,* then take your receipt to the person who makes the coffee. Refills are never free, except at hotel breakfasts.

When you're ordering coffee in bars in bigger cities, you'll notice that the price board (*lista dei prezzi*) clearly lists two price levels: the cheaper level for the stand-up bar and the more expensive for the *tavola* (table) or *terrazza* (out on the terrace or sidewalk).

Wine

I would like...	*Vorrei....*	vor-**reh**ee
We would like...	*Vorremo...*	vor-**ray**-moh
...a glass	*...un bicchiere*	oon bee-kee**ay**-ray
...a quarter liter	*...un quarto litro*	oon **kwar**-toh **lee**-troh
...a half liter	*...un mezzo litro*	oon **mehd**-zoh **lee**-troh
...a carafe	*...una caraffa*	**oo**-nah kah-**rah**-fah
...a half bottle	*...una mezza bottiglia*	**oo**-nah **mehd**-zah boh-**teel**-yah
...a bottle	*...una bottiglia*	**oo**-nah boh-**teel**-yah
...a 5-liter jug	*...una damigiana da cinque litri*	**oo**-nah dah-mee-**jah**-nah dah **cheeng**-kway **lee**-tree
...a barrel	*...un barile*	oon bah-**ree**-lay
...a vat	*...un tino*	oon **tee**-noh
...of red wine	*...di rosso*	dee **roh**-soh
...of white wine	*...di bianco*	dee bee**ahn**-koh
...of rosé wine	*...di rosato*	dee roh-**zah**-toh
...the wine list	*...la lista dei vini*	lah **lee**-stah **deh**ee **vee**-nee

Galileo once wrote, "Wine is light held together by water." It is certainly a part of the Italian culinary trinity—the vine, olive, and wheat. Visit an *enoteca* (wine shop or bar) to sample a variety of regional wines.

Wine Words

Italian wines are named by grape, place, descriptive term, or a combination of these. Below is a list of vocabulary to help you identify what you're looking for in a wine and where to find it.

| wine / wines | *vino / vini* | **vee**-noh / **vee**-nee |
| select wine (good year) | *vino selezionato* | **vee**-noh say-layt-seeoh-nah-toh |

EATING

table wine	vino da tavola	**vee**-noh dah **tah**-voh-lah
house wine	vino della casa	**vee**-noh **dehl**-lah **kah**-zah
local	locale	loh-**kah**-lay
of the region	della regione	**dehl**-lah ray-**joh**-nay
red	rosso	**roh**-soh
white	bianco	bee**ahn**-koh
rosé	rosato	roh-**zah**-toh
sparkling	frizzante	freed-**zahn**-tay
fruity	amabile	ah-**mah**-bee-lay
light / heavy	leggero / pesante	lay-**jay**-roh / pay-**zahn**-tay
sweet	dolce, abboccato	**dohl**-chay, ah-boh-**kah**-toh
medium	medio	**may**-deeoh
semi-dry	semi-secco	say-mee-**say**-koh
dry	secco	**say**-koh
very dry	molto secco	**mohl**-toh **say**-koh
full-bodied	pieno, corposo	pee**ay**-noh, kor-**poh**-zoh
mature	maturo	mah-**too**-roh
cork	tappo	**tah**-poh
corkscrew	cavitappi	kah-vee-**tah**-pee
grapes	uva	**oo**-vah
vintage	annata	ah-**nah**-tah
vineyard	vigneto	veen-**yay**-toh
wine-tasting	degustazione	day-goo-staht-see**oh**-nay
What is a good year?	Qual'è una buon'annata?	kwah-**leh oo**-nah bwoh-nah-**nah**-tah
What do you recommend?	Cosa raccomanda?	**koh**-zah rah-koh-**mahn**-dah

EATING

Wine Labels

DOCG	meets nationwide regulations for the highest quality wine (e.g., permitted grape varieties and minimum alcohol content)
DOC	meets national standards for high quality wine
IGT	meets regional standards

riserva	DOCG or DOC wine matured for a longer, specified time
classico	from a defined, select area
annata	year of harvest
vendemmia	harvest
imbottigliato dal produttore all'origin	bottled by producers

To save money, order *"Una caraffa di vino della casa"* (a carafe of the house wine). Red wine dominates in Italy. Many small-town Italians in the hotel business have a cellar or cantina that they are proud to show off. They'll often jump at any excuse to descend and drink. For a memorable and affordable adventure in Venice, have a "pub crawl" dinner. While *cicchetti* (bar munchies) aren't as common as they used to be, many bars (called *ciccheteria*) are still popular for their wide selection of often ugly, always tasty hors d'oeuvres on toothpicks. Ask for *un'ombra* (a small glass of wine) to wash them down.

Some wines to look for by region:

- The big, bold, dry reds of Piedmont: *Barbaresco, Barolo,* and *Barbera*
- From Tuscany, *Brunello di Montalcino* (smooth, dry red), *Chianti Classico* (not just Chianti in the basket bottle), *Montepulciano d'Abruzzo* (dry, medium-bodied red), *Vernaccia* (light white from the San Gimignano region), and the holy (dessert) wine, *Vin Santo*
- From the Veneto, *Bardolino* and *Amarone* (both full-bodied reds), *Valpolicella* (light red), *Soave* (dry white), and the bubbly white *Prosecco*
- From Umbria, *Orvieto Classico*, a golden, dry white
- From the Cinque Terre, *Bianca della Cinque Terre,* a light white wine, and *Sciacchetrà,* a sweet, potent after-dinner wine

Beer

beer	birra	**bee**-rah
bar	bar	bar

from the tap	*alla spina*	**ah**-lah **spee**-nah
glass of draft beer	*una birra*	**oo**-nah **bee**-rah
	alla spina	**ah**-lah **spee**-nah
20 cl draft beer	*una birra*	**oo**-nah **bee**-rah
	piccola	**pee**-koh-lah
33 cl draft beer	*una birra*	**oo**-nah **bee**-rah
	media	**may**-deeah
50 cl draft beer	*una birra*	**oo**-nah **bee**-rah
	grande	**grahn**-day
1 liter draft beer	*un litro di birra*	oon **lee**-troh dee **bee**-rah
	alla spina	**ah**-lah **spee**-nah
bottle	*bottiglia*	boh-**teel**-yah
light / dark	*chiara / scura*	kee**ah**-rah / **skoo**-rah
local / imported	*locale /*	loh-**kah**-lay /
	importata	eem-por-**tah**-tah
Italian beer	*birra*	**bee**-rah
	nazionale	naht-seeoh-**nah**-lay
German beer	*birra tedesca*	**bee**-rah tay-**dehs**-kah
Irish beer	*birra irlandese*	**bee**-rah eer-lahn-**day**-zay
small / large	*piccola / grande*	**pee**-koh-lah / **grahn**-day
low calorie	*leggera*	lay-**jay**-rah
cold	*fredda*	**fray**-dah
colder	*più fredda*	pew **fray**-dah

Bar Talk

Shall we go for a drink?	*Andiamo a prendere qualcosa da bere?*	ahn-dee**ah**-moh ah **prehn**-day-ray kwahl-**koh**-zah dah **bay**-ray
I'll buy you a drink	*Ti offro una bevanda.*	tee **oh**-froh **oo**-nah bay-**vahn**-dah
It's on me.	*Pago io.*	**pah**-goh ee**oh**
The next one's on me.	*Offro io la prossima.*	**oh**-froh ee**oh** lah **proh**-see-mah
What would you like?	*Che cosa prende?*	kay **koh**-zah **prehn**-day

I'll have...	Prendo...	**prehn**-doh
I don't drink.	Non bevo.	nohn **bay**-voh
alcohol-free	analcolica	ahn-ahl-**koh**-lee-kah
What is the local specialty?	Qual'è la specialità locale?	kwah-**leh** lah spay-chah-lee-**tah** loh-**kah**-lay
What is a good drink for a man / for a woman?	Qual'è una buona bevanda per un uomo / per una donna?	kwah-**leh** oo-nah **bwoh**-nah bay-**vahn**-dah pehr oon **woh**-moh / pehr **oo**-nah **doh**-nah
Straight.	Liscio.	**lee**-shoh
With / Without...	Con / Senza...	kohn / **sehnt**-sah
...alcohol.	...alcool.	**ahl**-kohl
...ice.	...ghiaccio.	gee**ah**-choh
One more.	Un altro.	oon **ahl**-troh
Cheers!	Cin cin!	cheen cheen
To your health!	Salute!	sah-**loo**-tay
Long life!	Lunga vita!	**loong**-gah **vee**-tah
Long live Italy!	Viva l'Italia!	**vee**-vah lee-**tahl**-yah
I'm feeling...	Mi sento...	mee **sehn**-toh
...tipsy.	...brillo[a].	**bree**-loh
...a little drunk.	...un po' ubriaco[a].	oon poh oo-bree**ah**-koh
...wasted.	...ubriaco[a] fradicio[a].	oo-bree**ah**-koh **frah**-dee-choh
I'm hung over.	Ho la sbornia.	oh lah **sbor**-neeah

Before dinner, try an *aperitivo* to stimulate your palate. There are many specialties, including the popular brands of vermouth, *Cinzano* and *Martini,* that come in red or white. Look for sweet or dry *Campari* (a dark-colored bitters with herbs and orange peel), *Cynar* (flavored with artichoke), *Americano* (vermouth with bitters, brandy, and lemon peel), *Bellini* (prosecco and white peach juice, a Venetian speciality), *Punt e Mes* (created from sweet red vermouth and red wine), and *spremuta di frutta* (freshly-squeezed fruit juice).

After dinner, try a *digestivo,* a liqueur thought to aid in digestion: *Amaro* (sweet, strong bitters; well-known brands are

Montenegro and *Fernet Branca*); *Grappa* (firewater distilled from grape skins and stems), *Sambuca* (syrupy anise-flavored liqueur), *Nocino* (walnut liqueur), *Amaretto* (almond-flavored liqueur), and *Frangelico* (hazelnut liqueur).

PICNICKING

At the Grocery

Is it self-service?	*È self-service?*	eh sehlf-**sehr**-vees
Ripe for today?	*Da mangiare oggi?*	dah mahn-**jah**-ray **oh**-jee
Does it need to be cooked?	*Bisogna cucinarlo prima di mangiarlo?*	bee-**zohn**-yah koo-chee-**nar**-loh **pree**-mah dee mahn-**jar**-loh
A little taste?	*Un assaggio?*	oon ah-**sah**-joh
Fifty grams.	*Cinquanta grammi.*	cheeng-**kwahn**-tah **grah**-mee
One hundred grams.	*Un etto.*	oon **eht**-toh
More. / Less.	*Più. / Meno.*	pew / **may**-noh
A piece.	*Un pezzo.*	oon **pehd**-zoh
A slice.	*Una fetta.*	**oo**-nah **fay**-tah
Four slices.	*Quattro fette.*	**kwah**-troh **fay**-tay
Sliced (fine).	*Tagliato (a fette sottili).*	tahl-**yah**-toh (ah **fay**-tay soh-**tee**-lee)
Half.	*Metà.*	may-**tah**
A small bag.	*Un sacchettino.*	oon sah-keht-**tee**-noh
A bag, please.	*Un sacchetto, per favore.*	oon sah-**keht**-toh pehr fah-**voh**-ray
Will you make... for me / us?	*Mi / Ci può fare...?*	mee / chee pwoh **fah**-ray
...a sandwich	*...un panino*	oon pah-**nee**-noh
...two sandwiches	*...due panini*	**doo**-ay pah-**nee**-nee
To take out.	*Da portar via.*	dah **por**-tar **vee**-ah
Can I / Can we use...?	*Posso / Possiamo usare...?*	**poh**-soh / poh-see**ah**-moh oo-**zah**-ray
...the microwave	*...il forno a microonde*	eel **for**-noh ah mee-kroh-**ohn**-day

EATING

May I borrow a...?	Posso prendere in prestito...?	**poh**-soh **prehn**-day-ray een preh-**stee**-toh
Do you have a...?	Ha per caso...?	ah pehr **kah**-zoh
Where can I buy / find a...?	Dove posso comprare / trovare un...?	**doh**-vay **poh**-soh kohm-**prah**-ray / troh-**vah**-ray oon
...corkscrew	...cavatappi	kah-vah-**tah**-pee
...can opener	...apriscatole	ah-pree-skah-**toh**-lay
Is there a park nearby?	C'è un parco qui vicino?	cheh oon **par**-koh kwee vee-**chee**-noh
Where is a good place to picnic?	Dov'è un bel posto per fare un picnic?	doh-**veh** oon behl **poh**-stoh pehr **fah**-ray oon **peek**-neek
Is picnicking allowed here?	Va bene fare un picnic qui?	vah **behn**-nay **fah**-ray oon **peek**-neek kwee
Enjoy your meal!	Buon appetito!	bwohn ah-pay-**tee**-toh

Tasty Picnic Words

picnic	picnic	**peek**-neek
open air market	mercato	mehr-**kah**-toh
grocery store	alimentari	ah-lee-mayn-**tah**-ree
supermarket	supermercato	soo-pehr-mehr-**kah**-toh
delicatessen	salumeria	sah-loo-may-**ree**-ah
bakery	panetteria, forno	pah-nay-tay-**ree**-ah, **for**-noh
sandwich shop	paninoteca	pah-nee-noh-**tay**-kah
pastry shop	pasticceria	pah-stee-chay-**ree**-ah
sandwich or roll	panino	pah-**nee**-noh
bread	pane	**pah**-nay
cured ham (pricey)	prosciutto crudo	proh-**shoo**-toh **kroo**-doh
cooked ham	prosciutto cotto	proh-**shoo**-toh **koh**-toh
sausage	salsiccia	sahl-**see**-chah
cheese	formaggio	for-**mah**-joh
mustard...	senape...	**say**-nah-pay
mayonnaise...	maionese...	mah-yoh-**nay**-zay
...in a tube	...in tubetto	een too-**bay**-toh

EATING

yogurt	*yogurt*	**yoh**-goort
fruit	*frutta*	**froo**-tah
box of juice	*cartone di succo*	kar-**toh**-nay dee **soo**-koh
	di frutta	dee **froo**-tah
spoon / fork...	*cucchiaio /*	koo-keeah-yoh /
	forchetta...	for-**kay**-tah
...made of plastic	*...di plastica*	dee **plah**-stee-kah
cup / plate...	*bicchiere /*	bee-keeay-ray /
	piatto...	peeah-toh
...made of paper	*...di carta*	dee **kar**-tah

Make your own sandwiches by getting the ingredients at a market. Order meat and cheese by the gram. One hundred grams (what the Italians call an *etto*) is about a quarter pound, enough for two sandwiches.

MENU
DECODER

ITALIAN/ENGLISH

This handy decoder won't list every word on the menu, but it will
help you get *trota* (trout) instead of *tripa* (tripe).

abbacchio	lamb (Rome)
abbacchio alla Romana	roasted spring lamb
abbocato	sweet (wine)
acciughe	anchovies
aceto	vinegar
acqua	water
acqua del rubinetto	tap water
acqua minerale	mineral water
affogato	poached
affumicato	smoked
After Eight	chocolate and mint (gelato)
aglio	garlic
agnello	lamb
agro	sour
ai funghi	with mushrooms
al cartoccio	steamed in parchment
al dente	not overcooked (pasta)
al forno	baked
al sangue	rare (meat)

al vapore	steamed
albicocca	apricot
alcool	alcohol
alfredo	butter, cream, cheese sauce
all'arrabbiata	with bacon, tomato—spicy hot
alla cacciatora	"hunter's style," with olive oil, rosemary, garlic, tomato
alla diavola	spicy
alla graticola	broiled
alla Parmigiana	with cheese and breadcrumbs
alla spina	from the tap (beer)
amabile	fruity (wine)
amatriciana	with bacon, tomato, and spices
analcolica	alcohol-free
ananas	pineapple
anatra	duck
animelle di vitello	sweetbreads
annata	vintage (wine)
antipasti	appetizers
antipasto misto	salami and marinated vegetables
aragosta	lobster
arancia	orange
aranciata	orange soda
aringa	herring
arrabiata	spicy tomato-chili sauce
arrosto	roasted
asiago	hard and spicy cheese
asparagi	asparagus
assortiti	assorted
assortito di carne arrosto	roasted assortment of meats
astice	male lobster
bacio	chocolate hazelnut candy
balani	barnacles
barbabietole	beets
basilico	basil
ben cotto	well-done (meat)
bevande	beverages

bianca, pizza	"white" pizza (no tomato sauce)
bianco	white
bibite	beverages
bicchiere	glass
bignole	cream puffs (Florence)
biologico	organic
birra	beer
biscotti	cookies
bistecca	steak
bistecca alle Fiorentina	T-bone steak
bocconcini	small balls of mozzarella
bollente	boiling hot
bollito	boiled
bollito misto	various boiled meats with sauces
Bolognese	meat and tomato sauce
bottiglia	bottle
branzino	bass
brasato	braised
brioche	roll
brodo	broth
bruschetta	toast with tomatoes and basil
bucatini	hollow, thick spaghetti
budino	pudding
burro	butter
burro d'arachidi	peanut butter
bustina di tè	tea bag
caciucco	Tuscan fish soup
caffè	coffee
caffè Americano	American-style coffee
caffè corretto	coffee and firewater
caffè con panna	coffee with whipped cream
caffè freddo	iced coffee
caffè latte	coffee with milk
caffè lungo	coffee with water
caffè macchiato	coffee with a little milk
caffè solubile	instant coffee
caffeina	caffeine

calamari	squid
caldo	hot
calzone	folded pizza
cannelloni	large tube-shaped noodles
cannoli	fried pastry tubes filled with ricotta, fruit, and chocolate
cantucci	Tuscan almond cookies
capesante	scallops
cappuccino	coffee with foam
capra	goat
caprese	mozzarella and tomato salad
capretto	baby goat
capricciosa	chef's choice
caprino	goat cheese
capriolo	venison
caraffa	carafe
caramelle	candy
carbonara	with meat sauce
carciofo	artichoke
carne	meat
carote	carrots
carpaccio	thinly sliced air-cured meat
casa	house
casalingo	homemade
cassa	cash register
cassata siciliana	Sicilian sponge cake
castagne	chestnut
cavatappi	corkscrew
cavolfiore	cauliflower
cavolini de Bruxelles	Brussels sprouts
cavolo	cabbage
ceci	chickpeas
cena	dinner
cereali	cereal
cervella	brains
cervo	venison
cetrioli	cucumber

Italian / English

MENU DECODER

cetriolini	pickles
ciabatta	crusty, flat, rustic bread
ciaccina, pizza	"white" pizza (no tomato sauce)
cibo	food
ciccheti	small appetizers
ciliegia	cherry
cinese	Chinese
cinghiale	wild boar
cioccolata	chocolate
cipolle	onions
cocomero	watermelon
colazione	breakfast
con	with
con panna	with whipped cream
coniglio	rabbit
cono	cone
contorni	side dishes
coperto	cover charge
coppa	small bowl
corretto	coffee and firewater
cornetto	croissant
corposo	full-bodied (wine)
costata	rib steak
cotoletta	cutlet
cotto	cooked; medium (meat)
cozze	mussels
crema	vanilla
crème caramel	caramelized topped custard
crescenza	mild cheese
crostata	pie with jam
crostini	toast with paté
crudo	raw
cucina	cuisine
cuoco	chef
da portar via	"to go"
datteri	dates
decaffeinato	decaffeinated

del giorno	of the day
della casa	of the house
di	of
digestivo	after-dinner drink
dolce	sweet
dolci	desserts
dragoncello	tarragon
e	and
emmenthal	Swiss cheese
entrecote	sirloin steak
erbe	herb
etto	one hundred grams
fagiano	pheasant
fagioli	beans
fagiolini	green beans
farcito	stuffed
farfalle	butterfly-shaped pasta
farinata	porridge
fatto in casa	homemade
fegato	liver
fegato alla Veneziana	liver and onions
fettina	slice
fettucine	long, flat noodles
fico	fig
filetto	fillet
filone	large unsalted bread
finocchio	fennel
fior di latte	milk (gelato flavor)
focaccia	flat bread
fontina	creamy, nutty, gruyere-style cheese
formaggio	cheese
fragola	strawberry
frangelico	hazelnut liqueur
frappè	milkshake
freddo	cold
fresco	fresh
frittata	omelet

fritto	fried
fritto misto	fried seafood
frizzante	sparkling
frumento	wheat
frutta	fruit
frutti di bosco	berries
frutti di mare	seafood
funghi	mushrooms
gamberetti	small shrimp
gamberi	shrimp
gamberoni	big shrimp
gassata	carbonated
gelatina	jelly
gelato	Italian ice cream
Genovese	with pesto sauce
ghiaccio	ice
giorno	day
gnocchi	potato noodles
gorgonzola	bleu cheese
granchione	crab
grande	large
granita	snow cone
granturco	corn
grappa	firewater
griglia	grilled
grissini	breadsticks
groviera	Swiss cheese
gusti	flavors
Haag	decaffeinated coffee
importato	imported
incluso	included
insalata	salad
insalata con uova	egg salad
insalata di mare	seafood salad
involtini	meat or fish filets with fillings
kasher	kosher
lampone	raspberry

latte	milk
latte fresco	fresh milk
latte intero	whole milk
latte macchiato	milk with a little coffee
latte magro	skim milk
latticini	small mozzarella balls
lattuga	lettuce
leggero	light
legumi	vegetables
lenticchie	lentils
lepre	hare
limonata	lemon soda
limone	lemon
lingua	tongue
linguine	thin, flat noodles
locale	local
lumache	snails
maccheroni	tube-shaped pasta
macedonia	fresh fruit salad
maiale	pork
maionese	mayonnaise
mame	giant artichokes
mandarino	tangerine
mandorle	almond
manzo	beef
margarina	margarine
Margherita	with cheese and tomato sauce (pizza)
marinara	tomato and garlic sauce
marmellata	jam
mascarpone	sweet, buttery dessert cheese
maturo	mature (wine)
mela	apple
melanzana	eggplant
melone	cantaloupe
melone verde	honeydew melon
menta	mint

menù del giorno	menu of the day
menù turistico	fixed-price meal
mercato	open-air market
merluzzo	cod
mezzo	half
miele	honey
Milanese	fried in breadcrumbs
millefoglie	layers of sweet, buttery pastry
minerale-acqua	mineral water
minestra	soup
minestrone	vegetable soup
mirtillo	blueberry
misto	mixed
molto	very
molto al sangue	very rare (meat)
mozzarella	handmade water-buffalo cheese
Napoletana	with cheese, anchovies, and tomato sauce (pizza)
nero	black
nero di seppie e polenta	cuttlefish cooked in its own ink
nocciola	hazelnut
noccioline	peanut
noce	walnut
noce di cocco	coconut
nocino	walnut liqueur
non	not
non fumare	non-smoking
non fumatori	non-smoking
o	or
olio	oil
olive	olives
omelette	omelet
orata	bream (fish)
orecchiette	small, ear-shaped pasta
organico	organic
ortolana	vegetarian (pizza)
ossobuca alla Genovese	veal shank braised in broth

ossobuco	bone marrow
ostriche	oysters
pallina	scoop
pancetta	salt-cured bacon
pane	bread
pane aromatico	herb or vegetable bread
pane casereccia	home-style bread
pane di olive	olive bread
pane di segale	rye bread
pane integrale	whole grain bread
pane scuro	brown bread
pane Toscano	rustic bread made without salt
paneficio	bakery
panettone	Milanese yeast fruitcake
panforte	fruitcake
panino	roll, sandwich
panna	cream, whipped cream
panna cotta	cooked cream with berries
pansotti	pasta stuffed with veggies
panzanella	bread and vegetable salad
parmigiano	Parmesan cheese
pasticceria	pastry shop; pastry
pasticcini	pastries
pastina	noodles
patate	potatoes
patate fritte	French fries
pecorino	sheep's cheese
penne	tube-shaped noodles
pepato	with pepper
pepe	pepper
peperonata	peppers with tomato sauce
peperoncino	paprika
peperoni	bell peppers
pera	pear
percorino	sheep cheese
pesante	heavy (wine)
pesca	peach

pescatora	seafood sauce
pesce	fish
pesce spada	swordfish
pesto	basil, pine nut, olive oil paste
petto (di___)	breast (of___)
pezzo	piece
piadina	stuffed, soft, flat bread
piatto	plate
piatto di formaggi misti	cheese plate
piccante	spicy hot
piccolo	small
pici	rough-cut thick twisted pasta
pieno	full-bodied (wine)
pinioli	pine nuts
piselli	peas
pistacchio	pistachio
poche calorie	low calorie
polenta	moist cornmeal
polipo	octopus
pollame	poultry
pollo	chicken
pollo alla cacciatora	chicken with olive oil, rosemary, garlic, and tomato
polpo	octopus
pomodoro	tomato
pompelmo	grapefruit
porchetta	roast suckling pig
porcini	porcini mushrooms
pranzo	lunch
prezzemolo	parsley
prima colazione	breakfast
primo piatto	first course
profiterole	cream-filled pastry with chocolate sauce
prosciutto	cured ham
prosciutto cotto	cooked ham
prosciutto crudo	dried, air-cured ham

prosciutto e melone / fichi	air-cured ham wrapped around melon / fresh figs
provolone	rich, firm aged cow's cheese
prugna	prune
puttanesca	zesty sauce
quattro	four
quattro formaggi	four cheeses
quattro stagioni	with four separate toppings (pizza)
radiattore	radiator-shaped pasta
ragù	meat and tomato sauce
ribollita	hearty bread and vegetable soup
ricivuta	receipt
ricotta	soft, airy cheese
rigatoni	tube-shaped noodles
ripieno	stuffed
riso	rice
risotto	saffron-flavored rice
rosato	rosé (wine)
rosmarino	rosemary
rosso	red
rotelli	wheel-shaped pasta
salame	pork sausage
salamino piccante	pepperoni
salato	salty
sale	salt
salmone	salmon
salsiccia	sausage
saltimbocca alla Romana	veal cutlet sautéed with sage, prosciutto, and white wine
salumi misti	assortment of sliced, cured meats
salvia	sage
sambuca	anise (licorice) liqueur
saporito	mild
sarde	sardines
scaloppine	thin-sliced veal
scampi	prawns
schiacciata	pizza-like flatbread

sciacchetra	sweet desert wine
secco	dry (wine)
secondo piatto	second course
selvaggina	game
senape	mustard
senza	without
seppie	cuttlefish, sometimes squid
servizio	service charge
servizio incluso	service included
servizio non incluso	service not included
sfogliatella	pastry filled with sweetened ricotta
sgombro	scad (like mackerel)
Siciliana	with capers and olives (pizza)
sogliola	sole
sono pieno	I'm stuffed
sorbetto	sherbet
specialità	specialty
spezzatino	meat, potato, tomato stew
spiedini alla griglia	grilled seafood on a skewer
spinaci	spinach
spizziccare	snack
spremuta	freshly squeezed juice
spuntino	snack
stagionato	aged, sharp, and hard (cheese)
stagioni	seasons (and pizza toppings)
stracchino	spreadable cheese
stracciatella	chocolate chips w/vanilla (gelato)
strangolapreti	twisted pasta
strapazzate	scrambled
stufato	stew
stuzzicadente	toothpick
succo	juice
sugo	sauce, usually tomato
susina	plum
tacchino	turkey
tagliatelle	flat noodles
taleggio	rich, creamy cheese

tartina	tart
tartufi	truffles
tartufo	super-chocolate ice cream
tavola calda	buffet-style
tavola	table
tazza	cup
tè	tea
tè alla frutta	fruit tea
tè alla menta	mint tea
tè freddo	iced tea
tiramisú	espresso-soaked cake with chocolate, cream, and marsala
tisana	herbal tea
tonno	tuna
torta	cake
torte	pie
tortellini	stuffed noodles
tovagliolo	napkin
tramezzini	small, crustless sandwiches
trippa	tripe
trota	trout
uova	eggs
uova fritte	fried eggs
uova strapazzate	scrambled eggs
uovo alla coque (molle / sodo)	boiled egg (soft / hard)
uva	grapes
vegetariano	vegetarian
veloce	fast
vendemmia	harvest (wine)
verde	green
verdure	vegetables
verza	cabbage
vigneto	vineyard
vino	wine
vino da tavola	table wine
vino della casa	house wine

vino selezionato	select wine (good year)
vino sfuso	house wine in a jug
vitello	veal
vitello tonato	thinly sliced veal with tuna-caper mayonnaise
vongole	clams
wurstel	hot dogs
zabaglione	egg and liquor cream
zucchero	sugar
zuppa	soup
zuppa di pesce	fish soup or stew
zuppa inglese	trifle

ENGLISH/ITALIAN

alcohol	alcool
alcohol-free	analcolica
almond	mandorle
anchovies	acciughe
and	e
appetizers	antipasti
appetizers, small	ciccheti
apple	mela
apricot	albicocca
artichoke	carciofo
artichokes, giant	mame
asparagus	asparagi
assorted	assortiti
bacon, salt-cured	pancetta
baked	al forno
bakery	paneficio
barnacles	balani
basil	basilico
bass	branzino
beans	fagioli
beef	manzo
beef steak	bistecca
beer	birra
beer from the tap	birra alla spina
beets	barbabietole
bell peppers	peperoni
berries	frutti di bosco
beverages	bevande, bibite
black	nero
bleu cheese	gorgonzola
blueberry	mirtillo
boar	cinghiale
boiled	bollito
boiled egg	uovo alla coque
(soft / hard)	(molle / sodo)

boiling hot	bollente
bone marrow	ossobuco
bottle	bottiglia
bowl, small (gelato)	coppa
brains	cervella
braised	brasato
bread	pane
bread, brown	pane scuro
bread, crusty, flat, rustic	ciabatta
bread, flat	focaccia
bread, herb or vegetable	pane aromatico
bread, home-style	pane casereccia
bread, olive	pane di olive
bread, rustic, without salt	pane Toscano
bread, rye	pane di segale
bread, stuffed, soft, flat	piadina
bread, unsalted	filone
bread, whole grain	pane integrale
breadsticks	grissini
breakfast	colazione, prima colazione
bream (fish)	orata
breast (of___)	petto (di___)
broiled	alla graticola
broth	brodo
Brussels sprouts	cavolini de Bruxelles
buffet-style	tavola calda
butter	burro
cabbage	cavolo, verza
caffeine	caffeina
cake	torta
candy	caramelle
cantaloupe	melone
carafe	caraffa
carbonated	gassata
carrots	carote
cash register	cassa
cauliflower	cavolfiore

cereal	cereali
cheese	formaggio
cheese plate	piatto di formaggi misti
chef	cuoco
cherry	ciliegia
chestnut	castagne
chicken	pollo
chickpeas	ceci
Chinese	cinese
chocolate	cioccolata
chocolate and mint (gelato)	After Eight
chocolate chips with vanilla (gelato)	stracciatella
chocolate hazelnut candy (also gelato)	bacio
chocolate, super- (gelato)	tartufo
clams	vongole
coconut	noce di cocco
cod	merluzzo
coffee	caffè
coffee and firewater	caffè corretto
coffee with a little milk	caffè macchiato
coffee with foam	cappuccino
coffee with milk	caffè latte
coffee with water	caffè lungo
coffee with whipped cream	caffè con panna
coffee, American-style	caffè Americano
coffee, iced	caffè freddo
coffee, instant	caffè solubile
cold	freddo
cone	cono
cooked	cotto
cookies	biscotti
corkscrew	cavatappi
corn	granturco
course, first	primo piatto
course, second	secondo piatto

English / Italian

MENU DECODER

cover charge	coperto
crab	granchione
cream	panna
cream puffs	bignole
croissant	cornetto
cucumber	cetrioli
cuisine	cucina
cup	tazza
cup (gelato)	coppa
cutlet	cotoletta
cuttlefish	seppie
cuttlefish cooked in its own ink	nero di seppie e polenta
dates	datteri
day	giorno
day, of the	del giorno
decaffeinated	decaffeinato
decaffeinated coffee	Haag
desserts	dolci
dinner	cena
dry (wine)	secco
duck	anatra
egg	uovo
egg salad	insalata con uova
egg, boiled (soft / hard)	uovo alla coque (molle / sodo)
eggplant	melanzana
eggs, fried	uova fritte
eggs, scrambled	uova strapazzate
fast	veloce
fennel	finocchio
fig	fico
fillet	filetto
firewater	grappa
first course	primo piatto
fish	pesce
fish soup	zuppa di pesce
fixed-price meal	menù turistico
flatbread	schiacciata

flavors	gusti
food	cibo
French fries	patate fritte
fresh	fresco
fried	fritto
fruit	frutta
fruit salad	macedonia
fruit tea	tè alla frutta
fruitcake	panforte
fruity (wine)	amabile
full, I'm	sono pieno
full-bodied (wine)	corposo, pieno
game	selvaggina
garlic	aglio
glass	bicchiere
goat	capra
goat cheese	caprino
goat, baby	capretto
grapefruit	pompelmo
grapes	uva
green	verde
green beans	fagiolini
grilled	griglia
half	mezzo
ham, cooked	prosciutto cotto
ham, cured	prosciutto
ham, dried, air-cured	prosciutto crudo
hare	lepre
harvest (wine)	vendemmia
hazelnut	nocciola
heavy (wine)	pesante
herb	erbe
herbal tea	tisana
herring	aringa
homemade	casalingo, fatto in casa
honey	miele
honeydew melon	melone verde

English	Italian
hot	caldo
hot dog	wurstel, salsiccia
house	casa
house wine	vino della casa, vino sfuso
house, of the	della casa
ice	ghiaccio
ice cream	gelato
iced coffee	caffè freddo
iced tea	tè freddo
imported	importato
included	incluso
instant coffee	caffè solubile
jam	marmellata
jelly	gelatina
juice	succo
juice, freshly squeezed	spremuta
kosher	kasher
lamb	agnello, abbacchio
large	grande
lemon	limone
lemon soda	limonata
lentils	lenticchie
lettuce	lattuga
light	leggero
liver	fegato
liver and onions	fegato alla Veneziana
lobster	aragosta
lobster (male)	astice
local	locale
low calorie	poche calorie
lunch	pranzo
margarine	margarina
mature (wine)	maturo
mayonnaise	maionese
meat	carne
meat and tomato sauce	Bolognese, ragù
medium (meat)	cotto

melon, honeydew	melone verde
menu of the day	menù del giorno
mild	saporito
milk	latte
milk (gelato flavor)	fior di latte
milk with a little coffee	latte macchiato
milk, fresh	latte fresco
milk, skim	latte magro
milk, whole	latte intero
milkshake	frappè
mineral water	acqua minerale, minerale-acqua
mint	menta
mint tea	tè alla menta
mixed	misto
mushrooms	funghi
mushrooms (porcini)	porcini
mussels	cozze
mustard	senape
napkin	tovagliolo
non-smoking	non fumatori, non fumare
noodles	pastina
not	non
octopus	polpo, polipo
of	di
of the day	del giorno
of the house	della casa
oil	olio
olives	olive
omelet	frittata, omelette
onions	cipolle
or	o
orange	arancia
orange soda	aranciata
organic	organico, biologico
oysters	ostriche
paprika	peperoncino
parchment, steamed in	al cartoccio

parsley	prezzemolo
pastry	pasticceria
pastry shop	pasticceria
peach	pesca
peanut	noccioline
peanut butter	burro d'arachidi
pear	pera
peas	piselli
pepper	pepe
pepperoni	salamino piccante
peppers with tomato sauce	peperonata
pheasant	fagiano
pickles	cetriolini
pie	torte
pie with jam	crostata
piece	pezzo
pig, roast suckling	porchetta
pine nuts	pinioli
pineapple	ananas
pistachio	pistacchio
pizza with capers and olives	pizza Siciliana
pizza with cheese and tomato sauce	pizza Margherita
pizza with cheese, anchovies, and tomato sauce	pizza Napoletana
pizza with four toppings	pizza quattro stagioni
pizza, "white" (no tomato sauce)	pizza bianca, pizza ciaccina
pizza, folded	calzone
pizza, vegetarian	pizza ortolana
pizza-like flatbread	schiacciata
plate	piatto
plum	susina
poached	affogato
pork	maiale
pork sausage	salame
porridge	farinata

potato noodles	gnocchi
potatoes	patate
poultry	pollame
prawns	scampi
prune	prugna
pudding	budino
rabbit	coniglio
rare (meat)	al sangue
raspberry	lampone
raw	crudo
receipt	ricivuta
red	rosso
rib steak	costata
rice	riso
rice, saffron-flavored	risotto
roasted	arrosto
roll	brioche, panino
rosé (wine)	rosato
rosemary	rosmarino
sage	salvia
salad	insalata
salad, bread and vegetable	panzanella
salad, egg	insalata con uova
salad, fruit	macedonia
salad, mozzarella and tomato	caprese
salad, seafood	insalata di mare
salmon	salmone
salt	sale
salty	salato
sandwich	panino
sandwiches, small, crustless	tramezzini
sardines	sarde
sauce of butter, cream, cheese	alfredo
sauce, seafood	pescatora
sauce, spicy tomato-chili	arrabiata
sauce, usually tomato	sugo

sauce, zesty	puttanesca
sausage	salsiccia
scad (like mackerel)	sgombro
scallops	capesante
scoop	pallina
scrambled	strapazzate
scrambled eggs	uova strapazzate
seafood	frutti di mare
seafood salad	insalata di mare
seafood sauce	pescatora
second course	secondo piatto
service charge	servizio
service (not) included	servizio (non) incluso
sheep cheese	pecorino
sherbet	sorbetto
shrimp	gamberi
shrimp, big	gamberoni
shrimp, small	gamberetti
side dishes	contorni
sirloin steak	entrecote
slice	fettina
small	piccolo
smoked	affumicato
snack	spuntino, spizziccare
snails	lumache
snow cone	granita
sole	sogliola
soup	zuppa, minestra
soup, fish	zuppa di pesce
soup, hearty bread and vegetable	ribollita
soup, vegetable	minestrone
sour	agro
sparkling (wine)	frizzante
specialty	specialità
spicy hot	piccante, alla diavola
spinach	spinaci

squid	calamari
steak	bistecca
steak, rib	costata
steak, sirloin	entrecote
steak, T-bone	bistecca alle Fiorentina
steamed	al vapore
stew	stufato
stew of meat, potato, tomato	spezzatino
strawberry	fragola
stuffed	ripieno, farcito
sugar	zucchero
sweet	dolce
sweet (wine)	abboccato
sweetbreads (calf pancreas)	animelle di vitello
Swiss cheese	emmenthal, groviera
swordfish	pesce spada
table	tavola
table wine	vino da tavola
tangerine	mandarino
tap water	acqua del rubinetto
tap, from the (beer)	alla spina
tarragon	dragoncello
tart	tartina
T-bone steak	bistecca alle Fiorentina
tea	tè
tea bag	bustina di tè
tea, herbal	tisana
tea, iced	tè freddo
tea, mint	tè alla menta
"to go"	da portar via
tomato	pomodoro
tomato and garlic sauce	marinara
tomato and meat sauce	Bolognese, ragù
tongue	lingua
toothpick	stuzzicadente
trifle	zuppa inglese
tripe	trippa

English / Italian

MENU DECODER

trout	trota
truffles	tartufi
tuna	tonno
turkey	tacchino
vanilla	crema
veal	vitello
vegetable soup	minestrone
vegetables	verdure, legumi
vegetarian	vegetariano
venison	cervo, capriolo
very	molto
very rare (meat)	molto al sangue
very well-done (meat)	completamente cotto
vinegar	aceto
vineyard	vigneto
vintage (wine)	annata
walnut	noce
water	acqua
water, mineral	acqua minerale, minerale-acqua
water, tap	acqua del rubinetto
watermelon	cocomero
well-done (meat)	ben cotto
wheat	frumento
whipped cream	panna
white	bianco
wine	vino
wine, dry	vino secco
wine, fruity	vino amabile
wine, full-bodied	vino corposo, vino pieno
wine, harvest	vino vendemmia
wine, heavy	vino pesante
wine, house	vino della casa, vino sfuso
wine, mature	vino maturo
wine, red	vino rosso
wine, rosé	vino rosato
wine, select (good year)	vino selezionato
wine, sparkling	vino frizzante

wine, sweet	vino abboccato
wine, table	vino da tavola
wine, vintage	vino annata
wine, white	vino bianco
with	con
without	senza
yogurt	yogurt

ACTIVITIES

SIGHTSEEING

Where?

English	Italian	Pronunciation
Where is...?	Dov'è...?	doh-**veh**
...the best view	...la vista più bella	lah **vee**-stah pew **behl**-lah
...the main square	...la piazza principale	lah pee**aht**-sah preen-chee-**pah**-lay
...the old town center	...il centro storico	eel **chehn**-troh **stoh**-ree-koh
...the museum	...il museo	eel moo-**zay**-oh
...the castle	...il castello	eel kah-**stehl**-loh
...the palace	...il palazzo	eel pah-**lahd**-zoh
...the ruins	...le rovine	lay roh-**vee**-nay
...an amusement park	...un parco dei divertimenti	oon **par**-koh **deh**ee dee-vehr-tee-**mehn**-tee
...tourist information	...l'ufficio informazioni	loo-**fee**-choh een-for-maht-see**oh**-nee
...the toilet	...la toilette	lah twah-**leht**-tay
...the entrance / exit	...l'entrata / l'uscita	lehn-**trah**-tah / loo-**shee**-tah
Is there a festival nearby?	C'è un festival qui vicino?	cheh oon fehs-tee-**vahl** kwee vee-**chee**-noh

Key Phrases: Sightseeing

Where is...?	Dov'è...?	doh-**veh**
How much is it?	Quanto costa?	**kwahn**-toh **koh**-stah
What time does this open / close?	A che ora apre / chiude?	ah kay **oh**-rah **ah**-pray / keeoo-day
Do you have a guided tour?	Avete un tour guidato?	ah-**vay**-tay oon toor gwee-**dah**-toh
When is the next tour in English?	Quando è il prossimo tour in inglese?	**kwahn**-doh eh eel **proh**-see-moh toor een een-**glay**-zay

At the Sight

Do you have...?	Avete...?	ah-**vay**-tay
...information...	...informazioni...	een-for-maht-see**oh**-nee
...a guidebook...	...una guida...	**oo**-nah **gwee**-dah
...in English	...in inglese	een een-**glay**-zay
Is it free?	È gratis?	eh **grah**-tees
How much is it?	Quanto costa?	**kwahn**-toh **koh**-stah
Is (the ticket) valid all day?	È valido per tutto il giorno?	eh **vah**-lee-doh pehr **too**-toh eel **jor**-noh
Can I get back in?	Posso rientrare?	**poh**-soh ree-ehn-**trah**-ray
What time does this open / close?	A che ora apre / chiude?	ah kay **oh**-rah **ah**-pray / keeoo-day
What time is the last entry?	Quand'è l'ultima entrata?	kwahn-**deh lool**-tee-mah ayn-**trah**-tah

Please

PLEASE let me / us in.	PER FAVORE, mi / ci faccia entrare.	pehr fah-**voh**-ray mee / chee **fah**-chah ayn-**trah**-ray
I've traveled all the way from ___.	Sono venuto[a] qui da ___.	**soh**-noh vay-**noo**-toh kwee dah
We've traveled all the way from ___.	Siamo venuti[e] qui da ___.	see**ah**-moh vay-**noo**-tee kwee dah

ACTIVITIES

I must leave tomorrow.	*Devo partire domani.*	**day**-voh par-**tee**-ray doh-**mah**-nee
We must leave tomorrow.	*Dobbiamo partire domani.*	doh-beeah-moh par-**tee**-ray doh-**mah**-nee
I promise I'll be fast.	*Prometto che sarò veloce.*	proh-**meht**-toh kay sah-**roh** vay-**loh**-chay
We promise we'll be fast.	*Promettiamo che saremo veloci.*	proh-meht-teeah-moh kay sah-**ray**-moh vay-**loh**-chee
It was my mother's dying wish that I see this.	*Ho promesso a mia madre sul letto di morte che avrei visto questo.*	oh proh-**mehs**-soh ah **mee**-ah **mah**-dray sool **leht**-toh dee **mor**-tay kay ah-**vray**ee **vee**-stoh **kweh**-stoh
I've / We've always wanted to see this.	*Ho / Abbiamo sempre desiderato vedere questo.*	oh / ah-bee**ah**-moh **sehm**-pray day-zee-day-**rah**-toh vay-**dehr**-ay **kweh**-stoh

Tours

Do you have...?	*Avete...?*	ah-**vay**-tay
...an audioguide	*...un'audioguida*	oo-now-deeoh-**gwee**-dah
...a guided tour	*...un tour guidato*	oon toor gwee-**dah**-toh
...a city walking tour	*...una visita guidata della città*	**oo**-nah vee-**zee**-tah gwee-**dah**-tah **dehl**-lah chee-**tah**
...in English	*...in inglese*	een een-**glay**-zay
When is the next tour in English?	*Quando è il prossimo tour in inglese?*	**kwahn**-doh eh eel **proh**-see-moh toor een een-**glay**-zay
Is it free?	*È gratis?*	eh **grah**-tees
How much is it?	*Quanto costa?*	**kwahn**-toh **koh**-stah
How long does it last?	*Quanto dura?*	**kwahn**-toh **doo**-rah
Can I / Can we join a tour in progress?	*Posso / Possiamo unirci ad un tour già iniziato?*	**poh**-soh / poh-see**ah**-moh oon-**eer**-chee ahd oon toor jah ee-neet-see**ah**-toh

ACTIVITIES

Entrance Signs

adulti	adults
giro guidato, tour	guided tour
mostra	special exhibit
siete qui	you are here (on map)

Discounts

You may be eligible for discounts at tourist sights, hotels, or on buses and trains—ask.

Is there a discount for...?	*Fate sconti per...?*	**fah**-tay **skohn**-tee pehr
...youth	*...giovani*	joh-**vah**-nee
...students	*...studenti*	stoo-**dehn**-tee
...families	*...famiglie*	fah-**meel**-yay
...seniors	*...anziani*	ahnt-seeah-nee
...groups	*...comitive*	koh-mee-**tee**-vay
I am...	*Sono...*	**soh**-noh
He / She is...	*Lui / Lei ha...*	lwee / **leh**ee ah
... ___ years old.	*... ___ anni.*	___ **ahn**-nee
...extremely old.	*...vecchissimo[a].*	vehk-**ee**-see-moh

In the Museum

Where is...?	*Dov'è...?*	doh-**veh**
I'd / We'd like to see...	*Mi / Ci piacerebbe vedere...*	mee / chee peeah-chay-**ray**-bay vay-**dehr**-ay
Photo / video O.K.?	*Foto / video è O.K.?*	**foh**-toh / **vee**-day-oh eh "O.K."
No flash / tripod.	*Vietato usare flash / trepiede.*	veeay-**tah**-toh oo-**zah**-ray flahsh / tray-peeay-day
I like it.	*Mi piace.*	mee peeah-chay
It's so...	*È così...*	eh koh-**zee**
...beautiful.	*...bello.*	**behl**-loh
...ugly.	*...brutto.*	**broo**-toh
...strange.	*...strano.*	**strah**-noh

ACTIVITIES

...boring.	...noioso.	noh-**yoh**-zoh
...interesting.	...interessante.	een-tay-ray-**sahn**-tay
...pretentious.	...presuntuoso.	pray-zoon-**twoh**-zoh
It's thought-provoking.	Fa pensare.	fah pehn-**sah**-ray
It's B.S.	È una stronzata.	eh **oo**-nah strohnt-**sah**-tah
I don't get it.	Non capisco.	nohn kah-**pees**-koh
Is it upside down?	È rovesciato?	eh roh-vay-**shah**-toh
Who did this?	Chi l'ha fatto?	kee lah **fah**-toh
How old is this?	Quanti anni ha?	**kwahn**-tee **ah**-nee ah
Wow!	Wow!	"Wow"
My feet hurt!	Mi fanno male i piedi!	mee **fah**-noh **mah**-lay ee peeay-dee
I'm exhausted!	Sono stanco[a] morto[a]!	**soh**-noh **stahn**-koh **mor**-toh
We're exhausted!	Siamo stanchi[e] morti[e]!	seeah-moh **stahn**-kee **mor**-tee

Be careful when planning your sightseeing. Many museums close in the afternoon from 1:00 P.M. until 3:00 or 4:00 P.M., and are closed all day on a weekday, usually Monday. Museums often stop selling tickets 45 minutes before closing. Historic churches usually open much earlier than museums.

Art and Architecture

art	arte	**ar**-tay
artist	artista	ar-**tee**-stah
painting	quadro	**kwah**-droh
self portrait	autoritratto	ow-toh-ree-**trah**-toh
sculptor	scultore	skool-**toh**-ray
sculpture	scultura	skool-**too**-rah
architect	architetto	ar-kee-**teht**-toh
architecture	architettura	ar-kee-teht-**too**-rah
original	originale	oh-ree-jee-**nah**-lay
restored	restaurato	ray-stow-**rah**-toh
B.C.	A.C.	ah chee

A.D.	D.C.	dee chee
century	secolo	**say**-koh-loh
style	stile	**stee**-lay
copy by ___	copia di ___	**koh**-peeah dee
after the style of ___	nello stile di ___	**nehl**-loh **stee**-lay dee
from the school of ___	della scuola di ___	**dehl**-lah **skwoh**-lah dee
abstract	Astratto	ah-**strah**-toh
ancient	Antico	ahn-**tee**-koh
Art Nouveau	Arte Nouveau	**ar**-tay **noo**-voh
Baroque	Barocco	bah-**roh**-koh
classical	Classico	**klah**-see-koh
Gothic	Gotico	**goh**-tee-koh
impressionist	Impressionista	eem-pray-seeoh-**nee**-stah
medieval	Medievale	may-deeay-**vah**-lay
modern	Moderno	moh-**dehr**-noh
Neoclassical	Neoclassico	nee-oh-**klah**-see-koh
Renaissance	Rinascimento	ree-nah-shee-**mayn**-toh
Romanesque	Romanico	roh-**mahn**-ee-koh
Romantic	Romantico	roh-**mahn**-tee-koh

The Italians refer to their three greatest centuries of art in an unusual way. The 1300s are called *tre cento* (300s). The 1400s (early Renaissance) are called *quattro cento* (400s), and the 1500s (High Renaissance) are *cinque cento* (500s).

Castles and Palaces

castle	castello	kah-**stehl**-loh
palace	palazzo	pah-**lahd**-zoh
hall	sala	**sah**-lah
kitchen	cucina	koo-**chee**-nah
cellar	cantina	kahn-**tee**-nah
dungeon	segrete	say-**gray**-tay
moat	fossato	foh-**sah**-toh
fortified walls	muri	**moo**-ree
	fortificati	for-tee-fee-**kah**-tee

tower	*torre*	**tor**-ray
fountain	*fontana*	fohn-**tah**-nah
garden	*giardino*	jar-**dee**-noh
king	*re*	ray
queen	*regina*	ray-**jee**-nah
knight	*cavaliero*	kah-vah-lee**ay**-roh

Religious Words

cathedral	*duomo*	**dwoh**-moh
church	*chiesa*	kee**ay**-zah
monastery	*monastero*	moh-nah-**stay**-roh
synagogue	*sinagoga*	see-nah-**goh**-gah
chapel	*cappella*	kah-**pehl**-lah
altar	*altare*	ahl-**tah**-ray
bells	*campane*	kahm-**pah**-nay
choir	*coro*	**kor**-oh
cloister	*chiostro*	kee**oh**-stroh
cross	*croce*	**kroh**-chay
crypt	*cripta*	**kreep**-tah
dome	*cupola*	**koo**-poh-lah
organ	*organo*	**or**-gah-noh
pulpit	*pulpito*	pool-**pee**-toh
relics	*reliquie*	ray-**lee**-kweeay
treasury	*tesoro*	tay-**zoh**-roh
baptistery	*battistero*	bah-tee-**stay**-roh
saint	*santo[a]*	**sahn**-toh
pope	*Papa*	**pah**-pah
God	*Dio*	**dee**-oh
Christian	*cristiano[a]*	kree-stee**ah**-noh
Protestant	*protestante*	proh-tay-**stahn**-tay
Catholic	*cattolico[a]*	kah-**toh**-lee-koh
Jewish	*ebreo*	ay-**bray**-oh
Muslim	*mussulmano[a]*	moo-sool-**mah**-noh
agnostic	*agnostico[a]*	ahn-**yoh**-stee-koh
atheist	*ateo[a]*	ah-**tay**-oh
When is the mass (service)?	*A che ora è la messa?*	ah kay **oh**-rah eh lah **may**-sah

ACTIVITIES

| Are there church concerts? | *Ci sono concerti in chiesa?* | chee **soh**-noh kohn-**chehr**-tee een kee**ay**-zah |

The piano was invented in Italy. Unlike a harpsichord, it could be played soft and loud, so it was called just that: *piano-forte* (soft-loud). Here are other Italian musical words you might know: *subito* (suddenly), *crescendo* (growing louder), *sopra* (over), *sotto* (under), *ritardando* (slowing down), and *fine* (finish).

SHOPPING

Italian Shops

Where is a...?	*Dov'è un...?*	doh-**veh** oon
antique shop	*negozio di antiquariato*	nay-**goht**-seeoh dee ahn-tee-kwah-ree**ah**-toh
art gallery	*galleria d'arte*	gah-lay-**ree**-ah **dar**-tay
bakery	*panificio*	pah-nee-**fee**-choh
barber shop	*barbiere*	bar-bee**ay**-ray
beauty salon	*parrucchiere*	pah-roo-kee**ay**-ray
book shop	*libreria*	lee-bray-**ree**-ah
camera shop	*foto-ottica*	foh-toh-**oh**-tee-kah
cell phone shop	*negozio di cellulari*	nay-**goht**-seeoh dee chehl-loo-**lah**-ree
clothing boutique	*boutique di abbigliamento*	boo-**teek** dee ah-beel-yah-**mehn**-toh
coffee shop	*bar*	bar
department store	*grande magazzino*	**grahn**-day mah-gahd-**zee**-noh
delicatessen	*salumeria*	sah-loo-may-**ree**-ah
flea market	*mercato delle pulci*	mehr-**kah**-toh **dehl**-lay **pool**-chee
flower market	*mercato dei fiori*	mehr-**kah**-toh **deh**ee fee-**oh**-ree
grocery store	*alimentari*	ah-lee-mayn-**tah**-ree
hardware store	*ferramenta*	fehr-rah-**mehn**-tah

Key Phrases: Shopping

Where can I buy...?	Dove posso comprare...?	**doh**-vay **poh**-soh kohm-**prah**-ray
Where is a...?	Dov'è un...?	doh-**veh** oon
grocery store	alimentari	ah-lee-mayn-**tah**-ree
department store	grande magazzino	**grahn**-day mah-gahd-**zee**-noh
Internet café	Internet café	**een**-tehr-neht kah-**fay**
launderette	lavanderia	lah-vahn-day-**ree**-ah
pharmacy	farmacia	far-mah-**chee**-ah
How much is it?	Quanto costa?	**kwahn**-toh **koh**-stah
I'm just browsing.	Sto solo guardando.	stoh **soh**-loh gwar-**dahn**-doh

Internet café	Internet café	**een**-tehr-neht kah-**fay**
jewelry shop	gioielliera	joh-yay-lee**ay**-rah
launderette	lavanderia	lah-vahn-day-**ree**-ah
leather shop	pelletteria	pehl-leht-teh-**ree**-ah
newsstand	giornalaio	jor-nah-**lah**-yoh
office supplies	cartoleria	kar-toh-lay-**ree**-ah
open air market	mercato	mehr-**kah**-toh
optician	ottico	**oh**-tee-koh
pastry shop	pasticceria	pah-stee-chay-**ree**-ah
pharmacy	farmacia	far-mah-**chee**-ah
photocopy shop	copisteria	koh-pee-stay-**ree**-ah
pottery shop	negozio di ceramica	nay-**goht**-seeoh dee chay-**rah**-mee-kah
shopping mall	centro commerciale	**chehn**-troh koh-mehr-**chah**-lay
souvenir shop	negozio di souvenir	nay-**goht**-seeoh dee **soo**-vay-neer
supermarket	supermercato	soo-pehr-mehr-**kah**-toh
sweets shop	negozio di dolciumi, pasticceria	nay-**goht**-seeoh dee dohl-chee**oo**-mee, pah-stee-chay-**ree**-ah

toy store	*negozio di giocattoli*	nay-**goht**-seeoh dee joh-**kah**-toh-lee
travel agency	*agenzia di viaggi*	ah-jehnt-**see**-ah dee veeah-jee
used bookstore	*negozio di libri usati*	nay-**goht**-seeoh dee **lee**-bree oo-**zah**-tee
...with books in English	*...che vende libri in inglese*	kay **vehn**-dray lee-bree een een-**glay**-zay
wine shop	*negozio di vini*	nay-**goht**-seeoh dee **vee**-nee

Most businesses are closed daily from 1:00 P.M. until 3:00 or 4:00 P.M. Many stores in the larger cities close for all or part of August—not a good time to plan a shopping spree.

Shop Till You Drop

opening hours	*orario d'apertura*	oh-**rah**-reeoh dah-pehr-**too**-rah
sale	*saldo*	**sahl**-doh
I'd like / We'd like...	*Vorrei / Vorremmo...*	vor-**reh**ee / vor-**ray**-moh
Where can I buy...?	*Dove posso comprare...?*	**doh**-vay **poh**-soh kohm-**prah**-ray
Where can we buy...?	*Dove possiamo comprare...?*	**doh**-vay poh-see**ah**-moh kohm-**prah**-ray
How much is it?	*Quanto costa?*	**kwahn**-toh **koh**-stah
I'm / We're...	*Sto / Stiamo...*	stoh / stee**ah**-moh
...just browsing.	*...solo guardando.*	**soh**-loh gwar-**dahn**-doh
Do you have something...?	*Avete qualcosa di...?*	ah-**vay**-tay kwahl-**koh**-zah dee
...cheaper	*...meno caro*	**may**-noh **kah**-roh
...better	*...miglior qualità*	**meel**-yor kwah-lee-**tah**
Better quality, please.	*Qualcosa di migliore qualità, per favore.*	kwahl-**koh**-zah dee **meel**-yoh-ray kwah-lee-**tah** pehr fah-**voh**-ray
genuine / imitation	*autentico / imitazione*	ow-**tehn**-tee-koh / ee-mee-taht-see**oh**-nay

Can I / Can we see more?	Posso / Possiamo vederne ancora?	**poh**-soh / poh-seeah-moh vay-**dehr**-nay ahn-**koh**-rah
This one.	Questo qui.	**kweh**-stoh kwee
Can I try it on?	Lo posso provare?	loh **poh**-soh proh-**vah**-ray
Do you have a mirror?	Ha uno specchio?	ah **oo**-noh **spay**-keeoh
Too...	Troppo...	**troh**-poh
...big.	...grande.	**grahn**-day
...small.	...piccolo.	**pee**-koh-loh
...expensive.	...caro.	**kah**-roh
It's too...	È troppo...	eh **troh**-poh
...short / long.	...corto / lungo.	**kor**-toh / **loon**-goh
...tight / loose.	...stretto / largo.	**streht**-toh / **lar**-goh
...dark / light.	...scuro / chiaro.	**skoo**-roh / keeah-roh
What is it made of?	Di che cosa è fatto?	dee kay **koh**-zah eh **fah**-toh
Is it machine washable?	Si può lavare in lavatrice?	see pwoh lah-**vah**-ray een lah-vah-**tree**-chay
Will it shrink?	Si ritira?	see ree-**tee**-rah
Will it fade in the wash?	Scolora quando si lava?	skoh-**loh**-rah **kwahn**-doh see **lah**-vah
Credit card O.K.?	Carta di credito è O.K.?	**kar**-tah dee **kray**-dee-toh eh "O.K."
Can you ship this?	Può spedirmelo?	pwoh spay-**deer**-may-loh
Tax-free?	Esente da tasse?	ay-**zehn**-tay dah **tah**-say
I'll think about it.	Ci penserò.	chee pehn-say-**roh**
What time do you close?	A che ora chiudete?	ah kay **oh**-rah keeoo-**day**-tay
What time do you open tomorrow?	A che ora aprite domani?	ah kay **oh**-rah ah-**pree**-tay doh-**mah**-nee

Street Markets

| Did you make this? | L'avete fatto voi questo? | lah-**vay**-tay **fah**-toh **voh**ee **kweh**-stoh |

Is that your final price?	È questo il prezzo finale?	eh **kweh**-stoh eel **prehd**-zoh fee-**nah**-lay
Cheaper?	Me lo dà a meno?	may loh dah ah **may**-noh
My last offer.	La mia ultima offerta.	lah **mee**-ah **ool**-tee-mah oh-**fehr**-tah
Good price.	Buon prezzo.	bwohn **prehd**-zoh
I'll take it.	Lo prendo.	loh **prehn**-doh
We'll take it.	Lo prendiamo.	loh prehn-dee**ah**-moh
I'm nearly broke.	Sono quasi al verde.	**soh**-noh **kwah**-zee ahl **vehr**-day
We're nearly broke.	Siamo quasi al verde.	see**ah**-moh **kwah**-zee ahl **vehr**-day
My male friend...	Il mio amico...	eel **mee**-oh ah-**mee**-koh
My female friend...	La mia amica...	lah **mee**-ah ah-**mee**-kah
My husband...	Mio marito...	**mee**-oh mah-**ree**-toh
My wife...	Mia moglie...	**mee**-ah **mohl**-yay
...has the money.	...ha i soldi.	ah ee **sohl**-dee

At street markets, it's common to bargain.

Clothes

For...	Per...	pehr
...a male / a female baby.	...un neonato / una neonata.	oon nay-oh-**nah**-toh / **oo**-nah nay-oh-**nah**-tah
...a male / a female child.	...un bambino / una bambina.	oon bahm-**bee**-noh / **oo**-nah bahm-**bee**-nah
...a male / a female teenager.	...un ragazzo / una ragazza.	oon rah-**gahd**-zoh / **oo**-nah rah-**gahd**-zah
...a man.	...un uomo.	oon **woh**-moh
...a woman.	...una donna.	**oo**-nah **doh**-nah
bathrobe	accappatoio	ah-kah-pah-**toh**-yoh
bib	bavaglino	bah-vahl-**yee**-noh
belt	cintura	cheen-**too**-rah
bra	reggiseno	ray-jee-**zay**-noh
clothing	vestiti	vehs-**tee**-tee
dress	vestito da donna	vehs-**tee**-toh dah **doh**-nah

flip-flops	ciabatte da piscina	chah-**bah**-tay dah pee-**shee**-nah
gloves	guanti	**gwahn**-tee
hat	cappello	kah-**pehl**-loh
jacket	giacca	**jah**-kah
jeans	jeans	"jeans"
nightgown	vestaglia	vehs-**tahl**-yah
nylons	collant	koh-**lahnt**
pajamas	pigiama	pee-**jah**-mah
pants	pantaloni	pahn-tah-**loh**-nee
raincoat	impermeabile	eem-pehr-may-**ah**-bee-lay
sandals	sandali	sahn-**dah**-lee
scarf	sciarpa, foulard	**shar**-pah, foo-**lard**
shirt...	camicia...	kah-**mee**-chah
...long-sleeved	...a maniche lunghe	ah mah-**nee**-kay **loong**-gay
...short-sleeved	...a maniche corte	ah mah-**nee**-kay **kor**-tay
...sleeveless	...senza maniche	**sehnt**-sah mah-**nee**-kay
shoelaces	lacci da scarpe	**lah**-chee dah **skar**-pay
shoes	scarpe	**skar**-pay
shorts	pantaloni corti	pahn-tah-**loh**-nee **kor**-tee
skirt	gonna	**goh**-nah
sleeper (for baby)	tutina (da neonato)	too-**tee**-nah (dah nay-oh-**nah**-toh)
slip	sottoveste	soh-toh-**vehs**-tay
slippers	ciabatte, pantofole	chah-**bah**-tay, pahn-**toh**-foh-lay
socks	calzini	kahlt-**see**-nee
sweater	maglione	mahl-yee**oh**-nay
swimsuit	costume da bagno	kohs-**too**-may dah **bahn**-yoh
tennis shoes	scarpe da ginnastica	**skar**-pay dah jee-**nah**-stee-kah
T-shirt	maglietta	mahl-**yay**-tah
underwear	mutande	moo-**tahn**-day
vest	gilè	jee-**lay**

ACTIVITIES

Colors

black	nero	**nay**-roh
blue	azzurro	ahd-**zoo**-roh
brown	marrone	mah-**roh**-nay
gray	grigio	**gree**-joh
green	verde	**vehr**-day
orange	arancio	ah-**rahn**-choh
pink	rosa	**roh**-zah
purple	viola	vee**oh**-lah
red	rosso	**roh**-soh
white	bianco	bee**ahn**-koh
yellow	giallo	**jah**-loh
dark / light	scuro / chiaro	**skoo**-roh / kee**ah**-roh
lighter	più chiaro	pew kee**ah**-roh
brighter	più brillante	pew bree-**lahn**-tay
darker	più scuro	pew **skoo**-roh

Materials

brass	ottone	oh-**toh**-nay
bronze	bronzo	**brohnt**-soh
ceramic	ceramica	chay-**rah**-mee-kah
copper	rame	**rah**-may
cotton	cotone	koh-**toh**-nay
glass	vetro	**vay**-troh
gold	oro	**oh**-roh
lace	pizzo	**peed**-zoh
leather	cuoio / pelle	**kwoh**-yoh / **pehl**-lay
linen	lino	**lee**-noh
marble	marmo	**mar**-moh
metal	metallo	may-**tah**-loh
nylon	nylon	**nee**-lohn
paper	carta	**kar**-tah
pewter	peltro	**pehl**-troh
plastic	plastica	**plah**-stee-kah
polyester	polyestere	poh-lee-ehs-**tay**-ray
porcelain	porcellana	por-chay-**lah**-nah

silk	seta	**say**-tah
silver	argento	ar-**jehn**-toh
velvet	velluto	vay-**loo**-toh
wood	legno	**layn**-yoh
wool	lana	**lah**-nah

Jewelry

bracelet	bracciale	brah-chee**ah**-lay
brooch	spilla	**spee**-lah
earrings	orecchini	oh-ray-**kee**-nee
jewelry	gioielli	joh-**yeh**-lee
necklace	collana	koh-**lah**-nah
ring	anello	ah-**nehl**-loh
Is this...?	Questo è...?	**kwehs**-toh eh
...sterling silver	...argento sterling	ar-**jehn**-toh **stehr**-leeng
...real gold	...oro zecchino	**oh**-roh tseh-**kee**-noh
...stolen	...rubato	roo-**bah**-toh

SPORTS

Bicycling

bicycle	bicicletta	bee-chee-**klay**-tah
mountain bike	mountain bike	"mountain bike"
I'd like to rent a bicycle.	Vorrei noleggiare una bicicletta.	vor-**reh**ee noh-leh-**jah**-ray **oo**-nah bee-chee-**klay**-tah
We'd like to rent two bicycles.	Vorremmo noleggiare due biciclette.	vor-**ray**-moh noh-leh-**jah**-ray **doo**-ay bee-chee-**klay**-tay
How much...?	Quanto...?	**kwahn**-toh
...per hour	...all'ora	ah-**loh**-rah
...per half day	...per mezza giornata	pehr **mehd**-zah jor-**nah**-tah
...per day	...al giorno	ahl **jor**-noh
Is a deposit required?	Ci vuole un deposito?	chee **vwoh**-lay oon day-**poh**-zee-toh

ACTIVITIES

deposit	deposito	day-**poh**-zee-toh
helmet	casco	**kahs**-koh
lock	lucchetto	loo-**keht**-toh
air / no air	aria /	**ah**-reeah /
	senza aria	**sehnt**-sah ah-reeah
tire	gomma	**goh**-mah
pump	pompa	**pohm**-pah
map	cartina	kar-**tee**-nah
How many gears?	Quante marce?	**kwahn**-tay **mar**-kay
What is a...route	Mi può	mee pwoh
of about ___	indicare un	een-dee-**kah**-ray oon
kilometers?	percorso... di	pehr-**kor**-soh... dee
	circa ___	**cheer**-kah ___
	chilometri?	kee-**loh**-may-tree
...good	...bello	**behl**-loh
...scenic	...panoramico	pah-noh-**rah**-mee-koh
...interesting	...interessante	een-tay-ray-**sahn**-tay
...easy	...facile	**fah**-chee-lay
How many	Quanti minuti /	**kwahn**-tee mee-**noo**-tee /
minutes / How	Quante ore	**kwahn**-tay **oh**-ray
many hours by	in bicicletta?	een bee-chee-**klay**-tah
bicycle?		
I (don't) like hills.	(Non) mi	(nohn) mee
	piacciono le	peeah-**choh**-noh lay
	salite.	sah-**lee**-tay
I brake for	Mi fermo	mee **fehr**-moh
bakeries.	ad ogni	ahd **ohn**-yee
	pasticceria.	pah-stee-chay-**ree**-ah

For more on route-finding, see "Finding Your Way," beginning on page 47 in the Traveling chapter.

Swimming and Boating

Where can I /	Dove posso /	**doh**-vay **poh**-soh /
can we rent...?	possiamo	poh-seeah-**moh**
	noleggiare...?	noh-leh-**jah**-ray

ACTIVITIES

...a paddleboat	...un pedalò	oon pay-dah-**loh**
...a rowboat	...una barca	**oo**-nah **bar**-kah
	a remi	ah **ray**-mee
...a boat	...una barca	**oo**-nah **bar**-kah
...a sailboat	...una barca	**oo**-nah **bar**-kah
	a vela	ah **vay**-lah
How much...?	Quanto...?	**kwahn**-toh
...per hour	...all'ora	ah-**loh**-rah
...per half day	...per mezza	pehr **mehd**-zah
	giornata	jor-**nah**-tah
...per day	...al giorno	ahl **jor**-noh
beach	spiaggia	spee**ah**-jah
nude beach	spiaggia	spee**ah**-jah
	nudista	noo-**dee**-stah
Where's a	Mi può	mee pwoh
good beach?	indicare una	een-dee-**kah**-ray **oo**-nah
	bella spiaggia?	**behl**-lah spee**ah**-jah
Is it safe for	È sicura per	eh see-**koo**-rah pehr
swimming?	nuotare?	nwoh-**tah**-ray
flip-flops	ciabatte da	chah-**bah**-tay dah
	piscina	pee-**shee**-nah
pool	piscina	pee-**shee**-nah
snorkel and mask	boccaglio e	boh-**kahl**-yoh ay
	maschera	mahs-**kay**-rah
sunglasses	occhiali da sole	oh-kee**ah**-lee dah **soh**-lay
sunscreen	protezione	proh-teht-see**oh**-nay
	solare	soh-**lah**-ray
surfboard	tavola da surf	**tah**-voh-lah dah soorf
surfer	surfer	**soorf**-er
swimsuit	costume da	kohs-**too**-may dah
	bagno	**bahn**-yoh
towel	asciugamano	ah-shoo-gah-**mah**-noh
waterskiing	sci acquatico	shee ah-**kwah**-tee-koh
windsurfing	windsurf	**weend**-soorf

ACTIVITIES

In Italy, nearly any beach is topless, but if you want to go to (or avoid) a nude beach, keep your eyes peeled for a *spiaggia nudista*.

Sports Talk

sports	gli sport	**lee**yee sport
game	partita	par-**tee**-tah
team	squadra	**skwah**-drah
championship	campionato	kahm-peeoh-**nah**-toh
soccer	football, calcio	**foot**-bahl, **kahl**-choh
basketball	basket	**bah**-skeht
hockey	hockey	**oh**-kee
American football	football Americano	**foot**-bahl ah-may-ree-**kah**-noh
baseball	baseball	**bahs**-bahl
tennis	tennis	**tehn**-nees
golf	golf	gohlf
skiing	sci	shee
gymnastics	ginnastica	jee-**nah**-stee-kah
jogging	jogging	**joh**-geeng
Olympics	le Olimpiadi	lay oh-leem-pee**ah**-dee
medal...	medaglia...	may-**dahl**-yah
...gold / silver / bronze	...oro / argento / bronzo	**oh**-roh / ar-**jehn**-toh / **brohnt**-soh
Which is your favorite sport / athlete?	Qual'è il suo sport / giocatore?	kwah-**leh** eel **soo**-oh sport / joh-kah-**toh**-ray
Which is your favorite team?	Qual'è la sua squadra?	kwah-**leh** lah **soo**-ah **skwah**-drah
Where can I see a game?	Dove posso vedere una partita?	**doh**-vay **poh**-soh vay-**day**-ray **oo**-nah par-**tee**-tah
Where's a good place to jog?	Dov'è un buon luogo per fare jogging?	doh-**veh** oon bwohn loo**oh**-goh pehr **fah**-ray **joh**-geeng

ENTERTAINMENT

What's happening tonight?	Che cosa succede stasera?	kay **koh**-zah soo-**chay**-day stah-**zay**-rah
What do you recommend?	Che cosa raccomanda?	kay **koh**-zah rah-koh-**mahn**-dah
Where is it?	Dov'è?	doh-**veh**
How do you get there?	Come ci si arriva?	**koh**-may chee see ah-**ree**-vah
Is it free?	È gratis?	eh **grah**-tees
Are there seats available?	Ci sono ancora dei posti?	chee **soh**-noh ahn-**koh**-rah **deh**ee poh-stee
Where can I buy a ticket?	Dove si comprano i biglietti?	**doh**-vay see kohm-**prah**-noh ee beel-**yay**-tee
Do you have tickets for today / tonight?	Ha dei biglietti per oggi / stasera?	ah **deh**ee beel-**yay**-tee pehr **oh**-jee / stah-**zay**-rah
When does it start?	A che ora comincia?	ah kay **oh**-rah koh-**meen**-chah
When does it end?	A che ora finisce?	ah kay **oh**-rah fee-**nee**-shay
Where's the best place to dance nearby?	Qual'è il posto migliore per ballare qui vicino?	kwah-**leh** eel **poh**-stoh meel-**yoh**-ray pehr bah-**lah**-ray kwee vee-**chee**-noh
Where do people stroll?	Dov'è la passeggiata?	doh-**veh** lah pah-say-**jah**-tah

Entertaining Words

movie...	cinema...	**chee**-nay-mah
...original version	...versione originale	vehr-see**oh**-nay oh-ree-jee-**nah**-lay
...in English	...in inglese	een een-**glay**-zay
...with subtitles	...con sottotitoli	kohn soh-toh-**tee**-toh-lee
...dubbed	...doppiato	doh-pee**ah**-toh
music...	musica...	**moo**-zee-kah

ACTIVITIES

...live	...dal vivo	dahl **vee**-voh
...classical	...classica	**klah**-see-kah
...folk	...folk	fohlk
...opera	...lirica	**lee**-ree-kah
...symphony	...sinfonica	seen-**foh**-nee-kah
...choir	...corale	koh-**rah**-lay
...traditional	...tradizionale	trah-deet-seeoh-**nah**-lay
old rock	rock vecchio stile	rohk **vehk**-eeoh **stee**-lay
jazz / blues	jazz / blues	jahz / "blues"
singer	cantante	kahn-**tahn**-tay
concert	concerto	kohn-**chehr**-toh
show	spettacolo	speht-**tah**-koh-loh
dancing	ballare	bah-**lah**-ray
folk dancing	danze	**dahnt**-say
	popolari	poh-poh-**lah**-ree
disco	discoteca	dee-skoh-**tay**-kah
bar with	locale con	loh-**kah**-lay kohn
live music	musica dal	**moo**-zee-kah dahl
	vivo	**vee**-voh
nightclub	locale notturno	loh-**kah**-lay noh-**toor**-noh
no cover charge	ingresso libero	een-**gray**-soh **lee**-bay-roh
sold out	tutto esaurito	**too**-toh ay-zow-**ree**-toh

For cheap entertainment, join the locals and take a *passeggiata* (stroll) through town. As you bump shoulders in the crowd, you'll know why it's also called *struscio* (rubbing). On workdays, Italians stroll between work and dinner. On holidays, they hit the streets after lunch. This is Italy on parade. People are strutting. If ever you could enjoy being forward, this is the time. Whispering a breathy *bella* (cute girl) or *bello* (cute guy) feels natural.

ACTIVITIES

CONNECT

PHONING

English	Italian	Pronunciation
I'd like to buy a...	Vorrei comprare una...	voh-**reh**ee kohm-**prah**-ray **oo**-nah
...telephone card.	...carta telefonica.	**kar**-tah tay-lay-**foh**-nee-kah
...cheap international telephone card.	...carta telefonica prepagate internazionali.	**kar**-tah tay-lay-**foh**-nee-kah pray-pah-**gah**-tay een-tehr-naht-seeoh-**nah**-lee
Where is the nearest phone?	Dov'è il telefono più vicino?	doh-**veh** eel tay-**lay**-foh-noh pew vee-**chee**-noh
It doesn't work.	Non funziona.	nohn foont-seeoh-nah
May I use your phone?	Posso usare il telefono?	**poh**-soh oo-**zah**-ray eel tay-**lay**-foh-noh
Can you talk for me?	Può parlare per me?	pwoh par-**lah**-ray pehr may
It's busy.	È occupato.	eh oh-koo-**pah**-toh
Will you try again?	Può riprovare?	pwoh ree-proh-**vah**-ray
Hello. (on phone)	Pronto.	**prohn**-toh
My name is ___.	Mi chiamo ___.	mee keeah-moh
Sorry, I speak only a little Italian.	Mi dispiace, parlo solo un po' d'italiano.	mee dee-spee**ah**-chay **par**-loh **soh**-loh oon poh dee-tah-lee**ah**-noh

Speak slowly	Parli lentamente	**par**-lee layn-tah-**mayn**-tay
and clearly.	e chiaramente.	ay keeah-rah-**mayn**-tay
Wait a moment.	Un momento.	oon moh-**mayn**-toh

In this book, you'll find the phrases you need to reserve a hotel room (page 52) or a table at a restaurant (page 70). To spell your name over the phone, refer to the code alphabet on page 56.

Make your calls using handy phone cards sold at post offices, train stations, **tabacchi** (tobacco shops), and from machines near phone booths. There are two kinds:

1) an insertable card (**carta telefonica**) that you slide into a phone in a phone booth (tear the corner off your phone card before using), and...

2) a cheaper-per-minute international phone card (with a scratch-off PIN code) that you can use from any phone, usually even from your hotel room. If a phone balks, change its setting from pulse to tone. To get a PIN card, ask for a **carta telefonica prepagate internazionali.**

You can also make phone calls from post offices, telephone offices, and metered phones in cafés and bars.

At phone booths, you'll encounter these words on the phone's message display: **sganciare** (which means either hang onto the phone...or hang up), **inserire una carta** (insert a card), **carta telefonica** (the phone acknowledges that you've inserted a phone card), then **selezionare** or **digitare numero** (dial your number). **Occupato** means busy. You'll see the **credito** (monetary value of your card) tick down after you connect. When you hang up, you'll see **attendere prego** (please wait), **ritirare la carta** (retrieve your card), and again **sganciare** (you're done or you can start again). There are some regional differences in the various messages, but the sequence is the same.

Italian phones are temperamental. At any time while you're dialing, you may hear a brusque recording: "*Telecom Italia informazione gratuita: Il numero selezionato è inesistente*" (Telecom Italia free information: The number you're dialing is nonexistent). If you get this message, try dialing again, slowly, as though the phone doesn't understand numbers very well. For more tips, see "Let's Talk Telephones" on page 275 in the appendix.

Telephone Words

telephone	*telefono*	tay-**lay**-foh-noh
telephone card	*carta*	**kar**-tah
	telefonica	tay-lay-**foh**-nee-kah
cheap	*carta*	**kar**-tah
international	*telefonica*	tay-lay-**foh**-nee-kah
telephone card	*prepagate in-*	pray-pah-**gah**-tay een-
	ternazionali	tehr-naht-seeoh-**nah**-lee
PIN code	*PIN*	peen
phone booth	*cabina*	kah-**bee**-nah
	telefonica	tay-lay-**foh**-nee-kah
out of service	*guasto*	gooah-stoh
metered phone	*telefono a*	tay-**lay**-foh-noh ah
	scatti	**skah**-tee
phone office	*posto*	**poh**-stoh
	telefonico	tay-lay-**foh**-nee-koh
	pubblico	**poob**-lee-koh
operator	*centralinista*	chayn-trah-lee-**nee**-stah
international	*assistenza per*	ah-see-**stehnt**-sah pehr
assistance	*chiamate inter-*	keeah-**mah**-tay een-tehr-
	nazionali	naht-seeoh-**nah**-lee
international call	*telefonata inter-*	tay-lay-foh-**nah**-tah een-tehr-
	nazionale	naht-seeoh-**nah**-lay
collect call	*telefonata a*	tay-lay-foh-**nah**-tah ah
	carico del	**kah**-ree-koh dayl
	desinatario	dehs-tee-nah-**tah**-reeoh
credit card call	*telefonata con*	tay-lay-foh-**nah**-tah kohn
	la carta di	lah **kar**-tah dee
	credito	**kray**-dee-toh
toll-free	*numero verde*	**noo**-may-roh **vehr**-day
fax	*fax*	fahks
country code	*prefisso per*	pray-**fee**-soh pehr
	il paese	eel pah-**ay**-zay
area code	*prefisso*	pray-**fee**-soh
extension	*numero interno*	**noo**-may-roh een-**tehr**-noh
telephone book	*elenco*	ay-**lehn**-koh
	telefonico	tay-lay-**foh**-nee-koh
yellow pages	*pagine gialle*	**pah**-jee-nay **jah**-lay

Cell Phones

Where is a cell phone shop?	Dov'è un negozio di cellulari?	doh-**veh** oon nay-**goht**-seeoh dee chehl-loo-**lah**-ree
I'd like / We'd like...	Vorrei / Vorremmo...	vor-**reh**ee / vor-**ray**-moh
...a cell phone.	...un telefono cellulare.	oon tay-**lay**-foh-noh chehl-loo-**lah**-ray
...a chip.	...una scheda.	**oo**-nah **skay**-dah
...to buy more time.	...una ricarica.	**oo**-nah ree-**kah**-ree-kah
How do you...?	Come si fa a...?	**koh**-may see fah ah
...make calls	...fare una chiamata	**fah**-ray **oo**-nah keeah-**mah**-tah
...receive calls	...ricevere una chiamata	ree-**chay**-vay-ray **oo**-nah keeah-**mah**-tah
Will this work outside this country?	Funziona anche all'estero?	foont-seeoh-nah **ahn**-kay ah-lehs-**tay**-roh
Where can I buy a chip for this service / phone?	Dove posso comprare una scheda per questo gestore / telefono?	**doh**-vay **poh**-soh kohm-**prah**-ray **oo**-nah **skay**-dah pehr **kweh**-stoh jehs-**toh**-ray / tay-**lay**-foh-noh

Many travelers now buy cell phones in Europe to make both local and international calls. You'll pay under €100 for a "locked" phone that works only in the country you buy it in (includes about €20 worth of calls). You can buy additional time at a newsstand or cell phone shop. An "unlocked" phone is more expensive, but it works all over Europe: when you cross a border, buy a SIM card at a cell phone shop and insert the pop-out chip, which comes with a new phone number. Pricier tri-band phones (*telefono tri-banda*) also work in North America.

EMAIL AND THE WEB

Email

My email address is___.	*Il mio indirizzo di posta elettronica è___.*	eel **mee**-oh een-dee-**reed**-zoh dee **poh**-stah ay-leht-**troh**-nee-kah eh
What's your email address?	*Qual è il suo indirizzo di posta elettronica?*	kwahl eh eel **soo**-oh een-dee-**reed**-zoh dee **poh**-stah ay-leht-**troh**-nee-kah
Can I use this computer to check my email?	*Posso usare il computer per controllare mia posta elettronica?*	**poh**-soh oo-**zah**-ray eel kohm-**poo**-ter pehr kohn-troh-**lah**-ray **mee**-ah **poh**-stah ay-leht-**troh**-nee-kah
Where can I / can we access the Internet?	*C'è un posto dove posso / possiamo accedere a Internet?*	cheh oon **poh**-stoh **doh**-vay **poh**-soh / poh-see**ah**-moh ah-**chay**-day-ray ah **een**-tehr-neht
Where is an Internet café?	*Dov'è un Internet café?*	doh-**veh** oon **een**-tehr-neht kah-**fay**
How much for...minutes?	*Quanto costa per... minuti?*	**kwahn**-toh **koh**-stah pehr... mee-**noo**-tee
...10	*...dieci*	dee**ay**-chee
...15	*...quindici*	**kween**-dee-chee
...30	*...trenta*	**trayn**-tah
...60	*...sessanta*	say-**sahn**-tah
Help me, please.	*Mi aiuti, per favore.*	mee ah-**yoo**-tee pehr fah-**voh**-ray
How do I...	*Come si fa a...*	**koh**-may see fah ah
...start this?	*...accendere questo?*	ah-**chehn**-day-ray **kweh**-stoh
...send a file?	*...mandare un file?*	mahn-**dah**-ray oon **fee**-lay

CONNECT

Key Phrases: Email and the Web

email	*posta elettronica*	**poh**-stah ay-leht-**troh**-nee-kah
Internet	*Internet*	**een**-tehr-neht
Where is the nearest Internet access point?	*Dov'è l'Internet più vicino?*	doh-veh **leen**-tehr-neht pew vee-**chee**-noh
I'd like to check my email.	*Vorrei controllare la mia posta elettronica.*	vor-**reh**ee kohn-troh-**lah**-ray lah **mee**-ah poh-stah ay-leht-**troh**-nee-kah

...print out a file?	*...stampare un file?*	stahm-**pah**-ray oon **fee**-lay
...make this symbol?	*...fare questo simbolo?*	**fah**-ray **kweh**-stoh **seem**-boh-loh
...type @?	*...fare la chiocciola?*	fah-ray lah kee**oh**-choh-lah
This isn't working.	*Non funziona.*	nohn foont-see**oh**-nah

Web Words

email	*posta elettronica*	**poh**-stah ay-leht-**troh**-nee-kah
email address	*indirizzo di posta elettronica*	een-dee-**reed**-zoh dee **poh**-stah ay-leht-**troh**-nee-kah
website	*sito Internet*	**see**-toh **een**-tehr-neht
Internet	*Internet*	**een**-tehr-neht
surf the Web	*navigare su Internet*	nah-vee-**gah**-ray soo **een**-tehr-neht
download	*scaricare*	shah-ree-**kah**-ray
@ sign	*chiocciola*	kee**oh**-choh-lah
dot	*punto*	**poon**-toh
hyphen (-)	*trattino*	trah-**tee**-noh

CONNECT

underscore (_)	*linea bassa*	**lee**-nay-ah **bah**-sah
modem	*modem*	**moh**-dehm

On Screen

aprire	open	salvare	save	
cancellare	delete	stampare	print	
documento	file	scrivere	write	
inviare	send	rispondere	reply	
messaggio	message			

MAILING

Where is the post office?	*Dov'è la Posta?*	doh-**veh** lah **poh**-stah
Which window for...?	*Qual'è lo sportello per...?*	kwah-**leh** loh spor-**tehl**-loh pehr
Is this the line for...?	*È questa la fila per...?*	eh **kweh**-stah lah **fee**-lah pehr
...stamps	*...francobolli*	frahn-koh-**boh**-lee
...packages	*...pacchi*	**pah**-kee
To the United States...	*Per Stati Uniti...*	pehr **stah**-tee oo-**nee**-tee
...by air mail.	*...per via aerea.*	pehr **vee**-ah ah-**ay**-ray-ah
...by surface mail.	*...via terra.*	**vee**-ah **tehr**-rah
...slow and cheap.	*...lento e economico.*	**lehn**-toh ay ay-koh-**noh**-mee-koh
How much is it?	*Quanto costa?*	**kwahn**-toh **koh**-stah
How much to send a letter / postcard to...?	*Quanto costa mandare una lettera / una cartolina a...?*	**kwahn**-toh **koh**-stah mahn-**dah**-ray **oo**-nah leht-**tay**-rah / **oo**-nah kar-toh-**lee**-nah ah
I need stamps for ___ postcards to...	*Ho bisogno di francobolli per ___ cartoline per...*	oh bee-**zohn**-yoh dee frahn-koh-**boh**-lee pehr ___ kar-toh-**lee**-nay pehr
...America / Canada.	*...gli Stati Uniti / il Canada.*	**lee**yee **stah**-tee oo-**nee**-tee / eel kah-nah-**dah**

Key Phrases: Mailing

post office	*ufficio postale*	oo-**fee**-choh poh-**stah**-lay
stamp	*francobollo*	frahn-koh-**boh**-loh
postcard	*cartolina*	kar-toh-**lee**-nah
letter	*lettera*	**leht**-tay-rah
air mail	*per via aerea*	pehr **vee**-ah ah-**ay**-ray-ah
Where is the post office?	*Dov'è la Posta?*	doh-**veh** lah **poh**-stah
I need stamps for ___ postcards / letters to America.	*Ho bisogno di francobolli per ___ cartoline / lettere per gli Stati Uniti.*	oh bee-**zohn**-yoh dee frahn-koh-**boh**-lee pehr ___ kar-toh-**lee**-nay / **leht**-tay-ray pehr **lee**yee **stah**-tee oo-**nee**-tee

Pretty stamps, please.	*Dei bei francobolli, per favore.*	**deh**ee **beh**ee frahn-koh-**boh**-lee pehr fah-**voh**-ray
I always choose the slowest line.	*Scelgo sempre la fila più lenta.*	**shehl**-goh **sehm**-pray lah **fee**-lah pew **lehn**-tah
How many days will it take?	*Quanti giorni ci vogliono?*	**kwahn**-tee **jor**-nee chee **vohl**-yoh-noh

In Italy, you can often get stamps at the corner *tabacchi* (tobacco shop). As long as you know which stamps you need, this is a great convenience. Unless you like to gamble, avoid mailing packages from Italy. The most reliable post offices are in the Vatican City.

Licking the Postal Code

Post & Telegraph Office	*Poste e Telegrafi*	**poh**-stay ay tay-**lay**-grah-fee
post office	*ufficio postale*	oo-**fee**-choh poh-**stah**-lay
stamp	*francobollo*	frahn-koh-**boh**-loh

CONNECT

postcard	*cartolina*	kar-toh-**lee**-nah
letter	*lettera*	**leht**-tay-rah
envelope	*busta*	**boo**-stah
package	*pacco*	**pah**-koh
box...	*scatola...*	**skah**-toh-lah
...cardboard	*...de cartone*	day kar-**toh**-nay
string	*filo*	**fee**-loh
tape	*scotch*	"scotch"
mailbox	*cassetta postale*	kah-**say**-tah poh-**stah**-lay
air mail	*per via aerea*	pehr **vee**-ah ah-**ay**-ray-ah
express	*espresso*	eh-**sprehs**-soh
surface mail	*via terra*	**vee**-ah **tehr**-rah
slow and cheap	*lento e economico*	**lehn**-toh ay ay-koh-**noh**-mee-koh
book rate	*prezzo di listino*	**prehd**-zoh dee lee-**stee**-noh
weight limit	*limite di peso*	lee-**mee**-tay dee **pay**-zoh
registered	*raccomandata*	rah-koh-mahn-**dah**-tah
insured	*assicurato*	ah-see-koo-**rah**-toh
fragile	*fragile*	frah-**jee**-lay
contents	*contenuto*	kohn-tay-**noo**-toh
customs	*dogana*	doh-**gah**-nah
sender	*mittente*	mee-**tehn**-tay
destination	*destinatario*	dehs-tee-nah-**tah**-reeoh
to / from	*da / a*	dah / ah
address	*indirizzo*	een-dee-**reed**-zoh
zip code	*codice postale*	koh-**dee**-chay poh-**stah**-lay
general delivery	*fermo posta*	**fehr**-moh **poh**-stah

CONNECT

HELP!

Help!	Aiuto!	ah-**yoo**-toh
Call a doctor!	Chiamate un dottore!	keeah-**mah**-tay oon doh-**toh**-ray
Call...	Chiamate...	keeah-**mah**-tay
...the police.	...la polizia.	lah poh-leet-**see**-ah
...an ambulance.	...un'ambulanza.	oo-nahm-boo-**lahnt**-sah
...the fire department.	...i vigili del fuoco.	ee **vee**-jee-lee dehl **fwoh**-koh
I'm lost.	Mi sono perso[a].	mee **soh**-noh **pehr**-soh
We're lost.	Ci siamo persi[e].	chee seeah-moh **pehr**-see
Thank you for your help.	Grazie dell'aiuto.	**graht**-seeay dehl-ah-**yoo**-toh
You are very kind.	Lei è molto gentile.	**leh**ee eh **mohl**-toh jehn-**tee**-lay

In Italy, call 118 if you have a medical emergency.

Theft and Loss

Stop, thief!	Fermatelo! Al ladro!	fehr-**mah**-tay-loh ahl **lah**-droh
I have been robbed.	Sono stato[a] derubato[a].	**soh**-noh **stah**-toh day-roo-**bah**-toh
We have been robbed.	Siamo stati[e] derubati[e].	seeah-moh **stah**-tee day-roo-**bah**-tee

171

HELP!

Key Phrases: Help!

accident	*incidente*	een-chee-**dehn**-tay
emergency	*emergenza*	ay-mehr-**jehnt**-sah
police	*polizia*	poh-leet-**see**-ah
Help!	*Aiuto!*	ah-**yoo**-toh
Call a doctor / the police!	*Chiamate un dottore / la polizia!*	keeah-**mah**-tay oon doh-**toh**-ray / lah poh-leet-**see**-ah
Stop, thief!	*Fermatelo! Al ladro!*	fehr-**mah**-tay-loh ahl **lah**-droh

A thief took...	*Un ladro ha preso...*	oon **lah**-droh ah **pray**-zoh
Thieves took...	*I ladri hanno preso...*	ee **lah**-dree **ah**-noh **pray**-zoh
I have lost my money.	*Ho perso i soldi.*	oh **pehr**-soh ee **sohl**-dee
We have lost our money.	*Abbiamo perso i soldi.*	ah-beeah-moh **pehr**-soh ee **sohl**-dee
I've lost my...	*Ho perso il mio...*	oh **pehr**-soh eel **mee**-oh
...passport.	*...passaporto.*	pah-sah-**por**-toh
...ticket.	*...biglietto.*	beel-**yay**-toh
...baggage.	*...bagaglio.*	bah-**gahl**-yoh
...wallet.	*...portafoglio.*	por-tah-**fohl**-yoh
I've lost...	*Ho perso...*	oh **pehr**-soh
...my purse.	*...la mia borsa.*	la **mee**-ah **bor**-sah
...my faith in humankind.	*...la fiducia nel prossimo.*	lah fee-**doo**-chah nayl **proh**-see-moh
We've lost our...	*Abbiamo perso i nostri...*	ah-beeah-moh **pehr**-soh ee **noh**-stree
...passports.	*...passaporti.*	pah-sah-**por**-tee
...tickets.	*...biglietti.*	beel-**yay**-tee
...baggage.	*...bagagli.*	bah-**gahl**-yee
I want to contact my embassy.	*Vorrei contattare la mia ambasciata.*	vor-**reh**ee kohn-tah-**tah**-ray lah **mee**-ah ahm-bah-shee**ah**-tah

I need to file a police report for my insurance.	*Devo fare una denuncia per la mia assicurazione.*	**day**-voh **fah**-ray **oo**-nah day-**noon**-chah pehr lah **mee**-ah ah-see-koo-raht-see**oh**-nay

Dialing 113 will connect you to English-speaking police help. See page 277 in the appendix for American and Canadian embassies and consulates in Italy.

HELP!

Helpful Words

ambulance	*ambulanza*	ahm-boo-**lahnt**-sah
accident	*incidente*	een-chee-**dehn**-tay
injured	*ferito*	fay-**ree**-toh
emergency	*emergenza*	ay-mehr-**jehnt**-sah
emergency room	*pronto soccorso*	**prohn**-toh soh-**kor**-soh
fire	*fuoco*	**fwoh**-koh
police	*polizia*	poh-leet-**see**-ah
smoke	*fumo*	**foo**-moh
thief	*ladro*	**lah**-droh
pickpocket	*borsaiolo*	bor-sah-**yoh**-loh

Help for Women

Leave me alone.	*Mi lasci in pace.*	mee **lah**-shee een **pah**-chay
I want to be alone.	*Voglio stare sola.*	**vohl**-yoh **stah**-ray **soh**-lah
I'm not interested.	*Non sono interessata.*	nohn **soh**-noh een-tay-ray-**sah**-tah
I'm married.	*Sono sposata.*	**soh**-noh spoh-**zah**-tah
I'm a lesbian.	*Sono lesbica.*	**soh**-noh **lehz**-bee-kah
I have a contagious disease.	*Ho una malattia contagiosa.*	oh **oo**-nah mah-lah-**tee**-ah kohn-tah-**joh**-zah
You are bothering me.	*Mi sta importunando.*	mee stah eem-por-too-**nahn**-doh
This man is bothering me.	*Questo uomo mi importuna.*	**kweh**-stoh **woh**-moh mee eem-por-**too**-nah

You are intrusive.	*Mi sta dando fastidio.*	mee stah **dahn**-doh fah-**stee**-deeoh
Don't touch me.	*Non mi tocchi.*	nohn mee **toh**-kee
You're disgusting.	*Tu sei disgustoso.*	too **seh**ee dees-goo-**stoh**-zoh
Stop following me.	*La smetta di seguirmi.*	lah **smay**-tah dee say-**gweer**-mee
Stop it!	*La smetta!*	lah **smay**-tah
Enough!	*Basta!*	**bah**-stah
Go away.	*Se ne vada.*	say nay **vah**-dah
Get lost!	*Sparisca!*	spah-**ree**-skah
Drop dead!	*Crepi!*	**kray**-pee
I'll call the police.	*Chiamo la polizia.*	kee**ah**-moh lah poh-leet-**see**-ah

Whenever macho males threaten to make leering a contact sport, local women stroll arm-in-arm or holding hands. Wearing conservative clothes and avoiding smiley eye contact also convey a "don't hustle me" message.

SERVICES

Laundry

Is a... nearby?	C'è una... qui vicino?	cheh **oo**-nah... kwee vee-**chee**-noh
...self-service laundry	...lavanderia self-service	lah-vahn-day-**ree**-ah sehlf-**sehr**-vees
...full-service laundry	...lavanderia	lah-vahn-day-**ree**-ah
Help me, please.	Mi aiuti, per favore.	mee ah-**yoo**-tee pehr fah-**voh**-ray
How does this work?	Come funziona?	**koh**-may foont-seeoh-nah
Where is the soap?	Dov'è il detersivo?	doh-**veh** eel day-tehr-**see**-voh
Are these yours?	Sono suoi questi?	**soh**-noh **swoh**-ee **kweh**-stee
This stinks.	Questo puzza.	**kweh**-stoh **pood**-zah
Smells...	Sente...	**sehn**-tay
...like spring time.	...del profumo di primavera.	dehl proh-**foo**-moh dee pree-mah-**vay**-rah
...like a locker room.	...d'uno spogliatoio.	**doo**-noh spohl-yah-**toh**-yoh
...like cheese.	...del formaggio.	dehl for-**mah**-joh
I need change.	Ho bisogno di moneta.	oh bee-**zohn**-yoh dee moh-**nay**-tah
Same-day service?	Servizio in giornata?	sehr-**veet**-seeoh een jor-**nah**-tah

175

SERVICES

By when do I need to drop off my clothes?	Quando devo portare qui i miei panni?	**kwahn**-doh **day**-voh por-**tah**-ray kwee ee mee-**ay**ee **pah**-nee
When will they be ready?	Quando saranno pronti?	**kwahn**-doh sah-**rah**-noh **prohn**-tee
Dried?	Asciutti?	ah-**shoo**-tee
Folded?	Piegati?	peeay-**gah**-tee
Hey there, what's spinning?	Salve, come gira?	**sahl**-vay **koh**-may **jee**-rah

Clean Words

wash / dry	lavare / asciugare	lah-**vah**-ray / ah-shoo-**gah**-ray
washer / dryer	lavatrice / asciugatrice	lah-vah-**tree**-chay / ah-shoo-gah-**tree**-chay
detergent	detersivo da bucato	day-tehr-**see**-voh dah boo-**kah**-toh
token	gettone	jeht-**toh**-nay
whites	il bianco	eel bee**ahn**-koh
colors	il colore	eel koh-**loh**-ray
delicates	delicato	day-lee-**kah**-toh
handwash	lavare a mano	lah-**vah**-ray ah **mah**-noh

Haircuts

Where is a barber / hair salon?	Dov'è un barbiere / parrucchiere?	doh-**veh** oon bar-bee**ay**-ray / pah-roo-kee**ay**-ray
I'd like...	Vorrei...	vor-**reh**ee
...a haircut.	...un taglio.	oon **tahl**-yoh
...a permanent.	...una permanente.	**oo**-nah pehr-mah-**nehn**-tay
...just a trim.	...solo una spuntatina.	**soh**-loh **oo**-nah spoon-tah-**tee**-nah
Cut about this much off.	Tagli tanto cosi.	**tahl**-yee **tahn**-toh **koh**-zee
Cut my bangs here.	Mi tagli la frangia qui.	mee **tahl**-yee lah **frahn**-jah kwee
Longer here.	Più lunghi qui.	pew **loong**-gee kwee

Shorter here.	*Più corti qui.*	pew **kor**-tee kwee
I'd like my hair...	*Vorrei...*	vor-**reh**ee
...short.	*...tagliarmi i capelli.*	tahl-**yar**-mee ee kah-**pay**-lee
...colored.	*...tingermi i capelli.*	teen-**jehr**-mee ee kah-**pay**-lee
...shampooed.	*...fare uno shampoo.*	**fah**-ray **oo**-noh **shahm**-poo
...blow dried.	*...una piega a phon.*	**oo**-nah pee**ay**-gah ah fohn
It looks good.	*Sta bene.*	stah **behn**-ay

SERVICES

Repair

These handy lines can apply to any repair, whether it's a ripped rucksack, bad haircut, or crabby camera.

This is broken.	*Questo è rotto.*	**kweh**-stoh eh **roh**-toh
Can you fix it?	*Lo può aggiustare?*	loh pwoh ah-joo-**stah**-ray
Just do the essentials.	*Faccia solamente le cose essenziali.*	**fah**-chah soh-lah-**mayn**-tay lay **koh**-zay ay-saynt-seeah-lee
How much will it cost?	*Quanto costa?*	**kwahn**-toh **koh**-stah
When will it be ready?	*Quando sarà pronta?*	**kwahn**-doh sah-**rah** **prohn**-tah
I need it by ___.	*Ne ho bisogno entro ___.*	nay oh bee-**zohn**-yoh **ayn**-troh
We need it by ___.	*Ci serve per___.*	chee **sehr**-vay pehr
Without it, I'm...	*Senza sono...*	**sehn**-sah **soh**-noh
...lost.	*...perso.*	**pehr**-soh
...ruined.	*...rovinato.*	roh-vee-**nah**-toh
...finished.	*...finito.*	fee-**nee**-toh

Filling out Forms

Signore / Signora / Signorina	Mr. / Mrs. / Miss
nome	first name
cognome	name
indirizzo	address
domicilio	address
strada	street
città	city
stato	state
paese	country
nazionalità	nationality
origine / destinazione	origin / destination
età	age
data di nascita	date of birth
luogo di nascita	place of birth
sesso	sex
sposato / sposata	married man / married woman
scapolo / nubile	single man / single woman
professione	profession
adulto	adult
bambino / ragazzo / ragazza	child / boy / girl
bambini	children
famiglia	family
firma	signature

When filling out dates, do it European-style: day/month/year.

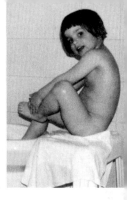

HEALTH

I am sick.	Sto male.	stoh **mah**-lay
I feel (very) sick.	Mi sento (molto) male.	mee **sehn**-toh (**mohl**-toh) **mah**-lay
My husband / My wife...	Mio marito / Mia moglie...	**mee**-oh mah-**ree**-toh / **mee**-ah **mohl**-yay
My son / My daughter...	Mio figlio / Mia figlia...	**mee**-oh **feel**-yoh / **mee**-ah **feel**-yah
My male friend / My female friend...	Il mio amico / La mia amica...	eel **mee**-oh ah-**mee**-koh / lah **mee**-ah ah-**mee**-kah
...feels (very) sick.	...si sente (molto) male.	see **sehn**-tay (**mohl**-toh) **mah**-lay
It's urgent.	È urgente.	eh oor-**jehn**-tay
I / We need a doctor...	Ho / Abbiamo bisogno di un dottore...	oh / ah-beeah-moh bee-**zohn**-yoh dee oon doh-**toh**-ray
...who speaks English	...che parli inglese.	kay **par**-lee een-**glay**-zay
Please call a doctor.	Per favore, chiami un dottore.	pehr fah-**voh**-ray keeah-mee oon doh-**toh**-ray
Could a doctor come here?	Puo venire qua un dottore?	pwoh vay-**nee**-ray kwah oon doh-**toh**-ray
I am...	Sono...	**soh**-noh
He / She is...	Lui / Lei è...	lwee / **leh**ee eh
...allergic to	...allergico[a] alla	ah-**lehr**-jee-koh **ah**-lah

179

HEALTH

penicillin / sulfa.	*pennicillina / ai sulfamidici.*	pehn-nee-chee-**lee**-nah / **ah**ee sool-fah-mee-**dee**-chee
I am diabetic.	*Ho il diabete.*	oh eel deeah-**bay**-tay
I have cancer.	*Ho il cancro.*	oh eel **kahn**-kroh
I had a heart attack ___ years ago.	*Ho avuto un infarto ___ anni fa.*	oh ah-**voo**-toh oon een-**far**-toh ___ **ah**-nee fah
It hurts here.	*Fa male qui.*	fah **mah**-lay kwee
I feel faint.	*Mi sento svenire.*	mee **sehn**-toh svay-**nee**-ray
It hurts to urinate.	*Fa male urinare.*	fah **mah**-lay oo-ree-**nah**-ray
I have body odor.	*Puzzo.*	**pood**-zoh
I'm going bald.	*Perdo i capelli.*	**pehr**-doh ee kah-**pay**-lee
Is it serious?	*È grave?*	eh **grah**-vay
Is it contagious?	*È contagioso?*	eh kohn-tah-**joh**-zoh
Aging sucks.	*Che schifo, invecchiare!*	kay **skee**-foh een-vehk-keeah-ray
Take one pill every ___ hours for ___ days before meals / with meals.	*Prenda una pillola ogni ___ ore per ___ giorni prima dei pasti / con i pasti.*	**prehn**-dah **oo**-nah peel-**oh**-lah **ohn**-yee ___ **oh**-ray pehr ___ **jor**-nee **pree**-mah **de**hee **pah**-stee / kohn ee **pah**-stee
I need a receipt for my insurance.	*Ho bisogno di una ricevuta per la mia assicurazione.*	oh bee-**zohn**-yoh dee **oo**-nah ree-chay-**voo**-tah pehr lah **mee**-ah ah-see-koo-raht-see**oh**-nay

Ailments

I have...	*Ho...*	oh
He / She has...	*Lui / Lei ha...*	lwee / **leh**ee ah
I / We need medication for...	*Ho / Abbiamo bisogno di un farmaco per...*	oh / ah-bee**ah**-moh bee-**zohn**-yoh dee oon far-**mah**-koh pehr
...arthritis.	*...l'artrite.*	lar-**tree**-tay

Key Phrases: Health

doctor	*dottore*	doh-**toh**-ray
hospital	*ospedale*	oh-spay-**dah**-lay
pharmacy	*farmacia*	far-mah-**chee**-ah
medicine	*medicina*	may-dee-**chee**-nah
I am sick.	*Mi sento male.*	mee **sehn**-toh **mah**-lay
I need a doctor	*Ho bisogno di*	oh bee-**zohn**-yoh dee
(who speaks	*un dottore (che*	oon doh-**toh**-ray (kay
English).	*parli inglese).*	**par**-lee een-**glay**-zay)
It hurts here.	*Fa male qui.*	fah **mah**-lay kwee

...asthma.	*...l'asma.*	**lahz**-mah
...athelete's foot (fungus).	*...piede d'atleta (fungo).*	peeay-day daht-**lay**-tah (**foong**-goh)
...bad breath.	*...l'alito cattivo.*	lah-**lee**-toh kah-**tee**-voh
...blisters.	*...vesciche.*	vay-**shee**-kay
...bug bites.	*...le punture d'insetto.*	lay poon-**too**-ray deen-**seht**-toh
...a burn.	*...una bruciatura.*	**oo**-nah broo-chah-**too**-rah
...chest pains.	*...dolore al petto.*	doh-**loh**-ray ahl **peht**-toh
...chills.	*...i brividi.*	ee bree-**vee**-dee
...a cold.	*...un raffreddore.*	oon rah-fray-**doh**-ray
...congestion.	*...una congestione.*	**oo**-nah kohn-jehs-teeoh-nay
...constipation.	*...la stitichezza.*	lah stee-tee-**kayd**-zah
...a cough.	*...la tosse.*	lah **toh**-say
...cramps.	*...i crampi*	ee krahm-pee
...diabetes.	*...il diabete.*	eel dee-ah-**bay**-tay
...diarrhea.	*...la diarrea.*	lah dee-ah-**ray**-ah
...dizziness.	*...capogiri.*	kah-poh-**jee**-ree
...earache.	*...il mal d'orecchi.*	eel mahl doh-**ray**-kee
...epilepsy.	*...l'epilessia.*	lay-pee-**lay**-seeah
...a fever.	*...la febbre.*	lah **feh**-bray
...the flu.	*...l'influenza.*	leen-floo-**ehnt**-sah

HEALTH

...food poisoning.	...l'avvelenamento da cibo.	lah-vehl-ehn-ah-**mehn**-toh dah **chee**-boh
...the giggles.	...la ridarella.	lah ree-dah-**ray**-lah
...hay fever.	...il raffreddore da fieno.	eel rah-fray-**doh**-ray dah fee**ay**-noh
...a headache.	...un mal di testa.	oon mahl dee **tehs**-tah
...a heart condition.	...i disturbi cardiaci.	ee dee-**stoor**-bee kar-dee**ah**-chee
...hemorrhoids.	...le emorroidi.	lay ay-moh-roh**ee**-dee
...high blood pressure.	...la pressione alta.	lah pray-see**oh**-nay **ahl**-tah
...indigestion.	...una indigestione.	**oo**-nah een-dee-jay-stee**oh**-nay
...an infection.	...una infezione.	**oo**-nah een-feht-see**oh**-nay
...inflammation.	...una infiammazione.	**oo**-nah een-feeah-maht-see**oh**-nay
...a migraine.	...l'emicrania.	lay-mee-**krah**-nee-ah
...nausea.	...la nausea.	lah **now**-zee-ah
...pneumonia.	...la bronco-polmonite.	lah brohn-koh-pohl-moh-**nee**-tay
...a rash.	...un'irritazione della pelle.	oo-nee-ree-taht-see**oh**-nay **dehl**-lah **pehl**-lay
...sinus problems.	...disturbi sinusali.	dee-**stoor**-bee see-noo-**zah**-lee
...a sore throat.	...il mal di gola.	eel mahl dee **goh**-lah
...a stomach ache.	...il mal di stomaco.	eel mahl dee **stoh**-mah-koh
...sunburn.	...una scottatura solare.	**oo**-nah skoh-tah-**too**-rah soh-**lah**-ray
...swelling.	...un gonfiore.	oon gohn-fee**oh**-ray
...a toothache.	...mal di denti.	mahl dee **dehn**-tee
...a urinary infection.	...infezione urinaria.	een-feht-see**oh**-nay oo-ree-**nah**-reeah
...a venereal disease.	...una malattia venerea.	**oo**-nah mah-lah-**tee**-ah vay-**nay**-ray-ah

...vicious sunburn.	...una grave scottatura solare.	oo-nah **grah**-vay skoh-tah-**too**-rah soh-**lah**-ray
...vomiting.	...il vomito.	eel **voh**-mee-toh
...worms.	...vermi.	**vehr**-mee

Women's Health

menstruation, period	le mestruazioni	lay may-stroo-aht-see**oh**-nee
menstrual cramps	i dolori mestruali	ee doh-**loh**-ree may-stroo-**ah**-lee
pregnancy (test)	(test di) gravidanza	(tehst dee) grah-vee-**dahnt**-sah
miscarriage	aborto spontaneo	ah-**bor**-toh spohn-**tah**-nay-oh
abortion	aborto	ah-**bor**-toh
birth control pills	pillole anti-concezionali	peel-**oh**-lay ahn-tee-kohn-chayt-seeoh-**nah**-lee
diaphragm	diaframma	deeah-**frah**-mah
condoms	preservativi	pray-zehr-vah-**tee**-vee
I'd like to see...	Vorrei vedere...	vor-**reh**ee vay-**dehr**-ay
...a female doctor.	...una dottoressa.	**oo**-nah doh-toh-**ray**-sah
...a female gynecologist.	...una ginecologa.	oo-nah jee-nay-koh-**loh**-gah
I've missed a period.	Ho saltato il ciclo mestruale.	oh sahl-**tah**-toh eel **chee**-kloh may-stroo-**ah**-lay
My last period started on ___.	L'ultima mestruazione è cominciata il ___.	**lool**-tee-mah may-stroo-aht-see**oh**-nay eh koh-meen-**chah**-tah eel
I am / She is... pregnant.	Sono / È incinta...	**soh**-noh / eh een-**cheen**-tah
...___ months	...di ___ mesi.	dee ___ **may**-zee

Parts of the Body

ankle	caviglia	kah-**veel**-yah
arm	braccio	**brah**-choh

HEALTH

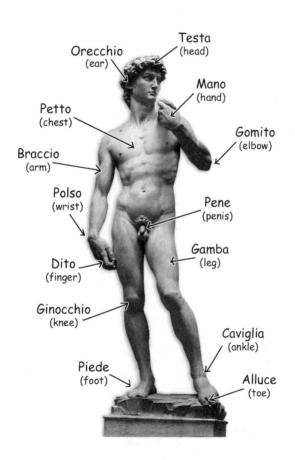

Testa
(head)

Orecchio
(ear)

Mano
(hand)

Petto
(chest)

Gomito
(elbow)

Braccio
(arm)

Polso
(wrist)

Pene
(penis)

Dito
(finger)

Gamba
(leg)

Ginocchio
(knee)

Caviglia
(ankle)

Piede
(foot)

Alluce
(toe)

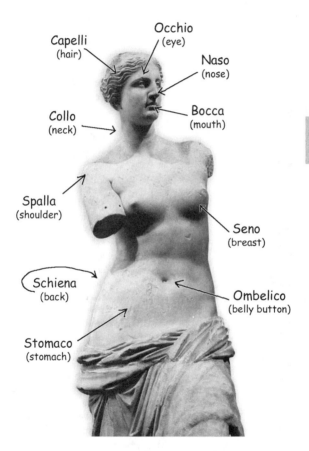

Capelli
(hair)

Occhio
(eye)

Naso
(nose)

Collo
(neck)

Bocca
(mouth)

Spalla
(shoulder)

Seno
(breast)

Schiena
(back)

Ombelico
(belly button)

Stomaco
(stomach)

back	schiena	skee**ay**-nah
bladder	vescica	vay-**shee**-kah
breast	seno	**say**-noh
buttocks	glutei	**gloo**-tehee
chest	petto	**pay**-toh
ear	orecchio	oh-**ray**-keeoh
elbow	gomito	goh-**mee**-toh
eye	occhio	**oh**-keeoh
face	faccia	**fah**-chah
finger	dito	**dee**-toh
foot	piede	pee**ay**-day
hair (head / body)	capelli / peli	kah-**pay**-lee / **pay**-lee
hand	mano	**mah**-noh
head	testa	**tehs**-tah
heart	cuore	**kwoh**-ray
intestines	intestino	een-tehs-**tee**-noh
knee	ginocchio	jee-**noh**-keeoh
leg	gamba	**gahm**-bah
lung	polmone	pohl-**moh**-nay
mouth	bocca	**boh**-kah
neck	collo	**koh**-loh
nose	naso	**nah**-zoh
penis	pene	**pay**-nay
rectum	retto	**ray**-toh
shoulder	spalla	**spah**-lah
stomach	stomaco	**stoh**-mah-koh
teeth	denti	**dehn**-tee
testicles	testicoli	tehs-**tee**-koh-lee
throat	gola	**goh**-lah
toe	alluce	ah-**loo**-chay
urethra	uretra	oo-**reht**-rah
uterus	utero	**oo**-tay-roh
vagina	vagina	vah-**jee**-nah
waist	vita	**vee**-tah
wrist	polso	**pohl**-soh

Healthy Words

24-hour pharmacy	farmacia aperta venti-quattro ore	far-mah-**chee**-ah ah-**pehr**-tah vayn-tee-**kwah**-troh **oh**-ray
bleeding	sanguinare	sahn-gwee-**nah**-ray
blood	sangue	**sahn**-gway
contraceptives	contraccettivi	kohn-trah-chay-**tee**-vee
dentist	dentista	dayn-**tee**-stah
doctor	dottore	doh-**toh**-ray
health insurance	assicurazione medica	ah-see-koo-raht-see-**oh**-nay **mehd**-ee-kah
hospital	ospedale	oh-spay-**dah**-lay
medical clinic	clinica	**klee**-nee-kah
medicine	medicina	may-dee-**chee**-nah
nurse	infermiera	een-fehr-mee-**ay**-rah
pain	dolore	doh-**loh**-ray
pharmacy	farmacia	far-mah-**chee**-ah
pill	pillola	**pee**-loh-lah
prescription	prescrizione	pray-skreet-see-**oh**-nay
unconscious	inconscio	een-**kohn**-shoh
X-ray	raggi x, radiografia	**rah**-jee eeks, rah-dee-oh-grah-**fee**-ah

HEALTH (vertical tab)

First-Aid Kit

antacid	antiacido	ahn-teeah-**chee**-doh
antibiotic	antibiotici	ahn-tee-beeoh-tee-chee
aspirin	aspirina	ah-spee-**ree**-nah
non-aspirin substitute	Saridon	**sah**-ree-dohn
bandage	benda	**behn**-dah
Band-Aids	cerotti	chay-**roh**-tee
cold medicine	medicina per il raffreddore	may-dee-**chee**-nah pehr eel rah-fray-**doh**-ray
cough drops	sciroppo per la tosse	skee-**roh**-poh pehr lah **toh**-say
decongestant	decongestio-nante	day-kohn-jehs-teeoh-**nahn**-tay

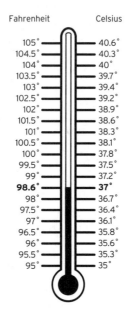

Fahrenheit   Celsius

Fahrenheit	Celsius
105°	40.6°
104.5°	40.3°
104°	40°
103.5°	39.7°
103°	39.4°
102.5°	39.2°
102°	38.9°
101.5°	38.6°
101°	38.3°
100.5°	38.1°
100°	37.8°
99.5°	37.5°
99°	37.2°
98.6°	**37°**
98°	36.7°
97.5°	36.4°
97°	36.1°
96.5°	35.8°
96°	35.6°
95.5°	35.3°
95°	35°

HEALTH

disinfectant	*disinfettante*	dee-seen-feht-**tahn**-tay
first-aid cream	*pomata*	proh-**mah**-tah
	antistaminica	ahn-tee-stah-**mee**-nee-kah
gauze / tape	*garza / nastro*	**gart**-sah / **nah**-stroh
laxative	*lassativo*	lah-sah-**tee**-voh
medicine for	*farmaco per*	far-**mah**-koh pehr
diarrhea	*la diarrea*	lah dee-ah-**ray**-ah
moleskin	*feltro, moleskin*	**fehl**-troh, "moleskin"
pain killer	*analgesico*	ah-nahl-**jehz**-ee-koh
Preparation H	*Preparazione*	pray-pah-raht-see**oh**-nay
	H	**ah**-kah
support bandage	*fascia di*	**fah**-shah dee
	sostegno	soh-**stehn**-yoh
thermometer	*termometro*	tehr-moh-**may**-troh

| Vaseline | vaselina | vah-zay-**lee**-nah |
| vitamins | vitamine | vee-tah-**mee**-nay |

Contacts and Glasses

glasses	occhiali	oh-kee**ah**-lee
sunglasses	occhiali da sole	oh-kee**ah**-lee dah **soh**-lay
prescription	prescrizione	pray-skreet-see**oh**-nay
contact lenses...	lenti a contatto	**lehn**-tee ah kohn-**tah**-toh
...soft	...morbide	**mor**-bee-day
...hard	...dure	**doo**-ray
cleaning solution	liquido disinfettante	**lee**-kwee-doh dee-seen-feht-**tahn**-tay
soaking solution	soluzione salina	soh-loot-see**oh**-nay sah-**lee**-nah
all-purpose solution	liquido unico per lenti a contatto	**lee**-kwee-doh **oo**-nee-koh pehr **lehn**-tee ah kohn-**tah**-toh
20/20 vision	visione perfetto	vee-zee**oh**-nay pehr-**feht**-toh
I've... a contact lens.	Ho... una lente a contatto.	oh... **oo**-nah **lehn**-tay ah kohn-**tah**-toh
...lost	...perso	**pehr**-soh
...swallowed	...inghiottito	een-goh-**tee**-toh

Toiletries

comb	pettine	pay-**tee**-nay
conditioner for hair	balsamo	**bahl**-sah-moh
condoms	preservativi	pray-zehr-vah-**tee**-vee
dental floss	filo interdentale	**fee**-loh een-tehr-dayn-**tah**-lay
deodorant	deodorante	day-oh-doh-**rahn**-tay
facial tissue	fazzoletto di carta	fahd-zoh-**lay**-toh dee **kar**-tah
hairbrush	spazzola per capelli	spahd-**zoh**-lah pehr kah-**pay**-lee
hand lotion	crema per le mani	**kray**-mah pehr lay **mah**-nee

HEALTH

lip salve	burro di cacao	boo-roh dee kah-kah-oh
mirror	specchio	spay-keeoh
nail clippers	tagliaunghie	tahl-yah-oong-geeay
razor	rasoio	rah-zoh-yoh
sanitary napkins	assorbenti	ah-sor-bayn-tee
	igienici	ee-jay-nee-chee
scissors	forbici	for-bee-chee
shampoo	shampoo	shahm-poo
shaving cream	crema da barba	kray-mah dah bar-bah
soap	sapone	sah-poh-nay
sunscreen	protezione	proh-tayt-seeoh-nay
	solare	soh-lah-ray
suntan lotion	crema	kray-mah
	abbronzante	ah-brohnt-sahn-tay
tampons	assorbenti	ah-sor-bayn-tee
	interni	een-tehr-nee
tissues	fazzoletti	fahd-zoh-leht-tee
	di carta	dee kar-tah
toilet paper	carta igienica	kar-tah ee-jay-nee-kah
toothbrush	spazzolino	spahd-zoh-lee-noh
	da denti	dah dayn-tee
toothpaste	dentifricio	dayn-tee-free-choh
tweezers	pinzette	peent-say-tay

Makeup

blush	fard	fard
eye shadow	ombretto	ohm-bray-toh
eyeliner	matita, eyeliner	mah-tee-tah, "eyeliner"
face cleanser	latte detergente	lah-tay day-tehr-jehn-tay
face powder	cipria	cheep-reeah
foundation	fondotinta	fohn-doh-teen-tah
lipstick	rossetto	roh-say-toh
makeup	trucco	troo-koh
mascara	mascara	mah-skah-rah
moisturizer...	crema	kray-mah
	idratante...	ee-drah-tahn-tay

HEALTH

...with sun block	...con protezione solare	kohn proh-tayt-see**oh**-nay soh-**lah**-ray
nail polish	smalto per le unghie	**smahl**-toh pehr lay **oong**-gay
nail polish remover	solvente per le unghie	sohl-**vehn**-tay pehr lay **oong**-gay
perfume	profumo	proh-**foo**-moh

For Babies

baby	neonato	nay-oh-**nah**-toh
baby food	cibo per neonati	**chee**-boh pehr nay-oh-**nah**-tee
bib	bavaglino	bah-vahl-**yee**-noh
bottle	biberon	**bee**-behr-ohn
diaper	pannolino	pah-noh-**lee**-noh
diapers	pannolini	pah-noh-**lee**-nee
diaper wipes	salviettine per neonati	sahl-veeay-**tee**-nay pehr nay-oh-**nah**-tee
diaper ointment	olio per neonati	**oh**-leeoh pehr nay-oh-**nah**-tee
formula...	formulazione...	for-moo-laht-see**oh**-nay
...powdered	...in polvere	een pohl-**vay**-ray
...liquid	...liquida	**lee**-kwee-dah
...soy	...di soia	dee **soh**-yah
medication for...	farmaco per la...	far-**mah**-koh pehr lah
...diaper rash	...dermatite da pannolone	dehr-mah-**tee**-tay dah pah-noh-**loh**-nay
...teething	...dentizione	dehn-teet-see**oh**-nay
nipple	capezzolo	kah-pehd-**zoh**-loh
pacifier	ciucio	**choo**-choh
Will you refrigerate this?	Può metterlo in frigo?	pwoh meht-**tehr**-loh een **free**-goh
Will you warm... for a baby?	Può riscaldare... per un neonato?	pwoh ree-skahl-**dah**-ray... pehr oon nay-oh-**nah**-toh
...this	...questo	**kweh**-stoh
...some water	...un po' d'acqua	oon poh **dah**-kwah

HEALTH

...some milk	...un po' di latte	oon poh dee **lah**-tay
Not too hot, please.	*Non troppo caldo,*	nohn **troh**-poh **kahl**-doh
	per favore.	pehr fah-**voh**-ray

More Baby Things

backpack to
  carry baby
	zaino per
	  portare i
	  neonati
		tsah**ee**-noh pehr
		  por-**tah**-ray ee
		  nay-oh-**nah**-tee

booster seat	*seggiolino per*
	  neonati
		say-joh-**lee**-noh pehr
		  nay-oh-**nah**-tee

car seat	*seggiolino per*
	  la macchina
		say-joh-**lee**-noh pehr
		  lah **mah**-kee-nah

high chair	*seggiolone*	say-joh-**loh**-nay
playpen	*box*	bohks
stroller	*passeggino*	pah-say-**jee**-noh

HEALTH

CHATTING

English	Italian	Pronunciation
My name is ___.	Mi chiamo ___.	mee kee**ah**-moh
What's your name?	Come si chiama?	**koh**-may see kee**ah**-mah
This is...	Le presento...	lay pray-**zehn**-toh
Pleased to meet you.	Piacere.	peeah-**chay**-ray
How are you?	Come sta?	**koh**-may stah
Very well, thanks.	Molto bene, grazie.	**mohl**-toh **behn**-ay **graht**-seeay
Where are you from?	Di dove è?	dee **doh**-vay eh
What city?	Da che città?	dah kay chee-**tah**
What country?	Da che paese?	dah kay pah-**ay**-zay
What planet?	Da che pianeta?	dah kay peeah-**nay**-tah
I'm...	Sono...	**soh**-noh
...American.	...Americano[a].	ah-may-ree-**kah**-noh
...Canadian.	...Canadese.	kah-nah-**day**-zay
...a pest.	...una peste.	**oo**-nah **pehs**-tay
Where are you going? (singular / plural)	Dove va? / Dove andate?	**doh**-vay vah / **doh**-vay ahn-**dah**-tay
I'm going / We're going to ___.	Vado / Andiamo a ___.	**vah**-doh / ahn-dee**ah**-moh ah
Will you take my / our photo?	Mi / ci fa una foto?	mee / chee fah **oo**-nah **foh**-toh
Can I take a photo of you?	Posso fare le una foto?	**poh**-soh **fah**-ray lay **oo**-nah **foh**-toh

193

| Smile! | Sorrida! / | soh-**ree**-dah / |
| (singular / plural) | Sorridete! | soh-ree-**day**-tay |

Nothing More Than Feelings...

I am / You are...	Sono / È...	**soh**-noh / eh
He / She is...	Lui / Lei è...	lwee / **leh**ee eh
...happy.	...felice.	fay-**lee**-chay
...sad.	...triste.	**tree**-stay
...tired.	...stanco[a].	**stahn**-koh
...lucky.	...fortunato[a].	for-too-**nah**-toh
I am / You are...	Ho / Ha...	oh / ah
He / She is...	Lui / Lei ha...	lwee / **leh**ee ah
...hungry.	...fame.	**fah**-may
...thirsty.	...sete.	**say**-tay
...homesick.	...nostalgia.	noh-**stahl**-jah
...cold.	...freddo.	**fray**-doh
...too warm.	...troppo caldo.	**troh**-poh **kahl**-doh

Who's Who

My... (m / f)	Mio / Mia...	**mee**-oh / **mee**-ah
...friend (m / f).	...amico / amica.	ah-**mee**-koh / ah-**mee**-kah
...boyfriend / girlfriend.	...ragazzo / ragazza.	rah-**gahd**-zoh / rah-**gahd**-zah
...husband / wife.	...marito / moglie.	mah-**ree**-toh / **mohl**-yay
...son / daughter.	...figlio / figlia.	**feel**-yoh / **feel**-yah
...brother / sister.	...fratello / sorella.	frah-**tehl**-loh / soh-**rehl**-lah
...father / mother.	...padre / madre.	**pah**-dray / **mah**-dray
...uncle / aunt.	...zio / zia.	**tsee**oh / **tsee**ah
...nephew or niece.	...nipote.	nee-**poh**-tay
...male / female cousin.	...cugino / cugina.	koo-**jee**-noh / koo-**jee**-nah
...grandfather / grandmother.	...nonno / nonna.	**noh**-noh / **noh**-nah
...grandchild.	...nipote.	nee-**poh**-tay

CHATTING

Key Phrases: Chatting

My name is ___.	*Mi chiamo ___.*	mee kee**ah**-moh
What's your name?	*Come si chiama?*	**koh**-may see kee**ah**-mah
Pleased to meet you.	*Piacere.*	peeah-**chay**-ray
Where are you from?	*Di dove è?*	dee **doh**-vay eh
I'm from ___.	*Sono da ___.*	**soh**-noh dah
Where are you going? (singular / plural)	*Dove va? / Dove andate?*	**doh**-vay vah / **doh**-vay ahn-**dah**-tay
I'm going to ___.	*Vado a ___.*	**vah**-doh ah
I like...	*Mi piace...*	mee pee**ah**-chay
Do you like...?	*Le piace...?*	lay pee**ah**-chay
Thank you very much.	*Molte grazie.*	**mohl**-tay **graht**-seeay
Have a good trip!	*Buon viaggio!*	bwohn vee**ah**-joh

Family

Are you married? (to a woman / a man)	*È sposata? / È sposato?*	eh spoh-**zah**-tah / eh spoh-**zah**-toh
Do you have children?	*Ha bambini?*	ah bahm-**bee**-nee
How many boys and girls?	*Quanti maschi e femmine?*	**kwahn**-tee **mahs**-kee ay fehm-**mee**-nay
Do you have photos?	*Ha delle foto?*	ah **dehl**-lay **foh**-toh
How old is your child?	*Quanti anni ha il suo bambino?*	**kwahn**-tee **ahn**-nee ah eel **soo**-oh bahm-**bee**-noh
Beautiful baby boy!	*Bel bambino!*	behl bahm-**bee**-noh
Beautiful baby girl!	*Bella bambina!*	**behl**-lah bahm-**bee**-nah
Beautiful children!	*Bei bambini!*	**beh**ee bahm-**bee**-nee

Work

English	Italian	Pronunciation
What is your job?	Che lavoro fa?	kay lah-**voh**-roh fah
Do you like your work?	Le piace il suo lavoro?	lay peeah-chay eel **soo**-oh lah-**voh**-roh
I work in...	Mi occupo...	mee oh-**koo**-poh
I'm studying to work in...	Studio per lavorare...	**stoo**-deeoh pehr lah-voh-**rah**-ray
I used to work in...	Lavoravo...	lah-voh-**rah**-voh
I want a job in...	Vorrei un lavoro...	vor-**reh**ee oon lah-**voh**-roh
...accounting.	...nella contabilità.	**nay**-lah kohn-tah-bee-lee-**tah**
...the medical field.	...nel campo medico.	nehl **kahm**-poh **may**-dee-koh
...social services.	...nell'assistenza sociale.	nay-lah-stee-**stehnt**-sah soh-**chah**-lay
...the legal profession.	...nel campo legale.	nehl **kahm**-poh lay-**gah**-lay
...banking.	...nel settore bancario.	nayl seht-**toh**-ray bahn-**kah**-reeoh
...business.	...in un'azienda.	een oo-naht-see**ehn**-dah
...government.	...nel governo.	nehl eel goh-**vehr**-noh
...engineering.	...nell'ingegneria.	nay-leen-jehn-**yay**-reeah
...public relations.	...nel relazioni pubbliche.	nehl ray-laht-see**oh**-nee poo-**blee**-kay
...science.	...nel campo scientifico.	nehl **kahm**-poh shee-ehn-**tee**-fee-koh
...teaching.	...come insegnante.	**koh**-may een-sayn-**yahn**-tay
...the computer field.	...nel settore informatico.	nayl seht-**toh**-ray een-for-**mah**-tee-koh
...the travel industry.	...nel settore turistico.	nayl seht-**toh**-ray too-**ree**-stee-koh
...the arts.	...nel campo artistico.	nehl **kahm**-poh ar-**tee**-stee-koh
...journalism.	...nel giornalismo.	nayl jor-nahl-**ees**-moh
...a restaurant.	...in un ristorante.	een oon ree-stoh-**rahn**-tay
...a store.	...in un negozio.	een oon nay-**goht**-seeoh

...a factory.	...in una fabbrica.	een **oo**-nah fah-**bree**-kah
I'm a professional traveler.	Sono turista di professione.	**soh**-noh too-**ree**-stah dee proh-fay-see**oh**-nay
I am / We are...	Sono / Siamo...	**soh**-noh / see**ah**-moh
...unemployed.	...disoccupato[a].	dee-zoh-koo-**pah**-toh
...retired.	...in pensione.	een payn-see**oh**-nay
Do you have a...?	Ha un...?	ah oon
Here is my / our...	Ecco il mio / il nostro...	**ay**-koh eel **mee**-oh / eel **noh**-stroh
...business card	...biglietto da visita	beel-**yay**-toh dah **vee**-zee-tah
...email address	...indirizzo di posta elettronica	een-dee-**reed**-zoh dee **poh**-stah ay-leht-**troh**-nee-kah

Chatting with Children

What's your name?	Come ti chiami?	**koh**-may tee kee**ah**-mee
My name is ___.	Mi chiamo ___.	mee kee**ah**-moh
How old are you?	Quanti anni hai?	**kwahn**-tee **ahn**-nee **ah**ee
Do you have brothers and sisters?	Hai fratelli e sorelle?	**ah**ee frah-**tehl**-lee ay soh-**rehl**-lay
Do you like school?	Ti piace la scuola?	tee pee**ah**-chay lah **skwoh**-lah
What are you studying?	Che cosa stai studiando?	kay **koh**-zah **stah**ee stoo-dee**ahn**-doh
I'm studying...	Sto studiando...	stoh stoo-dee**ahn**-doh
What's your favorite subject?	Qual'è la tua materia preferita?	kwah-**leh** lah **too**-ah mah-tay-**ree**-ah pray-fay-**ree**-tah
Do you have pets?	Hai animali domestici?	**ah**ee ah-nee-**mah**-lee doh-mehs-**tee**-chee
I have / We have a...	Ho / Abbiamo un...	oh / ah-bee**ah**-moh oon
...cat / dog / fish / bird.	...gatto / cane / pesce / uccello.	**gah**-toh / **kah**-nay / **peh**-shay / oo-**cheh**-loh
What is this / that?	Che cos'è questo / quello?	kay koh-**zeh kweh**-stoh / **kweh**-loh

Will you teach me / us...?	Mi / Ci insegni...?	mee / chee een-**sayn**-yee
...some Italian words	...delle parole in italiano	**dehl**-lay pah-**roh**-lay een ee-tah-lee**ah**-noh
...a simple Italian song	...una canzone italiana facile	**oo**-nah kahnt-**soh**-nay ee-tah-lee**ah**-nah **fah**-chee-lay
Guess which country I live in / we live in.	Indovina in quale paese vivo / viviamo.	een-doh-**vee**-nah een **kwah**-lay pah-**ay**-zay **vee**-voh / vee-vee**ah**-moh
How old am I?	Quanti anni ho?	**kwahn**-tee **ahn**-nee oh
I'm ___ years old.	Ho ___ anni.	oh ___ **ahn**-nee
Want to hear me burp?	Mi vuoi sentire ruttare?	mee **vwoh**ee sehn-**tee**-ray roo-**tah**-ray
Teach me a fun game.	Mi insegni un gioco divertente.	mee een-**sayn**-yee oon **joh**-koh dee-vehr-**tehn**-tay
Got any candy?	Hai una caramella?	**ah**ee **oo**-nah kah-rah-**mehl**-lah
Want to thumb-wrestle?	Vuoi fare la lotta con i pollici?	**vwoh**ee **fah**-ray lah **loh**-tah kohn ee poh-**lee**-chee
Gimme five. (hold up your hand)	Dammi un cinque.	**dah**-mee oon **cheeng**-kway

If you do break into song, try "Happy Birthday" (page 23) or "Volare" (page 272).

Travel Talk

I am / Are you...?	Sono / È...?	**soh**-noh / eh
...on vacation	...in vacanza	een vah-**kahnt**-sah
...on business	...qui per lavoro	kwee pehr lah-**voh**-roh
How long have you been traveling?	Da quanto tempo è in viaggio?	dah **kwahn**-toh **tehm**-poh eh een vee**ah**-joh
day / week	giorno / settimana	**jor**-noh / say-tee-**mah**-nah
month / year	mese / anno	**may**-zay / **ahn**-noh
When are you going home?	Quando ritorna a casa?	**kwahn**-doh ree-**tor**-nah ah **kah**-zah

This is my first time in __.	Questa è la mia prima volta in __.	**kweh**-stah eh lah **mee**-ah **pree**-mah **vohl**-tah een
This is our first time in __.	Questa è la nostra prima volta in __.	**kweh**-stah eh lah **noh**-strah **pree**-mah **vohl**-tah een
It is (not) a tourist trap.	(Non) è una trappola per turisti.	(nohn) eh **oo**-nah trah-**poh**-lah pehr too-**ree**-stee
The Italians are friendly / boring / rude.	Gli italiani sono amichevoli / noiosi / maleducati.	lee-yee ee-tah-lee**ah**-nee **soh**-noh ah-mee-kay-**voh**-lee / noh-**yoh**-zee / mah-lay-doo-**kah**-tee
Italy is fantastic.	L'Italia è fantastica.	lee-**tahl**-yah eh fahn-**tah**-stee-kah
So far...	Finora...	fee-**noh**-rah
Today...	Oggi...	**oh**-jee
...I have / we have seen __ and __.	...ho / abbiamo visto __ e __.	oh / ah-bee**ah**-moh **vee**-stoh __ ay
Next...	Dopo...	**doh**-poh
Tomorrow...	Domani...	doh-**mah**-nee
...I will see / we will see __.	...vedrò / vedremo __.	vay-**droh** / vay-**dray**-moh
Yesterday...	Ieri....	**yay**-ree
...I saw / we saw __.	...ho visto / abbiamo visto __.	oh **vee**-stoh / ah-bee**ah**-moh **vee**-stoh
My / Our vacation is __ days long. It began in __ and finishes in __.	La mia / La nostra vacanza dura __ giorni. Comincia a __ e finisce a __.	lah **mee**-ah / lah **noh**-strah vah-**kahnt**-sah **doo**-rah __ **jor**-nee koh-**meen**-chah ah __ ay fee-**nee**-shay ah
I'm happy here.	Sono felice qui.	**soh**-noh fay-**lee**-chay kwee
This is paradise.	Questo è il paradiso.	**kweh**-stoh eh eel pah-rah-**dee**-zoh
To travel is to live.	Viaggiare è vivere.	veeah-**jah**-ray eh vee-**vay**-ray
Travel is enlightening.	Viaggiare illumina.	veeah-**jah**-ray ee-**loo**-mee-nah

CHATTING

| I wish all (American) politicians traveled. | Vorrei che tutti i politici (americani) viaggiassero. | vor-**reh**ee kay **too**-tee ee poh-**lee**-tee-chee (ah-may-ree-**kah**-nee) veeah-jah-**say**-roh |
| Have a good trip! | Buon viaggio! | bwohn veeah-joh |

Map Musings

These phrases and maps will help you delve into family history and explore your travel dreams.

I live here.	Abito qui.	ah-**bee**-toh kwee
We live here.	Abitiamo qui.	ah-bee-teeah-moh kwee
I was born here.	Sono nato[a] qui.	**soh**-noh **nah**-toh kwee
My ancestors came from ___.	I miei antenati vennero da ___.	ee meeay-ee ahn-tay-**nah**-tee vay-**nay**-roh dah
I've traveled to ___.	Sono stato[a] a ___.	**soh**-noh **stah**-toh ah
We've traveled to___.	Siamo stati[e] a ___.	seeah-moh **stah**-tee ah
Next I'll go to ___.	Poi andrò a ___.	**poh**ee ahn-**droh** ah
Next we'll go to ___.	Poi andremo a ___.	**poh**ee ahn-**dray**-moh ah
I'd like / We'd like to go to ___.	Vorrei / Vorremmo andare a ____.	vor-**reh**ee / vor-**ray**-moh ahn-**dah**-ray ah
Where do you live?	Dove abita?	**doh**-vay ah-**bee**-tah
Where were you born?	Dove è nato[a]?	**doh**-vay eh **nah**-toh
Where did your ancestors come from?	Da dove vennero i suoi antenati?	dah **doh**-vay vay-**nay**-roh ee **swoh**-ee ahn-tay-**nah**-tee
Where have you traveled?	Dove è stato[a]?	**doh**-vay eh **stah**-toh
Where are you going?	Dove va?	**doh**-vay vah
Where would you like to go?	Dove vorrebbe andare?	**doh**-vay voh-**ray**-bay ahn-**dah**-ray

Italy

Europe

The United States

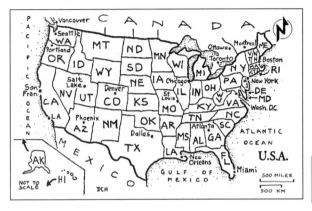

The World

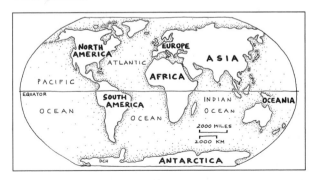

Favorite Things

What... do you like?	Qual'è il suo... preferito?	kwah-**leh** eel **soo**-oh... pray-fay-**ree**-toh
...art	...genere d'arte	**jay**-nay-ray **dar**-tay
...books	...genere di libri	**jay**-nay-ray dee **lee**-bree
...hobby	...passatempo	pah-sah-**tehm**-poh
...ice cream	...gelato	jay-**lah**-toh
...food	...cibo	**chee**-boh
...movie	...film	feelm
...music	...genere di musica	**jay**-nay-ray dee **moo**-zee-kah
...sport	...sport	sport
...vice	...vizio	**veet**-seeoh
...singer	...cantante	kahn-**tahn**-tay
...male movie star	...attore	ah-**toh**-ray
...male artist	...artista	ar-**tee**-stah
...male author	...autore	ow-**toh**-ray
...female movie star	...attrice	ah-**tree**-chay
...female artist	...artista	ar-**tee**-stah
...female author	...autrice	ow-**tree**-chay
Can you recommend a good...?	Può raccomandarmi un buon...?	pwoh rah-koh-mahn-**dar**-mee oon bwohn
...Italian CD	...CD italiano	chee-dee ee-tah-lee**ah**-noh
...Italian book translated in English	...libro italiano in traduzione inglese	**lee**-broh ee-tah-lee**ah**-noh een trah-doot-see**oh**-nay een-**glay**-zay

Weather

What will the weather be like tomorrow?	Come sarà il tempo domani?	**koh**-may sah-**rah** eel **tehm**-poh doh-**mah**-nee
sunny / cloudy	bello / nuvoloso	**behl**-loh / noo-voh-**loh**-zoh
hot / cold	caldo / freddo	**kahl**-doh / **fray**-doh
muggy / windy	umido / ventoso	**oo**-mee-doh / vehn-**toh**-zoh

CHATTING

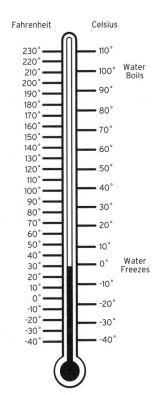

rain / snow	*pioggia / neve*	pee**oh**-jah / **nay**-vay
Should I bring	*Devo portare*	**day**-voh por-**tah**-ray
a jacket?	*una giacca?*	**oo**-nah **jah**-kah

Thanks a Million

Thank you	*Molte grazie.*	**mohl**-tay **graht**-seeay
very much.		
A thousand thanks.	*Grazie mille.*	**graht**-seeay **mee**-lay

This is great fun.	È un vero divertimento.	eh oon **vay**-roh dee-vehr-tee-**mayn**-toh
You are...	Lei è...	**leh**ee eh
...helpful.	...di aiuto.	dee ah-**yoo**-toh
...wonderful.	...meraviglioso[a].	may-rah-veel-**yoh**-zoh
...generous.	...generoso[a].	jay-nay-**roh**-zoh
...kind.	...gentile.	jayn-**tee**-lay
You spoil me / us.	Mi / Ci viziate.	mee / chee veet-see**ah**-tay
You've been a great help.	Lei è un grande aiuto.	**leh**ee eh oon **grahn**-day ah-**yoo**-toh
You are a saint.	Lei è un[a] santo[a].	**leh**ee eh oon **sahn**-toh
I will remember you...	Mi ricorderò di Lei...	mee ree-kor-day-**roh** dee **leh**ee
We will remember you...	Ci ricorderemo di Lei...	chee ree-kor-day-**ray**-moh dee **leh**ee
...always.	...sempre.	**sehm**-pray
...till Tuesday.	...fino a martedì.	**fee**-noh ah mar-tay-**dee**

CHATTING

Responses for All Occasions

I like that.	Mi piace.	mee pee**ah**-chay
We like that.	Ci piace.	chee pee**ah**-chay
I like you.	Lei mi piace.	**leh**ee mee pee**ah**-chay
We like you.	Lei ci piace.	**leh**ee chee pee**ah**-chay
Great!	Ottimo!	**oh**-tee-moh
Fantastic!	Fantastico!	fahn-**tah**-stee-koh
What a nice place.	Che bel posto.	kay behl **poh**-stoh
Perfect.	Perfetto.	pehr-**feht**-toh
Funny.	Divertente.	dee-vehr-**tehn**-tay
Interesting.	Interessante.	een-tay-ray-**sahn**-tay
Really?	Davvero?	dah-**vay**-roh
Wow!	Wow!	"Wow"
Congratulations!	Congratulazioni!	kohn-grah-too-laht-see**oh**-nee
Well done!	Bravo[a]!	**brah**-voh
You're welcome.	Prego.	**pray**-goh
Bless you! (after sneeze)	Salute!	sah-**loo**-tay

What a pity.	*Che peccato.*	kay pehk-**kah**-toh
That's life.	*È la vita!*	eh lah **vee**-tah
No problem.	*Non c'è problema.*	nohn cheh proh-**blay**-mah
O.K.	*Va bene.*	vah **behn**-ay
This is the	*Questa sì che*	**kweh**-stah see kay
good life!	*è vita!*	eh **vee**-tah
I feel like a	*Sto come*	stoh **koh**-may
pope! (happy)	*un papa!*	oon **pah**-pah
Have a good day!	*Buona giornata!*	**bwoh**-nah jor-**nah**-tah
Good luck!	*Buona fortuna!*	**bwoh**-nah for-**too**-nah
Let's go!	*Andiamo!*	ahn-dee**ah**-moh

Smoking

Do you smoke?	*Fuma?*	**foo**-mah
Do you smoke pot?	*Fuma*	**foo**-mah
	marijuana?	mah-ree-**wahn**-nah
I (don't) smoke.	*(Non) fumo.*	(nohn) **foo**-moh
We (don't) smoke.	*(Non) fumiano.*	(nohn) foo-mee**ah**-noh
I haven't any.	*Non ne ho.*	nohn nay oh
lighter	*accendino*	ah-chehn-**dee**-noh
cigarettes	*sigarette*	see-gah-**ray**-tay
marijuana	*marijuana*	mah-ree-**wahn**-nah
hash	*hashish*	hah-**sheesh**
joint	*canna*	**kah**-nah
stoned	*fumato, fatto*	foo-**mah**-toh, **fah**-toh
Wow!	*Wow!*	"Wow"

CHATTING

Conversing With Animals

rooster / cock-a-	*gallo /*	**gah**-loh /
doodle-doo	*chicchirichì*	kee-kee-ree-**kee**
bird / tweet tweet	*uccello /*	oo-**chehl**-loh /
	cip cip	cheep cheep
cat / meow	*gatto / miao*	**gah**-toh / **mee**-ow
dog / bark bark	*cane / bau bau*	**kah**-nay / bow bow
duck / quack quack	*oca / quac quac*	**oh**-kah / kwahk kwahk
cow / moo	*mucca / muu*	**moo**-kah / moo
pig / oink oink	*maiale / oinc oinc*	mah-**yah**-lay / oynk oynk

Profanity

People make animal noises, too. These words will help you understand what the more colorful locals are saying.

Go to hell!	*Vai al diavolo!*	**vah**ee ahl dee**ah**-voh-loh
Damn it.	*Dannazione.*	dah-naht-see**oh**-nay
bastard	*bastardo*	bah-**star**-doh
bitch	*cagna, troia*	**kahn**-yah, **troh**-yah
breasts (colloq.)	*tete*	**tay**-tay
penis (colloq.)	*cazzo*	**kahd**-zoh
butthole	*stronzo*	**strohnt**-soh
drunk	*ubriaco*	oo-bree**ah**-koh
idiot	*idiota*	ee-dee**oh**-tah
imbecile	*imbecille*	eem-bay-**chee**-lay
jerk	*scemo*	**shay**-moh
stupid	*stupido*	**stoo**-pee-doh
Did someone fart?	*Ma qualcuno*	mah kwahl-**koo**-noh
	ha fatto una	ah **fah**-toh **oo**-nah
	scoreggia?	skoh-**ray**-jah
I burped.	*Ho ruttato.*	oh roo-**tah**-toh
This sucks.	*Questo fa schifo.*	**kweh**-stoh fah **skee**-foh
Screw it.	*Vaffanculo.*	vah-fahn-**koo**-loh
Go take a shit.	*Va'a cagare.*	**vah**-ah kah-**gah**-ray
Shit.	*Merda.*	**mehr**-dah
Bullshit.	*Balle.*	**bah**-lay
Shove it up	*Mettitelo*	meht-tee-**tay**-loh
your ass.	*nel culo.*	nayl **koo**-loh
Stick it between	*Ficcatelo*	fee-kah-**tay**-loh
your teeth.	*tra i denti.*	trah ee **dayn**-tee
You are...	*Sei...*	seh**ee**
Don't be...	*Non essere...*	nohn ehs-**say**-ray
...a son of	*...un figlio di*	oon **feel**-yoh dee
a whore.	*puttana.*	poo-**tah**-nah
...an asshole.	*...uno stronzo.*	**oo**-noh **strohnt**-soh
...an idiot.	*...un idiota.*	oon ee-dee**oh**-tah
...a creep.	*...un deficiente.*	oon day-fee-chee-**ehn**-tay

| ...a cretin. | ...un cretino. | oon kray-**tee**-noh |
| ...a pig. | ...un porco. | oon **por**-koh |

Sweet Curses

My goodness.	Mamma mia.	**mah**-mah **mee**-ah
Good heavens.	Santo cielo.	**sahn**-toh chee**ay**-loh
Shoot.	Cavolo.	**kah**-voh-loh
Darn it!	Accidenti!	ah-chee-**dehn**-tee

CREATE YOUR OWN CONVERSATION

You can mix and match these words into a conversation. Make it as deep or silly as you want.

Who

I / you	io / Lei	**ee**oh / **leh**ee
he / she	lui / lei	lwee / **leh**ee
we / they	noi / loro	**noh**ee / **loh**-roh
my / your...	mio / suo...	**mee**-oh / **soo**-oh
...parents / children	...genitori / figli	jay-nee-**toh**-ree / **feel**-yee
men / women	uomini / donne	woh-**mee**-nee / **doh**-nay
rich / poor people	ricchi / poveri	**ree**-kee / **poh**-vay-ree
young / old people	giovani / anziani	joh-**vah**-nee / ahnt-seeah-nee
middle-aged people	persone di mezza età	pehr-**soh**-nay dee **mehd**-za ay-**tah**
Italians	italiani	ee-tah-leeah-nee
Austrians	austriaci	ow-stree**ah**-chee
Belgians	belgi	**bayl**-jee
Czech	cechi	**chay**-kee
French	francesi	frahn-**chay**-zee
Germans	tedeschi	tay-**dehs**-kee
Spanish	spagnoli	span-**yoh**-lee
Swiss	svizzeri	sveed-**zeh**-ree

Europeans	europei	ay-oo-roh-**pay**-ee
EU	UE	oo ay
(European Union)	(Unione	(oon-ee-**ohn**-ay
	Europeo)	ay-oo-roh-**pay**-oh)
Americans	americani	ah-may-ree-**kah**-nee
liberals	liberali	lee-bay-**rah**-lee
conservatives	conservatori	kohn-sehr-vah-**toh**-ree
radicals	radicali	rah-dee-**kah**-lee
terrorists	terroristi	tehr-roh-**ree**-stee
politicians	politici	poh-**lee**-tee-chee
big business	grande affare	**grahn**-day ah-**fah**-ray
multinational	multi-	mool-tee-
corporations	nazionale	naht-seeoh-**nah**-lay
military	militare	mee-lee-**tah**-ray
mafia	mafia	"mafia"
refugees	profughi	proh-**foo**-gee
travelers	viaggiatori	veeah-jah-**toh**-ree
God	Dio	**dee**oh
Christian	cristiano	kree-stee**ah**-noh
Catholic	cattolico	kah-**toh**-lee-koh
Protestant	protestante	proh-tay-**stahn**-tay
Jew	ebreo	ay-**bray**-oh
Muslim	musulmano	moo-sool-**mah**-noh
everyone	tutti	**too**-tee

What

buy / sell	comprare /	kohm-**prah**-ray /
	vendere	vehn-**day**-ray
have / lack	avere /	ah-**vay**-ray /
	non avere	nohn ah-**vay**-ray
help / abuse	aiutare /	ah-yoo-**tah**-ray /
	abusare	ah-boo-**zah**-ray
learn / fear	imparare /	eem-pah-**rah**-ray /
	temere	tay-**may**-ray
love / hate	amare / odiare	ah-**mah**-ray / oh-dee**ah**-ray
prosper / suffer	prosperare /	proh-spay-**rah**-ray /
	soffrire	soh-**free**-ray

take / give	prendere / dare	**prehn**-day-ray / **dah**-ray
want / need	volere /	voh-**lay**-ray /
	aver bisogno	**ah**-vehr bee-**zohn**-yoh
work / play	lavorare /	lah-voh-**rah**-ray /
	giocare	joh-**kah**-ray

Why

(anti-)	(anti-) globaliz-	(**ahn**-tee-) gloh-bah-leed-
globalization	zazione	zaht-see**oh**-nay
class warfare	conflitto	kohn-**flee**-toh
	di classe	dee **klah**-say
corruption	corruzione	koh-root-see**oh**-nay
democracy	democrazia	day-moh-kraht-**see**-ah
education	istruzione	een-stroot-see**oh**-nay
family	famiglia	fah-**meel**-yah
food	cibo	**chee**-boh
guns	armi	**ar**-mee
happiness	felicità	fay-lee-chee-**tah**
health	salute	sah-**loo**-tay
hope	speranza	spay-**rahnt**-sah
imperialism	imperialismo	eem-pehr-eeahl-**ees**-moh
lies	bugie	boo-**jee**-ay
love / sex	amore / sesso	ah-**moh**-ray / **sehs**-soh
marijuana	marijuana	mah-ree-**wahn**-nah
money / power	denaro /	day-**nah**-roh /
	potere	poh-**tay**-ray
pollution	inquinamento	een-kwee-nah-**mayn**-toh
racism	razzismo	rahd-**zeez**-moh
regime change	cambio di	**kahm**-beeoh dee
	regime	ray-**jee**-may
relaxation	rilassamento	ree-lah-sah-**mayn**-toh
religion	religione	ray-lee-**joh**-nay
respect	rispetto	ree-**spay**-toh
taxes	tasse	**tah**-say
television	televisione	tay-lay-vee-zee**oh**-nay
violence	violenza	vee-oh-**lehnt**-sah

CHATTING

work	lavoro	lah-**voh**-roh
war / peace	guerra / pace	**gwehr**-rah / **pah**-chay
global perspective	prospettiva	proh-spay-**tee**-vah
	globale	gloh-**bah**-lay

You Be the Judge

(no) problem	(non c'è) problema	(nohn cheh) proh-**blay**-mah
(not) good	(non) bene	(nohn) **behn**-ay
(not) dangerous	(non) pericoloso	(nohn) pay-ree-koh-**loh**-zoh
(not) fair	(non) giusto	(nohn) **joo**-stoh
(not) guilty	(non) colpevole	(nohn) kohl-pay-**voh**-lay
(not) powerful	(non) potente	(nohn) poh-**tehn**-tay
(not) stupid	(non) stupido	(nohn) **stoo**-pee-doh
(not) happy	(non) felice	(nohn) fay-**lee**-chay
because / for	perchè / per	pehr-**keh** / pehr
and / or / from	e / o / da	ay / oh / dah
too much	troppo	**troh**-poh
(never) enough	(mai)	(**mah**ee)
	abbastanza	ah-bah-**stahnt**-sah
same	stesso	**stay**-soh
better / worse	meglio / peggio	**mehl**-yoh / **peh**-joh
here / everywhere	qui / ovunque	kwee / oh-**voon**-kway

Beginnings and Endings

I like...	Mi piace...	mee pee**ah**-chay
We like...	Ci piace...	chee pee**ah**-chay
I don't like...	Non mi piace...	nohn mee pee**ah**-chay
We don't like...	Non ci piace...	nohn chee pee**ah**-chay
Do you like...?	Le piace...?	lay pee**ah**-chay
In the past...	In passato...	een pah-**sah**-toh
When I was	Quando ero	**kwahn**-doh **ay**-roh
younger,	più giovane,	pew joh-**vah**-nay
I thought...	credevo...	cray-**day**-voh
Now, I think...	Ora penso...	**oh**-rah pehn-soh
I am / Are you...?	Sono / È...?	**soh**-noh / eh
...an optimist /	...ottimista /	oh-tee-**mee**-stah /
pessimist	pessimista	pay-see-**mee**-stah

CHATTING

I believe...	Credo...	**kray**-doh
I don't believe...	Non credo...	nohn **kray**-doh
Do you believe...?	Lei crede...?	**leh**ee **kray**-day
...in God	...in Dio	een **dee**oh
...in life after death	...nella vita ultraterrena	**nay**-lah **vee**-tah ool-trah-tay-**ray**-nah
...in extraterrestrial life	...negli extraterrestri	**nayl**-yee ehk-strah-tehr-**rehs**-tree
...in Santa Claus	...in Babbo Natale	een **bah**-boh nah-**tah**-lay
Yes. / No.	Sì. / No.	see / noh
Maybe. / I don't know.	Forse. / Non lo so.	**for**-say / nohn loh soh
What's most important in life?	Qual'è la cosa più importante nella vita?	kwah-**leh** lah **koh**-zah pew eem-por-**tahn**-tay **nay**-lah **vee**-tah
The problem is...	Il problema è...	eel proh-**blay**-mah eh
The answer is...	La risposta è...	lah ree-**spoh**-stah eh
We have solved the world's problems.	Abbiamo risolto i problemi del mondo.	ah-bee**ah**-moh ree-**zohl**-toh ee proh-**blay**-mee dayl **mohn**-doh

AN ITALIAN ROMANCE

Words of Love

I / me / you / we	io / mi / ti / noi	**ee**oh / mee / tee / **noh**ee
flirt	flirtare	fleer-**tah**-ray
kiss	bacio	**bah**-choh
hug	abbraccio	ah-**brah**-choh
love	amore	ah-**moh**-ray
make love	fare l'amore	**fah**-ray lah-**moh**-ray
condom	preservativo	pray-zehr-vah-**tee**-voh
contraceptive	contraccetivo	kohn-trah-chay-**tee**-voh
safe sex	sesso sicuro	**sehs**-soh see-**koo**-roh
sexy	sensuale	sayn-soo**ah**-lay

cozy	accogliente	ah-kohl-**yehn**-tay
romantic	romantico	roh-**mahn**-tee-koh
honey bunch	dolce come	**dohl**-chay **koh**-may
	il miele	eel mee**ay**-lay
cupcake	pasticcino	pah-stee-**chee**-noh
sugar pie	zuccherino	tsoo-kay-**ree**-noh
pussy cat	gattino[a]	gah-**tee**-noh

Ah, Amore

What's the matter?	Qual'è il	kwah-**leh** eel
	problema?	proh-**blay**-mah
Nothing.	Niente.	nee**ehn**-tay
I am / Are you...?	Sono / È...?	**soh**-noh / eh
...straight	...normale	nor-**mah**-lay
...gay	...gay	gay
...bisexual	...bisessuale	bee-sehs-soo**ah**-lay
...undecided	...indeciso[a]	een-day-**chee**-zoh
...prudish	...pudico[a]	**poo**-dee-koh
...horny	...allupato[a]	ah-loo-**pah**-toh
We are on our	Siamo in luna	see**ah**-moh een **loo**-nah
honeymoon.	di miele.	dee mee**ay**-lay
I have...	Ho...	oh
...a boyfriend.	...il ragazzo.	eel rah-**gahd**-zoh
...a girlfriend.	...la ragazza.	lah rah-**gahd**-zah
I'm married.	Sono sposato[a].	**soh**-noh spoh-**zah**-toh
I'm married	Sono sposato[a]	**soh**-noh spoh-**zah**-toh
(but...).	(ma...).	(mah)
I'm not married.	Non sono	nohn **soh**-noh
	sposato[a].	spoh-**zah**-toh
Do you have a	Ha il ragazzo /	ah eel rah-**gahd**-zoh /
boyfriend /	la ragazza?	lah rah-**gahd**-zah
a girlfriend?		
I'm	Sono	**soh**-noh
adventurous.	avventuroso.	ah-vehn-too-**roh**-zoh
I'm lonely.	Sono solo[a].	**soh**-noh **soh**-loh
I'm lonely tonight.	Sono solo[a]	**soh**-noh **soh**-loh
	stasera.	stah-**zay**-rah

English	Italian	Pronunciation
I'm rich and single.	Sono ricco[a] e single.	soh-noh ree-koh ay seeng-glay
Do you mind if I sit here?	Le dispiace se mi siedo qui?	lay dee-speeah-chay say mee seeay-doh kwee
Would you like a drink?	Vuole qualcosa da bere?	vwoh-lay kwahl-koh-zah dah bay-ray
Will you go out with me?	Vuole uscire con me?	vwoh-lay oo-shee-ray kohn may
Would you like to go out tonight for...?	Vuole uscire stasera per...?	vwoh-lay oo-shee-ray stah-zay-rah pehr
...a walk	...una passeggiata	oo-nah pah-say-jah-tah
...dinner	...cena	chay-nah
...a drink	...qualcosa da bere	kwahl-koh-zah dah bay-ray
Where's the best place to dance nearby?	C'è un bel locale da ballo qui vicino?	cheh oon behl loh-kah-lay dah bah-loh kwee vee-chee-noh
Do you want to dance?	Vuole ballare?	vwoh-lay bah-lah-ray
I have no diseases.	Non ho malattie.	nohn oh mah-lah-tee-ay
I have many diseases.	Ho molte malattie.	oh mohl-tay mah-lah-tee-ay
I have only safe sex.	Faccio solo sesso sicuro.	fah-choh soh-loh sehs-soh see-koo-roh
Let's have a wild and crazy night!	Passiamo una notte di fuoco!	pah-seeah-moh oo-nah noh-tay dee fwoh-koh
Can I take you home?	Posso accompagnarti a casa?	poh-soh ah-kohm-pahn-yar-tee ah kah-zah
Why not?	Perché no?	pehr-kay noh
How can I change your mind?	Posso farti cambiare idea?	poh-soh far-tee kahm-beeah-ray ee-day-ah
Kiss me.	Baciami.	bah-cheeah-mee
May I kiss you?	Posso baciarti?	poh-soh bah-chee-ar-tee
Can I see you again?	Ti posso rivedere?	tee poh-soh ree-vay-day-ray

CHATTING

CHATTING

Your place or mine?	A casa tua o a casa mia?	ah **kah**-zah **too**-ah oh ah **kah**-zah **mee**-ah
How does this feel?	Ti piace questo?	tee pee**ah**-chay **kweh**-stoh
Is this an aphrodisiac?	È un afrodisiaco questo?	eh oon ah-froh-dee-**zee**-ah-koh **kweh**-stoh
This is (not) my first time.	Questa (non) è la mia prima volta.	**kweh**-stah (nohn) eh lah **mee**-ah **pree**-mah **vohl**-tah
You are my most beautiful souvenir.	Sei il mio più bel ricordo.	**seh**ee eel **mee**-oh pew behl ree-**kor**-doh
Do you do this often?	Lo fai spesso?	loh **fah**ee **speh**-soh
How's my breath?	Com'è il mio alito?	koh-**meh** eel **mee**-oh ah-**lee**-toh
Let's just be friends.	Solo amici.	**soh**-loh ah-**mee**-chee
I'll pay for my share.	Pago per la mia parte.	**pah**-goh pehr lah **mee**-ah **par**-tay
Would you like a massage...?	Vorresti un massaggio...?	vor-**ray**-stee oon mah-**sah**-joh
...for your back	...alla schiena	**ah**-lah shee**ay**-nah
...for your feet	...ai piedi	**ah**ee peeay-dee
Why not?	Perchè no?	pehr-**keh** noh
Try it.	Provalo.	**proh**-vah-loh
It tickles.	Fa solletico.	fah soh-**lay**-tee-koh
Oh my God!	Oh mio Dio!	oh **mee**-oh **dee**-oh
I love you.	Ti amo.	tee **ah**-moh
Darling, will you marry me?	Cara, mi vuoi sposare?	**kah**-rah mee **vwoh**ee spoh-**zah**-ray

DICTIONARY

ITALIAN/ENGLISH

You'll see some of the words in the dictionary listed like this: *aggressivo[a]*. Use the *a* ending (pronounced "ah") if you're talking about a woman.

A

a	to; at
abbastanza	enough
abbigliamento, boutique di	clothing boutique
abbronzarsi	sunbathe
abbronzatura	suntan (n)
aborto	abortion
aborto spontaneo	miscarriage
abusare	abuse (v)
accappatoio	bathrobe
accendino	lighter (n)
accessibile con la sedia a rotelle	wheelchair-accessible
accesso a Internet	Internet access
acerbo	sour
acqua	water
acqua del rubinetto	tap water
acqua minerale	mineral water
acqua potabile	drinkable water
adattatore elettrico	electrical adapter
adesso	now
adolescente	teenager
adulto	adult
aeroplano	plane
aeroporto	airport
affamato	hungry
affari	business
affascinante	charming
affittare	rent (v)
Africa	Africa
agenzia di viaggi	travel agency
aggiustare	fix (v)
aggressivo[a]	aggressive
agnello	lamb
agnostico[a]	agnostic

ago	needle
agosto	August
aiutare	help (v)
aiuto	help (n)
aiuto, di	helpful
ala	wing
alba	sunrise
albero	tree
alcool	alcohol
alimentari	grocery store
aliscafo	hydrofoil
alito	breath
all'aria aperta	outdoors
allergico[a]	allergic
allergie	allergies
alt	stop (n, sign)
altare	altar
alto	tall; high
altro	other
altro, un	another
amante	lover
amare	love (v)
ambasciata	embassy
ambulanza	ambulance
amicizia	friendship
amico	friend
amore	love (n)
anabbaglianti	headlights
analgesico	pain killer
ancora	more; again
andare	go
andata	one way (ticket)
andicappato	handicapped
anello	ring (n)
angolo	corner
animale	animal
animale domestico	pet (n)

anno	year
annullare	cancel
antenato[a]	ancestor
antiacido	antacid
antibiotico	antibiotic
antichità	antiques
antico	ancient
antipasti	appetizers
anziani	seniors
aperto	open (adj)
appartamento	apartment
appendiabiti	coat hanger
appuntamento	appointment
aprile	April
aprire	open (v)
apriscatola	can opener
arancia	orange (fruit)
arancione	orange (color)
arcobaleno	rainbow
argento	silver
aria	air
aria condizionata	air-conditioned
armadietti	lockers
aroma	flavor (n)
arrabbiato[a]	angry
arrivare	arrive
arrivederci	goodbye
arrivi	arrivals
arte	art; crafts
artificiale	artificial
artigianato	handicrafts
artista	artist
artrite	arthritis
ascensore	elevator
asciugamano	towel
asciugare	dry (v)

DICTIONARY

Italian / English

asciugatrice	dryer
asciutto	dry (adj)
ascoltare	listen
asino	donkey
asma	asthma
aspettare	wait
aspirina	aspirin
assaggiare	taste (v)
assegno	check (n)
assetato	thirsty
assicurato	insured
assicurazione	insurance
assicurazione medica	health insurance
assolato	sunny
assonnato[a]	sleepy
assorbenti igienici	sanitary napkins
assorbenti interni	tampons
Astratto	abstract
ateo[a]	atheist
attraente	handsome
attraversare	go through
attraverso	through
audioguida	audioguide
autista	driver
autobus	bus (city)
autostop	hitchhike
autostrada	highway
autunno	autumn
avere	have
avere bisogno di	need
avere fretta	hurry (v)
avvelenamento da cibo	food poisoning
avvocato	lawyer

B

Babbo Natale	Santa Claus
bacio	kiss
baffi	moustache
bagaglio	luggage
bagaglio a mano	carry-on luggage
bagnato	wet
bagno	bathroom; bath
balcone	balcony
ballare	dance (v)
balsamo	conditioner (hair)
bambinaia	babysitter
bambini	children
bambino[a]	child
bambola	doll
banca	bank
bancomat	cash machine
bandiera	flag
bar	coffee shop
barba	beard
barbiere	barber, barber shop
barca	boat
barca a remi	rowboat
basket	basketball
Bassi, Paesi	Netherlands
basso	low
batteria	battery
battito cardiaco	pulse
bavaglino	bib
Belgio	Belgium
bello[a]	beautiful; nice
benda	bandage
bene	fine (good)
benvenuto	welcome
benzina	gas
benzinaio	gas station

Italian	English
bere	drink (v)
berretto	cap
bevanda	drink (n)
bianchetto	white-out
bianco	white
biblioteca	library
bicchiere	glass
bicicletta	bicycle
biglietto	ticket
biglietto da visita	business card
binario	platform; track (train)
biondo[a]	blond
birra	beer
bisogno di, avere	need (v)
blocco note	notebook
blu	blue
bocca	mouth
boccaglio	snorkel
boccia	bowl
bollito	boiled
bollitore	kettle
bomba	bomb
borotalco	talcum powder
borsa	purse
borsaiolo	pickpocket
bottiglia	bottle
bottone	button
boutique di abbigliamento	clothing boutique
box	playpen
braca a vela	sailboat
braccialetto	bracelet
braccio	arm
Britannia	Britain
brividi	chills

Italian	English
broncopolmonite	pneumonia
bronzo	bronze
bruciatura	burn (n)
bruciatura del sole	sunburn
brutto[a]	ugly
buco	hole
bugie	lies
bulbo	bulb
buon giorno	good day
buono	good
burro di cacao	lip salve
busta	envelope
busta de plastica sigillabile	Ziplock bag

C

Italian	English
cabina telefonica	phone booth
cacciaviti	screwdriver
cadere	fall (v)
caffè	coffee
calcio	soccer
caldo	hot
calendario	calendar
calorie	calorie
calzini	socks
camare libere	vacancy (hotel)
cambiare	change (v); transfer (v)
cambio	change (n); exchange (n)
camera	room
camera da letto	bedroom
camerata	dormitory
cameriera	waitress
cameriere	waiter
camicetta	blouse

camicia	shirt	carta di credito	credit card
camminare	walk (v)	carta igienica	toilet paper
campagna	countryside	carta telefonica	telephone card
campane	bells		
campeggio	camping	carte	cards (deck)
camper	R.V.	cartina	card; map
campionato	championship	cartoleria	office supplies store
campo	field	cartolina	postcard
canale	canal	casa	house
cancellare	delete	casalingo	homemade
candela	candle	cascata	waterfall
candele	sparkplugs	caseficio	cheese shop
cane	dog	cassetta	tape (cassette)
canna	joint (marijuana)	cassiere	cashier
canoa	canoe	castello	castle
cantante	singer	cattedrale	cathedral
cantare	sing	cattivo	bad
cantina	cellar	cattolico[a]	Catholic (adj)
canzone	song	cavaliero	knight
capelli	hair	cavallo	horse
capire	understand	cavatappi	corkscrew
capitano	captain	caviglia	ankle
capo	boss	cena	dinner
capogiri	dizziness	centralinista	operator, receptionist
cappella	chapel		
cappello	hat	centro	center; downtown
caraffa	carafe	centro commerciale	shopping mall
caramella	candy	ceramica	ceramic
carino[a]	pretty	cerotto	Band-Aid
carne	meat	cestino	basket
caro	expensive	che cosa	what
carro attrezzi	tow truck	che peccato	it's a pity
carrozza letto	sleeper car (train)	check-in bagagli	baggage check
carrozza ristorante	dining car (train)	chi	who
carta	paper	chiaro	clear

chiave	key
chiesa	church
chiocciola	"at" sign (@)
chiostro	cloister
chitarra	guitar
chiudere	lock (v)
chiuso	closed
chiusura lampo	zipper
ciabatte	slippers
ciabatte da piscina	flip-flops
ciao	hello
cibo	food
cibo per neonati	baby food
cielo	sky; heaven
cinghia del ventilatore	fan belt
cintura	belt
cioccolato	chocolate
cipria	face powder
città	city, town
classe	class
classe, prima	first class
classe, seconda	second class
Classico	classical
clinica	medical clinic
coda	tail
codice postale	zip code
codice segreto	PIN code
coincidenza	connection (train)
colazione	breakfast
collana	necklace
collant	nylons (panty hose)
collina	hill
collo	neck
colori	colors
colpevole	guilty
coltello	knife

combattere	fight (v)
come	how
cominciare	begin
commercialista	accountant
compleanno	birthday
completo	no vacancy
complicato	complicated
comprare	buy
con	with
concerto	concert
conchiglia	shell
conduttore	conductor
confermare	confirm
confortevole	comfortable
congestione	congestion (sinus)
congratulazioni	congratulations
coniglio	rabbit
contadino[a]	farmer
contagioso	contagious
contante	cash
contento[a]	happy
conto	bill (payment)
contraccettivi	contraceptives
coperta	blanket
copia	copy
copisteria	photocopy shop
corda	rope
coro	choir
corpo	body
corrente	stream (n)
correre	run (v)
corridoio	aisle
corriera	long-distance bus
corruzione	corruption
corto[a]	short
cosa	thing

cosa, che	what	**denti, mal di**	toothache
coscia	thigh	**dentifricio**	toothpaste
costa	coast	**dentista**	dentist
costare	cost (v)	**dentizione**	teething (baby)
costruzioni	construction (sign)	**dentro**	inside
costume da bagno	swimsuit	**deodorante**	deodorant
cotone	cotton	**deposito**	deposit
crampi	cramps	**dermatite da**	diaper rash
crema da barba	shaving cream	**pannolone**	
crema idratante	moisturizer	**derubato**	robbed
crema per il sole	suntan lotion	**desiderare**	wish (v)
crema per le mani	hand lotion	**destra**	right (direction)
cripta	crypt	**detersivo da bucato**	laundry
cristiano[a]	Christian (adj)		detergent
croce	cross	**deviazione**	detour
crudo	raw	**di**	of
cuccetta	berth (train)	**di aiuto**	helpful
cucchiaio	spoon	**di sopra**	upstairs
cucina	kitchen	**diabete**	diabetes
cucinare	cook (v)	**diabetico[a]**	diabetic
cugino[a]	cousin	**diaframma**	diaphragm
cuore	heart		(birth control)
cupola	dome	**diamante**	diamond
cuscino	pillow	**diarrea**	diarrhea
		dicembre	December
		dichiarare	declare (customs)
D		**dietro**	behind
d'accordo	agree, OK	**difficile**	difficult
da	from	**dimenticare**	forget
dare	give	**Dio**	God
decongestion-	decongestant	**diretto**	direct
ante		**direttore**	manager
delizioso	delicious	**direzione**	direction
democrazia	democracy	**dirupo**	cliff
dente	tooth	**disinfettante**	disinfectant
denti	teeth	**disoccupato[a]**	unemployed
		dispiace, mi	sorry

disturbare	disturb
disturbi cardiaci	heart condition
disturbi sinusali	sinus problems
dito	finger
dito del piede	toe
divertente	funny
divertimento	fun
divertirsi	enjoy
divorziato[a]	divorced
dizionario	dictionary
doccia	shower
dogana	customs
dolce	sweet
dolci	dessert
dolore	pain
dolore al petto	chest pains
dolori mestruali	menstrual cramps
domanda	question (n)
domandare	ask
domani	tomorrow
domenica	Sunday
donne	women
dopo	after
dopobarba	aftershave
dopodomani	day after tomorrow
doppio	double
dormire	sleep (v)
dottore	doctor
dove	where
dozzina	dozen
dritto	straight
duro	hard

E

e	and
è	is
ebreo	Jewish
eccellente	excellent
eccetto	except
economico	cheap
edificio	building
emergenza	emergency
emicrania	migraine
emorroidi	hemorrhoids
entrata	entry
epilessia	epilepsy
equitazione	horse riding
errore	mistake
esattamente	exactly
esausto	exhausted
esempio	example
est	east
estate	summer
età	age
Europa	Europe

F

fabbrica	factory
faccia	face
facile	easy
falso	false
famiglia	family
famoso[a]	famous
fantastico[a]	fantastic
fard	blush (makeup)
fare	make (v)
fare spese	shopping
fare una gita	hike
farmacia	pharmacy

farmaco per la diarrea	diarrhea medicine
fascia di sostegno	support bandage
fatto	stoned
fattoria	farm
fazzoletto di carta	facial tissue
febbraio	February
febbre	fever
felicità	happiness
feltro	moleskin
femmina	female
fermare	stop (v)
fermata	stop (n, train or bus)
ferramenta	hardware store
festa	party
fettina	slice
fiammiferi	matches
figlia	daughter
figlio	son
film	movie
filo	string
filo interdentale	dental floss
finestra	window
finire	finish (v)
finito	over (finished)
fiore	flower
firma	signature
fiume	river
folla	crowd (n)
fondo	bottom
fondotinta	foundation (makeup)
fontana	fountain
football	soccer
football Americano	American football

footing	jogging
forbici	scissors
forchetta	fork
formaggio	cheese
formulazione	baby formula
forno	oven
forse	maybe
forte	strong; loud
fortuna	luck
fossato	moat
foto	photo
fotocopia	photocopy
foto-ottica	camera shop
Francia	France
francobolli	stamps
fratello	brother
freccia	turn signal
freddo	cold (adj)
freni	brakes
fresco	fresh; cool
fretta, avere	hurry (v)
frizzante	fizzy
frontiera	border
frutta	fruit
frutti di mare	seafood
fumare	smoking
fumato	stoned
fumo	smoke (n)
funerale	funeral
fuochi d'artificio	fireworks
fuoco	fire
fusibili	fuses
futuro	future

G

galleria	gallery
galleria d'arte	art gallery

Italian	English
gamba	leg
garantito	guarantee
garza	gauze
gatto	cat
gelato	ice cream
gemelli	twins
generoso[a]	generous
genitori	parents
gennaio	January
gentile	kind
genuino	genuine
Germania	Germany
gettone	token
ghiaccio	ice
già	already
giallo	yellow
giardinaggio	gardening
giardino	garden
ginecologa	gynecologist
ginnastica	gymnastics
ginocchio	knee
giocare	play (v)
giocatore	athlete
giocattolo	toy
giochi, parco	playground
gioco	game
gioielli	jewelry
gioielliera	jewelry shop
giornalaio	newsstand
giornale	newspaper
giorno	day
giorno festivo	holiday
giorno, buon	good day (hello)
giovane	young
giovani	youths
giovedì	Thursday
gioventù,	youth

Italian	English
ostello della	hostel
giro	tour
gita, fare una	hike
giù	down
giubbotto	jacket
giugno	June
giusto	fair (just)
glutei	buttocks
gola	throat
gola, mal di	sore throat
gomito	elbow
gomma	tire (n)
gomma	eraser
da cancellare	
gomma	gum
da masticare	
gommone	raft
gonfiore	swelling (n)
gonna	skirt
Gotico	Gothic
graffetta	paper clip
grammatica	grammar
Gran Bretagna	Great Britain
grande	big
grande magazzino	department store
grassi	fat (n)
grasso[a]	fat (adj); greasy
gratis	free (no cost)
gravidanza	pregnancy
grazie	thanks
Grecia	Greece
grigio	gray
grotta	cave
guaio	trouble
guanti	gloves
guardare	look, watch (v)

guerra	war
guida	guide; guidebook
guidare	drive (v)
gusto	taste (n)

I

ieri	yesterday
igienico	hygienic
il migliore	best
imbarazzante	embarrassing
immediatamente	immediately
imparare	learn
impermeabile	raincoat
importante	important
importato	imported
Impressionista	Impressionist
improvvisamente	suddenly
in	in; by (train, car, etc.)
in pensione	retired
incartare	wrap
incastrato	stuck
incidente	accident
incinta	pregnant
incluso	included
incomprensione	misunderstanding
inconscio	unconscious
incredibile	incredible
incrocio	intersection
indicare	point (v)
indigestione	indigestion
indipendente	independent
indirizzo	address
indirizzo di posta elettronica	email address
industria	industry

infermiera	nurse
infezione	infection
infezione urinaria	urinary infection
infiammazione	inflammation
influenza	flu
informazioni	information
infortunato	injured
ingeniere	engineer
inglese	English
ingoiare	swallow (v)
ingresso	entrance
innocente	innocent
inquinamento	pollution
insalata	salad
insegnante	teacher
insetto	insect
insieme	together
insolazione	sunstroke
intelligente	intelligent
interessante	interesting
intestino	intestines
invece	instead
inverno	winter
invito	invitation
iol	
iodio	iodine
Irlanda	Ireland
irritazione della pelle	rash
isola	island
isolato	block
istante	instant
istruzione	education
Italia	Italy

L

labbro	lip
lacci da scarpe	shoelaces
ladro	thief
lago	lake
lampadina	light bulb
lana	wool
lassativo	laxative
latte detergente	face cleanser
lattina	can (n)
lavanderia	launderette
lavandino	sink
lavare	wash
lavatrice	washer
lavorare	work (v)
lavoro	work (n); occupation
legno	wood
legumi	vegetables
lei	she
Lei	you (formal)
lenti a contatto	contact lenses
lento	slow
lenzuolo	sheet
lettera	letter
letti a castello	bunk beds
lettino	cot
letto	bed
letto, camera da	bedroom
letto, carrozza	sleeper car (train)
libere, camare	vacancy (hotel)
libero	vacant
libreria	book shop
libro	book
linea aerea	airline
linea bassa	underscore (_)
lingua	language

lino	linen
liquidazione	sale
liquido della trasmissione	transmission fluid
lista	list
litro	liter
locale	local
lontano	far
lotta	fight (n)
lozione anti-zanzare	insect repellant
luce	light (n)
luci posteriori	tail lights
luglio	July
lui	he
luna	moon
luna di miele	honeymoon
lunedì	Monday

M

macchina	car
macchina fotografica	camera
madre	mother
maggio	May
maglietta	T-shirt
maglione	sweater
magro[a]	skinny
mai	never
maiale	pig
mal d'orecchi	earache
mal di denti	toothache
mal di gola	sore throat
mal di stomaco	stomachache
mal di testa	headache
malato[a]	sick
malattia	disease

DICTIONARY

Italian / English

malattia venerea	venereal disease	mercato delle pulci	flea market
mangiare	eat	mercoledì	Wednesday
maniche	sleeves	merendina	snack
manico	handle (n)	mese	month
mano	hand	messa	church service
mano, bagaglio a	carry-on luggage	messaggio	message
		mestruazioni	menstruation; period (woman's)
manzo	beef		
marca	clothesline	metallo	metal
marcio	rotten	metropolitana	subway
mare	sea	mezzanotte	midnight
marito	husband	mezzogiorno	noon
marmo	marble (material)	mi dispiace	sorry
marrone	brown	mi scusi	excuse me
martedì	Tuesday	mia	my
marzo	March	migliore, il	best
mascara	mascara	militare	military
mascella	jaw	minerale, acqua	mineral water
maschio	male	minimo	minimum
massimo	maximum	minuti	minutes
matita	pencil; eyeliner	mio	my
matrimonio	wedding	misto	mix (n)
mattina	morning	mobili	furniture
maturo	ripe	moda	fashion
meccanico	mechanic	moderno	modern
medicina	medicine	moglie	wife
medicina per il raffreddore	cold medicine	molti	many
		molto	much; very
medio	medium	momento	moment
meglio	better	monastero	monastery
mela	apple	mondo	world
meno, più o	approximately	monete	coins
menù	menu	montagna	mountain
mercato	market	monumento	monument
mercato dei fiori	flower market	morire	die
		morso	bite (n)

morto	dead
moschea	mosque
mostrare	show (v)
motocicletta	motorcycle
motorino	motor scooter
mucca	cow
muri fortificati	fortified wall
muscolo	muscle
museo	museum
musica	music
mussulmano[a]	Muslim (adj)
mutande	underwear
mutandine	underpants
mutandoni	briefs

N

naso	nose
nastro adesivo	scotch tape
Natale	Christmas
natura	nature
naturale	natural
nave	ship (n)
nazionalità	nationality
nebbia	fog
necessario	necessary
negozio	shop (n)
negozio di antiquariato	antiques shop
negozio di cellulari	cell phone shop
negozio di dolciumi	sweets shop
negozio di giocattoli	toy store
negozio di souvenir	souvenir shop
negozio di vini	wine shop

neonato[a]	baby
nero	black
nervoso[a]	nervous
niente	nothing
nipote	grandchild; nephew; niece
no	no
noi	we; us
nome	name
non	not
nonna	grandmother
nonno	grandfather
nord	north
normale	normal
nostalgico[a]	homesick
notte	night
novembre	November
nubile	single (female)
nudo[a]	naked
numero verde	toll-free
nuotare	swim
nuovo	new
nuvoloso	cloudy
nylon	nylon (material)

O

o	or
obliterare	validate
occhiali	glasses (eye)
occhiali da sole	sunglasses
occhio	eye
occupato	occupied
oceano	ocean
odiare	hate (v)
odore	smell (n)
oggi	today

ogni	each; every	Paesi Scandinavi	Scandinavia
Olimpiadi	Olympics	pagare	pay
olio	oil (n)	pagina	page
ombrello	umbrella	palazzo	palace
ombretto	eye shadow	palla	ball
omosessuale	gay	panciotto	vest
onesto[a]	honest	pane	bread
ora	hour	panificio	bakery
orario	timetable	panino	sandwich
orario d'apertura	opening hours	panna	cream; whipped cream
orecchi, mal d'	earache	pannolino	diaper
orecchini	earrings	pantaloncini	shorts
orecchio	ear	pantaloni	pants
organo	organ	pantofole	slippers
originale	original	papà	dad
oro	gold	paradiso	heaven
orologio	clock, watch (n)	parcheggiare	park (v)
orribile	horrible	parcheggio	parking lot
ospedale	hospital	parco	park (garden)
ospite	guest	parco giochi	playground
ostello della gioventù	youth hostel	parlare	talk
		parola	word
ottico	optician	parrucchiere	beauty salon
ottimo	great	partenze	departures
ottobre	October	partire	leave
ottone	brass	Pasqua	Easter
ovest	west	passaporto	passport
		passato	past
P		passeggero[a]	passenger
		passeggino	stroller
pacco	package	pasticceria	pastry; pastry shop
pace	peace		
padre	father	pastiglie per la gola	lozenges
padrone	owner	pattinaggio	skating
paese	country	pattini a rotelle	roller skates
Paesi Bassi	Netherlands	peccato, che	it's a pity

pedaggio	toll
pedalò	paddleboat
pedone	pedestrian
peggio	worse
peggiore	worst
pelle	skin; leather
pelletteria	leather shop
peltro	pewter
pene	penis
penna	pen
pensare	think
pensione, in	retired
pepe	pepper
per	for
per favore	please
percentuale	percent
perchè	why (question); because (answer)
perfetto	perfect (adj)
pericolo	danger
pericoloso	dangerous
periodo	period (of time)
perso[a]	lost
persona	person
persone	people
pesante	heavy
pescare	fish (v)
pesce	fish (n)
peso	weight
pettine	comb (n)
petto	chest
pezzo	piece
piacere	like (v)
piangere	cry (v)
pianta	plant
piatto	plate
piazza	square

piazzuola	campsite
picchetti della tenda	tent pegs
piccolo[a]	small
piede	foot
piede d'atleta	athlete's foot
pietra	rock (n)
pigiama	pajamas
pigro[a]	lazy
pillola	pill
pillole anticoncezionali	birth control pills
pinzatrice	stapler
pinzette	pliers; tweezers
pioggia	rain (n)
piscina	swimming pool
pistola	gun
più	more
più o meno	approximately
più tardi	later; afterwards
pizzo	lace
plastica	plastic
po', un	some
poco	few
politici	politicians
polizia	police
pollo	chicken
polmoni	lungs
polso	wrist
polyestere	polyester
pomata antistaminica	first-aid cream
pomeriggio	afternoon
pompa	pump (n)
ponte	bridge
porcellana	porcelain
porco	pork
porta	door

portacenere	ashtray
portafoglio	wallet
portar via	take out (food)
portare	carry
porto	harbor
Portogallo	Portugal
possedere	own (v)
possibile	possible
posta	mail (n)
posta elettronica	email
posto	seat
posto in vagone letto	sleeper (train)
potabile, acqua	drinkable water
potente	powerful
potere	can (v); power
povero	poor
pratico[a]	practical
prendere	take; catch (v)
prendere in prestito	borrow
prenotare	reserve
prenotazione	reservation
prescrizione	prescription
preservativo	condom
pressione alta	high blood pressure
prestare	lend
presto	early
prete	priest
previsioni del tempo	weather forecast
prezzo	price
prima	before
prima classe	first class
primavera	spring

primo	first
primo soccorso	first aid
principale	main
privato	private
problema	problem
professione	profession
profughi	refugees
profumo	perfume
proibito	prohibited
pronto	ready
pronto soccorso	emergency room
pronuncia	pronunciation
prosperare	prosper
prossimo	next
protestante	Protestant (adj)
protestare	complain
protezione solare	sunscreen
prudente	careful
prurito	itch (n)
pubblico	public
pulce	flea
pulito[a]	clean (adj)
pullman	long-distance bus
pulpito	pulpit
punto	dot (computer)
puntuale	on time

Q

quadro	painting
qualcosa	something
qualità	quality
quando	when
quanti	how many
quanto costa	how much ($)
quarto	quarter (¼)
qui	here

R

raccomandare	recommend
raccordo anulare	ring road
radiatore	radiator
radiografia	X-ray
raffreddore	cold (n)
raffreddore da fieno	hay fever
ragazza	girl
ragazzo	boy
raggi x	X-ray
ragno	spider
rame	copper
rasoio	razor
razzismo	racism
re	king
regalo	gift
reggiseno	bra
regina	queen
religione	religion
reliquie	relic
Repubblica Ceca	Czech Republic
resistente	sturdy
retto	rectum
ricco[a]	rich
ricetta	recipe
ricevere	receive
ricevuta	receipt
ricordare	remember
ridere	laugh (v)
riempire	refill (v)
rilassamento	relaxation
rimborso	refund (n)
Rinascimento	Renaissance
riparare	repair (v)
riposare	relax (v)
rispetto	respect

risposta	answer
ritardo	delay (n)
ritiro bagagli	baggage claim
ritornare	return
ritorno	round trip
rivista	magazine
Romanico	Romanesque
Romantico	Romantic
romantico[a]	romantic
rosa	pink
rossetto	lipstick
rosso	red
rotaie	railway
rotonda	roundabout
rotto	broken
rovine	ruins
rubinetto	faucet
rubinetto, acqua del	tap water
rumoroso[a]	noisy
ruota	wheel
russare	snore

S

sabato	Saturday
sacchetto	bag
sacchetto di plastica	plastic bag
sacco a pelo	sleeping bag
sala d'aspetto	waiting room
sala di attesa	waiting room
salone	hall (big room)
saltare	jump (v)
salumeria	delicatessen
salute	health
Salute!	Cheers!
salvare	save (computer)

salvietta	napkin	scrivere	write
sandali	sandals	scultore	sculptor
sandali infradito	thongs	scultura	sculpture
sangue	blood	scuola	school
sanguinare	bleeding	scuro	dark
sano	healthy	scuse	apology
santo[a]	saint	scusi, mi	excuse me
sapere	know	se	if
sapone	soap	secchio	bucket
Saridon	non-aspirin substitute	secco	dry (adj)
scala	ladder	secolo	century
scaldare	heat (v)	seconda classe	second class
scale	stairs	sedia	chair
scandaloso	scandalous	sedia a rotelle,	wheelchair-
Scandinavi, Paesi	Scandinavia	accessibile con la	accessible
scapolo	single (male)	seggiolino per	car seat (baby)
scarafaggi	cockroach	la macchina	
scaricare	download	seggiolino per	booster seat
scarpe	shoes	neonati	
scarpe da ginnastica	tennis	seggiolone	highchair
	shoes	segno	sign
scarpe da tennis	tennis shoes	segrete	dungeon
scarpe, lacci da	shoelaces	segreto	secret
scatola	box	selvaggio[a]	wild
scherzo	joke (n)	semaforo	stoplight
schiena	back	seminterrato	basement
sci	skiing	semplice	simple, plain
sci acquatico	waterskiing	sempre	always
sciare	ski (v)	seno	breast
sciarpa	scarf	senso unico	one way (street)
scienza	science	senza	without
scienziato[a]	scientist	separato	separate (adj)
sciopero	strike (stop work)	sera	evening
sciroppo	cough drop	serio	serious
scivoloso	slippery	serratura	lock (n)
sconto	discount	servizio	service
scotch	tape (adhesive)	sesso	sex

Italian	English
seta	silk
settembre	September
settimana	week
sfortunatamente	unfortunately
si	yes
sicuro	safe
sigarette	cigarette
Signora	Mrs.
signore	gentleman (singular); ladies (plural)
Signore	Mr.
signore	sir
Signorina	Miss
silenzio	silence
simile	similar
sinagoga	synagogue
sinistra	left (direction)
sintetico	synthetic
sito Internet	website
smalto per le unghie	nail polish
soccorso, primo	first aid
soccorso, pronto	emergency room
soffrire	suffer
sognare	dream (v)
sogno	dream (n)
soldi	money
sole	sun; sunshine
sole, bruciatura del	sunburn
sole, occhiali da	sunglasses
solo	only
solo[a]	alone
solvente per le unghie	nail polish remover
sopra	above
sopra, di	upstairs
soprannome	nickname
sorella	sister
sorpresa	surprise (n)
sorriso	smile (n)
sottile	thin
sotto	under, below
sottoveste	slip
Spagna	Spain
spalle	shoulder
spaventato[a]	afraid
spazzolino da denti	toothbrush
specchio	mirror
specialità	specialty
specialmente	especially
spedire	send
spendere	spend
speranza	hope
spese, fare	shopping
spesso	thick
spettacolo	show (n)
spiaggia	beach
spiegare	explain
spilla	pin; brooch
spilla da balia	safety pin
spingere	push
sporco	dirty
sposato[a]	married
squadra	team
stampare	print
stanco	tired
stanotte	tonight
starnuto	sneeze (n)
Stati Uniti	United States
stato	state
stazione	station
stazione degli autobus	bus station

stazione della metropolitana	subway station
stella	star (in sky)
stesso	same
stile	style
stitichezza	constipation
stivali	boots
stoffa	cloth
stomaco	stomach
stomaco, mal di	stomachache
storia	history; story (floor)
strada	street
straniero	foreign
strano[a]	strange (odd)
stretto	tight; narrow
studente	student
stupido[a]	stupid
stuzzicadenti	toothpick
su	on; up
subito	soon
succhiotto	pacifier
succo	juice
sud	south
sudare	sweat (v)
suocera	mother-in-law
supermercato	supermarket
supplemento	supplement
sveglia	alarm clock
svegliarsi	wake up
Svizzera	Switzerland

T

taglia	size
tagliaunghie	nail clippers
taglio di capelli	haircut
tappeto	carpet; rug
tappi per le orecchie	earplugs
tappo	cork; sink stopper
tardi	late
tardi, più	later; afterwards
tasca	pocket
tassametro	taxi meter
tasse	tax
tavola da surf	surfboard
tavola	table
tavolo	desk
tazza	cup
teatro	theater; play (n)
telefono	telephone
telefono cellulare	cell phone
televisione	television
temere	fear (v)
temperatura	temperature
tempo	weather
tempo, previsioni del	weather forecast
temporale	storm
tenda	tent
tenere	keep
tenero	tender
tergicristalli	windshield wipers
termometro	thermometer
terra	earth
terroristi	terrorists
tesoro	treasury
test di gravidanza	pregnancy test
testa	head
testa, mal di	headache
testicoli	testicles
tetto	roof
tiepido	lukewarm
timbrare	validate

timido[a]	shy
tirare	pull; throw
toilette	toilet
torcia	flashlight
torre	tower
tosse	cough (n)
tossire	cough (v)
totale	total
tour guidato	guided tour
tradizionale	traditional
tradurre	translate
traffico	traffic
traghetto	ferry
tramonto	sunset
tranquillo	quiet
trattino	hyphen (-)
treno	train
trepiede	tripod
triste	sad
troppo	too
trucco	makeup
tu	you (informal)
Turchia	Turkey
turista	tourist
tutto	everything

U

ubriaco	drunk
uccello	bird
uccidere	kill
udire	hear
ufficio	office
ultimo	last
umido	muggy
un altro	another
un po'	some

una volta	once
unghie	fingernail
unico, senso	one way (street)
università	university
uomini	men
uomo	man
uretra	urethra
urgente	urgent
usare	use
uscita	exit
uscita d'emergenza	emergency exit
utero	uterus

V

vacanza	vacation
vagone	train car
valido	valid
valigia	suitcase
valle	valley
vasca da bagno	bathtub
vaselina	Vaseline
vecchio[a]	old
vedere	see
vedova	widow
vedovo	widower
vela	sailing
velluto	velvet
velocità	speed
vendere	sell
venerdì	Friday
venire	come
vento	wind
ventoso	windy
verde	green
vescica	bladder

DICTIONARY

vesciche	blisters
vestaglia	nightgown
vestiti	clothes
vestito	dress (n)
via aerea	air mail
viaggi, agenzia di	travel agency
viaggiare	travel
viaggiatori	travelers
viaggio	trip
vicino	near
video registratore	video recorder
vietato	forbidden
vietato fumare	non-smoking
vigneto	vineyard
villaggio	village
vino	wine
viola	purple
violenza	violence
violenza carnale	rape (n)
visita	visit (n)

visita, biglietto da	business card
visitare	visit (v)
vista	view
vita	life; waist
vitamine	vitamins
vivere	live (v)
voce	voice
volare	fly (v)
volere	want
volo	flight
volta, una	once
vomitare	vomit (v)
vuoto	empty

Z

zainetto	backpack
zaino	rucksack
zanzara	mosquito
zia	aunt
zio	uncle

Italian / English

English / Italian

DICTIONARY

ENGLISH/ITALIAN

You'll see some of the words in the dictionary listed like this: *aggressivo[a].* Use the *a* ending (pronounced "ah") if you're talking about a woman.

A

abortion	aborto
above	sopra
abstract	Astratto
abuse (v)	abusare
accident	incidente
accountant	commercialista
adapter, electrical	adattatore elettrico
address	indirizzo
address, email	indirizzo di posta elettronica
adult	adulto
afraid	spaventato[a]
Africa	Africa
after	dopo
afternoon	pomeriggio
aftershave	dopobarba
afterwards	più tardi
again	ancora
age	età
aggressive	aggressivo[a]
agnostic	agnostico[a]
agree	d'accordo
AIDS	AIDS
air	aria
air mail	via aerea
air-conditioned	aria condizionata
airline	linea aerea
airplane	aeroplano
airport	aeroporto
aisle	corridoio
alarm clock	sveglia
alcohol	alcool
allergic	allergico[a]
allergies	allergie
alone	solo[a]
already	già
altar	altare
always	sempre
ambulance	ambulanza
ancestor	antenato[a]
ancient	antico
and	e
angry	arrabbiato[a]
animal	animale
ankle	caviglia
another	un altro
answer	risposta
antacid	antiacido
antibiotic	antibiotico
antiques	antichità
antiques shop	negozio di antiquariato
apartment	appartamento
apology	scuse
appetizers	antipasti
apple	mela
appointment	appuntamento
approximately	più o meno
April	aprile

arm	braccio	back	schiena
arrivals	arrivi	backpack	zainetto
arrive	arrivare	bad	cattivo
art	arte	bag	sacchetto
art gallery	galleria d'arte	bag, plastic	sacchetto di
Art Nouveau	Arte Nouveau		plastica
arthritis	artrite	bag, Ziplock	busta de plastica
artificial	artificiale		sigillabile
artist	artista	baggage	bagaglio
ashtray	portacenere	baggage check	check-in
ask	domandare		bagagli
aspirin	aspirina	baggage claim	ritiro bagagli
asthma	asma	bakery	panificio
at	a	balcony	balcone
"at" sign (@)	chiocciola	ball	palla
atheist	ateo[a]	banana	banana
athlete	giocatore	bandage	benda
athlete's foot	piede d'atleta	bandage, support	fascia di
attractive	bello[a]		sostegno
audioguide	audioguida	Band-Aid	cerotto
August	agosto	bank	banca
aunt	zia	barber	barbiere
Austria	Austria	barber shop	barbiere
autumn	autunno	baseball	baseball
		basement	seminterrato

B

		basket	cestino
baby	neonato[a]	basketball	basket
baby booster seat	seggiolino	bath	bagno
	per neonati	bathrobe	accappatoio
baby car seat	seggiolino pe	bathroom	bagno
	la macchina	bathtub	vasca da bagno
baby food	cibo per neonati	battery	batteria
baby formula	formulazione	beach	spiaggia
babysitter	bambinaia	beard	barba
babysitting service	servizio di	beautiful	bello[a]
	baby sitter	beauty salon	parrucchiere
		because	perchè

English	Italian
bed	letto
bedbugs	insetti
bedroom	camera da letto
bedsheet	lenzuolo
beef	manzo
beer	birra
before	prima
begin	cominciare
behind	dietro
Belgium	Belgio
bells	campane
below	sotto
belt	cintura
berth (train)	cuccetta
best	il migliore
better	meglio
bib	bavaglino
bicycle	bicicletta
big	grande
bill (payment)	conto
bird	uccello
birth control pills	pillole anticoncezionali
birthday	compleanno
bite (n)	morso
black	nero
bladder	vescica
blanket	coperta
bleeding	sanguinare
blisters	vesciche
block	isolato
blond	biondo[a]
blood	sangue
blood pressure, high	pressione alta
blouse	camicetta
blue	blu
blush (makeup)	fard
boat	barca
body	corpo
boiled	bollito
bomb	bomba
book	libro
book shop	libreria
booster seat	seggiolino per neonati
boots	stivali
border	frontiera
borrow	prendere in prestito
boss	capo
bottle	bottiglia
bottom	fondo
boutique, clothing	boutique di abbigliamento
bowl	boccia
box	scatola
boy	ragazzo
bra	reggiseno
bracelet	braccialetto
brakes	freni
brass	ottone
bread	pane
breakfast	colazione
breast	seno
breath	alito
bridge	ponte
briefs	mutandoni
Britain	Britannia
broken	rotto
bronze	bronzo
brooch	spilla
brother	fratello
brown	marrone
bucket	secchio

building	edificio
bulb, light	lampadina
bunk beds	letti a castello
burn (n)	bruciatura
bus	autobus
bus station	stazione degli autobus
bus stop	fermata
bus, city	autobus
bus, long-distance	pullman, corriera
business	affari
business card	biglietto da visita
buttocks	glutei
button	bottone
buy	comprare
by (train, car, etc.)	in

C

calendar	calendario
calorie	calorie
camera	macchina fotografica
camera shop	foto-ottica
camper	camper
camping	campeggio
campsite	piazzuola
can (n)	lattina
can (v)	potere
can opener	apriscatola
Canada	Canada
canal	canale
cancel	annullare
candle	candela
candy	caramella
canoe	canoa

cap	berretto
captain	capitano
car	macchina
car (train)	vagone
car seat (baby)	seggiolino per la macchina
car, dining (train)	carrozza ristorante
car, sleeper (train)	carrozza letto
carafe	caraffa
card	cartina
card, telephone	carta telefonica
cards (deck)	carte
careful	prudente
carpet	tappeto
carry	portare
carry-on luggage	bagaglio a mano
cash	contante
cash machine	bancomat
cashier	cassiere
cassette	cassetta
castle	castello
cat	gatto
catch (v)	prendere
cathedral	cattedrale
Catholic (adj)	cattolico[a]
cave	grotta
cell phone	telefono cellulare
cell phone shop	negozio di cellulari
cellar	cantina
center	centro
century	secolo
ceramic	ceramica
chair	sedia

English	Italian
championship	campionato
change (n)	cambio
change (v)	cambiare
chapel	cappella
charming	affascinante
cheap	economico
check (n)	assegno
Cheers!	Salute!
cheese	formaggio
cheese shop	caseficio
chest	petto
chest pains	dolore al petto
chicken	pollo
child	bambino[a]
children	bambini
chills	brividi
Chinese	cinese
chocolate	cioccolato
choir	coro
Christian (adj)	cristiano[a]
Christmas	Natale
church	chiesa
church service	messa
cigarette	sigarette
cinema	cinema
city	città
class	classe
class, first	prima classe
class, second	seconda classe
classical	Classico
clean (adj)	pulito[a]
clear	chiaro
cliff	dirupo
clinic, medical	clinica
clock	orologio
clock, alarm	sveglia
cloister	chiostro

English	Italian
closed	chiuso
cloth	stoffa
clothes	vestiti
clothes pins	spilla
clothesline	marca
clothing boutique	boutique di abbigliamento
cloudy	nuvoloso
coast	costa
coat hanger	appendiabiti
cockroach	scarafaggi
coffee	caffè
coffee shop	bar
coins	monete
cold (adj)	freddo
cold (n)	raffreddore
cold medicine	medicina per il raffreddore
colors	colori
comb (n)	pettine
come	venire
comfortable	confortevole
compact disc	compact disc
complain	protestare
complicated	complicato
computer	computer
concert	concerto
conditioner (hair)	balsamo
condom	preservativo
conductor	conduttore
confirm	confermare
congestion (sinus)	congestione
congratulations	congratulazioni
connection (train)	coincidenza
constipation	stitichezza

construction (sign)	costruzioni
contact lenses	lenti a contatto
contagious	contagioso
contraceptives	contraccettivi
cook (v)	cucinare
cool	fresco
copper	rame
copy	copia
copy shop	copisteria
cork	tappo
corkscrew	cavatappi
corner	angolo
corridor	corridoio
corruption	corruzione
cost (v)	costare
cot	lettino
cotton	cotone
cough (n)	tosse
cough (v)	tossire
cough drop	sciroppo
country	paese
countryside	campagna
cousin	cugino[a]
cow	mucca
cozy	confortevole
crafts	arte
cramps	crampi
cramps, menstrual	dolori mestruali
cream	panna
cream, first-aid	pomata antistaminica
credit card	carta di credito
cross	croce
crowd (n)	folla
cry (v)	piangere

crypt	cripta
cup	tazza
customs	dogana
Czech Republic	Repubblica Ceca

D

dad	papà
dance (v)	ballare
danger	pericolo
dangerous	pericoloso
dark	scuro
dash (-)	trattino
daughter	figlia
day	giorno
day after tomorrow	dopodomani
dead	morto
December	dicembre
declare (customs)	dichiarare
decongestant	decongestionante
delay (n)	ritardo
delete	cancellare
delicatessen	salumeria
delicious	delizioso
democracy	democrazia
dental floss	filo interdentale
dentist	dentista
deodorant	deodorante
depart	partire
department store	grande magazzino
departures	partenze
deposit	deposito
dessert	dolci

detergent	detersivo da bucato	dot (computer)	punto
detour	deviazione	double	doppio
diabetes	diabete	down	giù
diabetic	diabetico[a]	download	scaricare
diamond	diamante	downtown	centro
diaper	pannolino	dozen	dozzina
diaper rash	dermatite da	dream (n)	sogno
	pannolone	dream (v)	sognare
diaphragm	diaframma	dress (n)	vestito
(birth control)		drink (n)	bevanda
diarrhea	diarrea	drink (v)	bere
diarrhea	farmaco per	drive (v)	guidare
medicine	la diarrea	driver	autista
dictionary	dizionario	drunk	ubriaco
die	morire	dry (adj)	secco, asciutto
difficult	difficile	dry (v)	asciugare
dining car (train)	carrozza	dryer	asciugatrice
	ristorante	dungeon	segrete
dinner	cena	duty free	duty free
direct	diretto		
direction	direzione	**E**	
dirty	sporco		
discount	sconto	each	ogni
disease	malattia	ear	orecchio
disease, venereal	malattia	earache	mal d'orecchi
	venerea	early	presto
disinfectant	disinfettante	earplugs	tappi per le orecchie
disturb	disturbare	earrings	orecchini
divorced	divorziato[a]	earth	terra
dizziness	capogiri	east	est
doctor	dottore	Easter	Pasqua
dog	cane	easy	facile
doll	bambola	eat	mangiare
dome	cupola	education	istruzione
donkey	asino	elbow	gomito
door	porta	electrical adapter	adattatore
dormitory	camerata		elettrico
		elevator	ascensore

email	posta elettronica
email address	indirizzo di posta elettronica
embarrassing	imbarazzante
embassy	ambasciata
emergency	emergenza
emergency exit	uscita d'emergenza
emergency room	pronto soccorso
empty	vuoto
engineer	ingeniere
English	inglese
enjoy	divertirsi
enough	abbastanza
entrance	ingresso
entrance (road)	entrata
entry	entrata
envelope	busta
epilepsy	epilessia
eraser	gomma da cancellare
especially	specialmente
Europe	Europa
evening	sera
every	ogni
everything	tutto
exactly	esattamente
example	esempio
excellent	eccellente
except	eccetto
exchange (n)	cambio
excuse me	mi scusi
exhausted	esausto
exit	uscita
exit, emergency	uscita d'emergenza
expensive	caro
explain	spiegare
eye	occhio
eye shadow	ombretto
eyeliner	matita, eyeliner

F

face	faccia
face cleanser	latte detergente
face powder	cipria
facial tissue	fazzoletto di carta
factory	fabbrica
fair (just)	giusto
fall (v)	cadere
false	falso
family	famiglia
famous	famoso[a]
fan belt	cinghia del ventilatore
fantastic	fantastico[a]
far	lontano
farm	fattoria
farmer	contadino[a]
fashion	moda
fat (adj)	grasso[a]
fat (n)	grassi
father	padre
faucet	rubinetto
fax	fax
fear (v)	temere
February	febbraio
female	femmina
ferry	traghetto
fever	febbre
few	poco
field	campo
fight (n)	lotta

English	Italian
fight (v)	combattere
fine (good)	bene
finger	dito
fingernail	unghie
finish (v)	finire
fire	fuoco
fireworks	fuochi d'artificio
first	primo
first aid	primo soccorso
first class	prima classe
first-aid cream	pomata antistaminica
fish (n)	pesce
fish (v)	pescare
fix (v)	aggiustare
fizzy	frizzante
flag	bandiera
flash (camera)	flash
flashlight	torcia
flavor (n)	aroma
flea	pulce
flea market	mercato delle pulci
flight	volo
flip-flops	ciabatte da piscina
floss, dental	filo interdentale
flower	fiore
flower market	mercato dei fiori
flu	influenza
fly (v)	volare
fog	nebbia
food	cibo
food poisoning	avvelenamento da cibo
foot	piede
football (soccer)	football, calcio
football, American	football Americano
for	per
forbidden	vietato
foreign	straniero
forget	dimenticare
fork	forchetta
formula (for baby)	formulazione
foundation (makeup)	fondotinta
fountain	fontana
fragile	fragile
France	Francia
free (no cost)	gratis
fresh	fresco
Friday	venerdì
friend	amico
friendship	amicizia
frisbee	frisbee
from	da
fruit	frutta
fun	divertimento
funeral	funerale
funny	divertente
furniture	mobili
fuses	fusibili
future	futuro

G

English	Italian
gallery	galleria
game	gioco
garage	garage
garden	giardino
gardening	giardinaggio
gas	benzina

DICTIONARY

English / Italian

gas station	benzinaio
gauze	garza
gay	omosessuale
generous	generoso[a]
gentleman	signore
genuine	genuino
Germany	Germania
gift	regalo
girl	ragazza
give	dare
glass	bicchiere
glasses (eye)	occhiali
gloves	guanti
go	andare
go through	attraversare
God	Dio
gold	oro
golf	golf
good	buono
good day	buon giorno
goodbye	arrivederci
Gothic	Gotico
grammar	grammatica
grandchild	nipote
grandfather	nonno
grandmother	nonna
gray	grigio
greasy	grasso
great	ottimo
Great Britain	Gran Bretagna
Greece	Grecia
green	verde
grocery store	alimentari
guarantee	garantito
guest	ospite
guide	guida
guidebook	guida

guided tour	tour guidato
guilty	colpevole
guitar	chitarra
gum	gomma da masticare
gun	pistola
gymnastics	ginnastica
gynecologist	ginecologa

H

hair	capelli
haircut	taglio di capelli
hall (big room)	salone
hand	mano
hand lotion	crema per le mani
handicapped	andicappato
handicrafts	artigianato
handle (n)	manico
handsome	attraente
happiness	felicità
happy	contento[a]
harbor	porto
hard	duro
hardware store	ferramenta
hash (drug)	hashish
hat	cappello
hate (v)	odiare
have	avere
hay fever	raffreddore da fieno
he	lui
head	testa
headache	mal di testa
headlights	anabbaglianti
health	salute
health insurance	assicurazione medica

English	Italian
healthy	sano
hear	udire
heart	cuore
heart condition	disturbi cardiaci
heat (n)	calore
heat (v)	scaldare
heaven	paradiso
heavy	pesante
hello	ciao
help (n)	aiuto
help (v)	aiutare
helpful	di aiuto
hemorrhoids	emorroidi
here	qui
hi	ciao
high	alto
high blood pressure	pressione alta
highchair	seggiolone
highway	autostrada
hike	fare una gita
hill	collina
history	storia
hitchhike	autostop
hobby	hobby
hockey	hockey
hole	buco
holiday	giorno festivo
homemade	casalingo
homesick	nostalgico[a]
honest	onesto[a]
honeymoon	luna di miele
hope	speranza
horrible	orribile
horse	cavallo
horse riding	equitazione
hospital	ospedale
hot	caldo
hotel	hotel
hour	ora
house	casa
how	come
how many	quanti
how much ($)	quanto costa
hungry	affamato
hurry (v)	avere fretta
husband	marito
hydrofoil	aliscafo
hyphen (-)	trattino

I

English	Italian
I	io
ice	ghiaccio
ice cream	gelato
if	se
ill	malato[a]
immediately	immediatamente
important	importante
imported	importato
impossible	impossibile
Impressionist	Impressionista
in	in
included	incluso
incredible	incredibile
independent	indipendente
indigestion	indigestione
industry	industria
infection	infezione
infection, urinary	infezione urinaria
inflammation	infiammazione
information	informazioni

injured	infortunato	job	lavoro
innocent	innocente	jogging	footing
insect	insetto	joint (marijuana)	canna
insect repellant	lozione anti-zanzare	joke (n)	scherzo
inside	dentro	journey	viaggio
instant	istante	juice	succo
instead	invece	July	luglio
insurance	assicurazione	jump (v)	saltare
insurance, health	assicurazione medica	June	giugno
insured	assicurato		
intelligent	intelligente	**K**	
interesting	interessante	keep	tenere
Internet	Internet	kettle	bollitore
Internet access	accesso a Internet	key	chiave
		kill	uccidere
Internet café	Internet café	kind	gentile
intersection	incrocio	king	re
intestines	intestino	kiss	bacio
invitation	invito	kitchen	cucina
iodine	iodio	kitchenette	cucina
Ireland	Irlanda	knee	ginocchio
is	è	knife	coltello
island	isola	knight	cavaliero
Italy	Italia	know	sapere
itch (n)	prurito		
		L	
J		lace	pizzo
jacket	giubbotto	ladder	scala
January	gennaio	ladies	signore
jaw	mascella	lady	signora
jeans	jeans	lake	lago
jewelry	gioielli	lamb	agnello
jewelry shop	gioielliera	language	lingua
Jewish	ebreo	large	grande
		last	ultimo
		late	tardi

later	più tardi	lockers	armadietti
laugh (v)	ridere	look	guardare
launderette	lavanderia	lost	perso[a]
laundry soap	detersivo	lotion, hand	crema per
	da bucato		le mani
lawyer	avvocato	loud	forte
laxative	lassativo	love (n)	amore
lazy	pigro[a]	love (v)	amare
learn	imparare	lover	amante
leather	pelle	low	basso
leather shop	pelletteria	lozenges	pastiglie
leave	partire		per la gola
left (direction)	sinistra	luck	fortuna
leg	gamba	luggage	bagaglio
lend	prestare	luggage, carry-on	bagaglio
lenses, contact	lenti a		a mano
	contatto	lukewarm	tiepido
letter	lettera	lungs	polmoni
library	biblioteca		
lies	bugie	**M**	
life	vita		
light (n)	luce	macho	macho
light bulb	lampadina	mad	arrabbiato[a]
lighter (n)	accendino	magazine	rivista
like (v)	piacere	mail (n)	posta
linen	lino	main	principale
lip	labbro	make (v)	fare
lip salve	burro di cacao	makeup	trucco
lipstick	rossetto	male	maschio
list	lista	mall (shopping)	centro
listen	ascoltare		commerciale
liter	litro	man	uomo
little (adj)	piccolo	manager	direttore
live (v)	vivere	many	molti
local	locale	map	cartina
lock (n)	serratura	marble (material)	marmo
lock (v)	chiudere	March	marzo
		marijuana	marijuana

DICTIONARY

English / Italian

market	mercato	Miss	Signorina
market, flea	mercato delle pulci	mistake	errore
		misunder- standing	incomprensione
market, flower	mercato dei fiori	mix (n)	misto
market, open-air	mercato	moat	fossato
married	sposato[a]	modern	moderno
mascara	mascara	moisturizer	crema idratante
matches	fiammiferi	moleskin	feltro, moleskin
maximum	massimo	moment	momento
May	maggio	monastery	monastero
maybe	forse	Monday	lunedì
meat	carne	money	soldi
mechanic	meccanico	month	mese
medicine	medicina	monument	monumento
medicine for a cold	medicina per il raffreddore	moon	luna
		more	ancora
medicine, non-aspirin substitute	Saridon	morning	mattina
		mosque	moschea
medieval	Medievale	mosquito	zanzara
medium	medio	mother	madre
men	uomini	mother-in-law	suocera
menstrual cramps	dolori mestruali	motor scooter	motorino
		motorcycle	motocicletta
menstruation	mestruazioni	mountain	montagna
menu	menù	moustache	baffi
message	messaggio	mouth	bocca
metal	metallo	movie	film
meter, taxi	tassametro	Mr.	Signore
midnight	mezzanotte	Mrs.	Signora
migraine	emicrania	much	molto
military	militare	muggy	umido
mineral water	acqua minerale	muscle	muscolo
minimum	minimo	museum	museo
minutes	minuti	music	musica
mirror	specchio	Muslim (adj)	mussulmano[a]
miscarriage	aborto spontaneo	my	mio / mia

N

nail (finger)	unghie
nail clippers	tagliaunghie
nail polish	smalto per le unghie
nail polish remover	solvente per le unghie
naked	nudo[a]
name	nome
napkin	salvietta
narrow	stretto
nationality	nazionalità
natural	naturale
nature	natura
nausea	nausea
near	vicino
necessary	necessario
neck	collo
necklace	collana
need (v)	avere bisogno di
needle	ago
Neoclassical	Neoclassico
nephew	nipote
nervous	nervoso[a]
Netherlands	Paesi Bassi
never	mai
new	nuovo
newspaper	giornale
newsstand	giornalaio
next	prossimo
nice	bello[a]
nickname	soprannome
niece	nipote
night	notte
nightgown	vestaglia
no	no
no vacancy	completo
noisy	rumoroso[a]
non-aspirin substitute	Saridon
non-smoking	vietato fumare
noon	mezzogiorno
normal	normale
north	nord
nose	naso
not	non
notebook	blocco note
nothing	niente
November	novembre
now	adesso
nurse	infermiera
nylon (material)	nylon
nylons (panty hose)	collant

O

occupation	lavoro
occupied	occupato
ocean	oceano
October	ottobre
of	di
office	ufficio
office supplies store	cartoleria
oil (n)	olio
OK	d'accordo
old	vecchio[a]
Olympics	Olimpiadi
on	su
on time	puntuale
once	una volta
one way (street)	senso unico
one way (ticket)	andata
only	solo

open (adj)	aperto	park (garden)	parco
open (v)	aprire	park (v)	parcheggiare
open-air market	mercato	parking lot	parcheggio
opening hours	orario	party	festa
	d'apertura	passenger	passeggero[a]
opera	opera	passport	passaporto
operator	centralinista	past	passato
optician	ottico	pastry shop	pasticceria
or	o	pay	pagare
orange (color)	arancione	peace	pace
orange (fruit)	arancia	pedestrian	pedone
organ	organo	pen	penna
original	originale	pencil	matita
other	altro	penis	pene
outdoors	all'aria aperta	people	persone
oven	forno	pepper	pepe
over (finished)	finito	percent	percentuale
own (v)	possedere	perfect (adj)	perfetto
owner	padrone	perfume	profumo
		period (of time)	periodo
		period (woman's)	mestruazioni

P

		person	persona
pacifier	succhiotto	pet (n)	animale domestico
package	pacco	pewter	peltro
paddleboat	pedalò	pharmacy	farmacia
page	pagina	phone	telefono
pail	secchio	phone booth	cabina
pain	dolore		telefonica
pain killer	analgesico	phone, mobile	telefono
pains, chest	dolore al petto		cellulare
painting	quadro	photo	foto
pajamas	pigiama	photocopy	fotocopia
palace	palazzo	photocopy shop	copisteria
panties	mutande	pickpocket	borsaiolo
pants	pantaloni	picnic	picnic
paper	carta	piece	pezzo
paper clip	graffetta	pig	maiale
parents	genitori		

pill	pillola
pillow	cuscino
pills, birth control	pillole anticoncezionali
pin	spilla
PIN code	codice segreto
pink	rosa
pity, it's a	che peccato
plain	semplice
plane	aeroplano
plant	pianta
plastic	plastica
plastic bag	sacchetto di plastica
plate	piatto
platform (train)	binario
play (n)	teatro
play (v)	giocare
playground	parco giochi
playpen	box
please	per favore
pliers	pinzette
pneumonia	broncopolmonite
pocket	tasca
point (v)	indicare
police	polizia
politicians	politici
pollution	inquinamento
polyester	polyestere
poor	povero
porcelain	porcellana
pork	porco
Portugal	Portogallo
possible	possibile
postcard	cartolina
poster	poster
power	potere

powerful	potente
practical	pratico[a]
pregnancy	gravidanza
pregnancy test	test di gravidanza
pregnant	incinta
Preparation H	Preparazione H
prescription	prescrizione
present (gift)	regalo
pretty	carino[a]
price	prezzo
priest	prete
print	stampare
private	privato
problem	problema
profession	professione
prohibited	proibito
pronunciation	pronuncia
prosper	prosperare
Protestant (adj)	protestante
public	pubblico
pull	tirare
pulpit	pulpito
pulse	battito cardiaco
pump (n)	pompa
punctual	puntuale
purple	viola
purse	borsa
push	spingere

Q

quality	qualità
quarter (¼)	quarto
queen	regina
question (n)	domanda
quiet	tranquillo

DICTIONARY

English / Italian

R

R.V.	camper
rabbit	coniglio
racism	razzismo
radiator	radiatore
radio	radio
raft	gommone
railway	rotaie
rain (n)	pioggia
rainbow	arcobaleno
raincoat	impermeabile
rape (n)	violenza carnale
rash	irritazione della pelle
rash, diaper	dermatite da pannolone
raw	crudo
razor	rasoio
ready	pronto
receipt	ricevuta
receive	ricevere
receptionist	centralinista
recipe	ricetta
recommend	raccomandare
rectum	retto
red	rosso
refill (v)	riempire
refugees	profughi
refund (n)	rimborso
relax (v)	riposare
relaxation	rilassamento
relic	reliquie
religion	religione
remember	ricordare
Renaissance	Rinascimento
rent (v)	affittare
repair (v)	riparare
reservation	prenotazione
reserve	prenotare
respect	rispetto
retired	in pensione
return	ritornare
rich	ricco[a]
right (direction)	destra
ring (n)	anello
ring road	raccordo anulare
ripe	maturo
river	fiume
robbed	derubato
rock (n)	pietra
roller skates	pattini a rotelle
Romanesque	Romanico
Romantic	Romantico
romantic	romantico[a]
roof	tetto
room	camera
rope	corda
rotten	marcio
round trip	ritorno
roundabout	rotonda
rowboat	barca a remi
rucksack	zaino
rug	tappeto
ruins	rovine
run (v)	correre
Russia	Russia

S

sad	triste
safe	sicuro
safety pin	spilla da balia
sailboat	barca a vela
sailing	vela
saint	santo[a]

English	Italian
sale	liquidazione
same	stesso
sandals	sandali
sandwich	panino
sanitary napkins	assorbenti igienici
Santa Claus	Babbo Natale
Saturday	sabato
save (computer)	salvare
scandalous	scandaloso
Scandinavia	Paesi Scandinavi
scarf	sciarpa
school	scuola
science	scienza
scientist	scienziato[a]
scissors	forbici
scotch tape	nastro adesivo
screwdriver	cacciaviti
sculptor	scultore
sculpture	scultura
sea	mare
seafood	frutti di mare
seat	posto
second class	seconda classe
secret	segreto
see	vedere
self-service	self-service
sell	vendere
send	spedire
seniors	anziani
separate (adj)	separato
September	settembre
serious	serio
service	servizio
service, church	messa
sex	sesso
sexy	sexy
shampoo	shampoo
shaving cream	crema da barba
she	lei
sheet	lenzuolo
shell	conchiglia
ship (n)	nave
shirt	camicia
shoelaces	lacci da scarpe
shoes	scarpe
shoes, tennis	scarpe da ginnastica
shop (n)	negozio
shop, antique	negozio di antiquariato
shop, barber	barbiere
shop, camera	foto-ottica
shop, cell phone	negozio di cellulari
shop, cheese	caseficio
shop, coffee	bar
shop, jewelry	gioielliera
shop, leather	pelletteria
shop, pastry	pasticceria
shop, photocopy	copisteria
shop, souvenir	negozio di souvenir
shop, sweets	pasticceria, negozio di dolciumi
shop, wine	negozio di vini
shopping	fare spese
shopping mall	centro commerciale
short	corto[a]
shorts	pantaloncini
shoulder	spalle
show (n)	spettacolo

show (v)	mostrare
shower	doccia
shy	timido[a]
sick	malato[a]
sign	segno
signature	firma
silence	silenzio
silk	seta
silver	argento
similar	simile
simple	semplice
sing	cantare
singer	cantante
single (m / f)	scapolo / nubile
sink	lavandino
sink stopper	tappo
sinus problems	disturbi sinusali
sir	signore
sister	sorella
size	taglia
skating	pattinaggio
ski (v)	sciare
skiing	sci
skin	pelle
skinny	magro[a]
skirt	gonna
sky	cielo
sleep (v)	dormire
sleeper (train)	posto in vagone letto
sleeper car (train)	carrozza letto
sleeping bag	sacco a pelo
sleepy	assonnato[a]
sleeves	maniche
slice	fettina
slip	sottoveste

slippers	ciabatte, pantofole
slippery	scivoloso
slow	lento
small	piccolo[a]
smell (n)	odore
smile (n)	sorriso
smoke	fumo
smoking	fumare
snack	merendina
sneeze (n)	starnuto
snore	russare
snorkel	boccaglio
soap	sapone
soap, laundry	detersivo da bucato
soccer	calcio
socks	calzini
some	un po'
something	qualcosa
son	figlio
song	canzone
soon	subito
sore throat	mal di gola
sorry	mi dispiace
sour	acerbo
south	sud
souvenir shop	negozio di souvenir
Spain	Spagna
sparkplugs	candele
speak	parlare
specialty	specialità
speed	velocità
spend	spendere
spider	ragno
spoon	cucchiaio

English / Italian

DICTIONARY

English	Italian
sport	sport
spring	primavera
square	piazza
stairs	scale
stamps	francobolli
stapler	pinzatrice
star (in sky)	stella
state	stato
station	stazione
stomach	stomaco
stomachache	mal di stomaco
stoned	fumato, fatto
stop (n, sign)	stop, alt
stop (n, train or bus)	fermata
stop (v)	fermare
stoplight	semaforo
stopper, sink	tappo
store	negozio
store, department	grande magazzino
store, hardware	ferramenta
store, office supplies	cartoleria
store, toy	negozio di giocattoli
storm	temporale
story (floor)	storia
straight	dritto
strange (odd)	strano[a]
stream (n)	corrente
street	strada
strike (stop work)	sciopero
string	filo
stroller	passeggino
strong	forte
stuck	incastrato
student	studente

English	Italian
stupid	stupido[a]
sturdy	resistente
style	stile
subway	metropolitana
subway entrance	entrata
subway exit	uscita
subway map	cartina
subway station	stazione della metropolitana
subway stop	fermata
suddenly	improvvisamente
suffer	soffrire
suitcase	valigia
summer	estate
sun	sole
sunbathe	abbronzarsi
sunburn	bruciatura del sole
Sunday	domenica
sunglasses	occhiali da sole
sunny	assolato
sunrise	alba
sunscreen	protezione solare
sunset	tramonto
sunshine	sole
sunstroke	insolazione
suntan (n)	abbronzatura
suntan lotion	crema per il sole
supermarket	supermercato
supplement	supplemento
surfboard	tavola da surf
surfer	surfer
surprise (n)	sorpresa
swallow (v)	ingoiare
sweat (v)	sudare
sweater	maglione
sweet	dolce

DICTIONARY

English / Italian

sweets shop	pasticceria, negozio di dolciumi
swelling (n)	gonfiore
swim	nuotare
swim trunks	costume d a bagno
swimming pool	piscina
swimsuit	costume da bagno
Switzerland	Svizzera
synagogue	sinagoga
synthetic	sintetico

T

table	tavola
tail	coda
tail lights	luci posteriori
take	prendere
take out (food)	portar via
talcum powder	borotalco
talk	parlare
tall	alto
tampons	assorbenti interni
tape (adhesive)	scotch
tape (cassette)	cassetta
taste (n)	gusto
taste (v)	assaggiare
tax	tasse
taxi meter	tassametro
teacher	insegnante
team	squadra
teenager	adolescente
teeth	denti
teething (baby)	dentizione
telephone	telefono

telephone card	carta telefonica
television	televisione
temperature	temperatura
tender	tenero
tennis	tennis
tennis shoes	scarpe da ginnastica
tent	tenda
tent pegs	picchetti della tenda
terrible	terribile
terrorists	terroristi
testicles	testicoli
thanks	grazie
theater	teatro
thermometer	termometro
thick	spesso
thief	ladro
thigh	coscia
thin	sottile
thing	cosa
think	pensare
thirsty	assetato
thongs	sandali infradito
thread	filo
throat	gola
through	attraverso
throw	tirare
Thursday	giovedì
ticket	biglietto
tight	stretto
time, on	puntuale
timetable	orario
tire (n)	gomma
tired	stanco

tissue, facial	fazzoletto di carta
to	a
today	oggi
toe	dito del piede
together	insieme
toilet	toilette
toilet paper	carta igienica
token	gettone
toll	pedaggio
toll-free	numero verde
tomorrow	domani
tonight	stanotte
too	troppo
tooth	dente
toothache	mal di denti
toothbrush	spazzolino da denti
toothpaste	dentifricio
toothpick	stuzzicadenti
total	totale
tour	giro
tour, guided	tour guidato
tourist	turista
tow truck	carro attrezzi
towel	asciugamano
tower	torre
town	città
toy	giocattolo
toy store	negozio di giocattoli
track (train)	binario
traditional	tradizionale
traffic	traffico
train	treno
train car	vagone
transfer (v)	cambiare
translate	tradurre

transmission fluid	liquido della trasmissione
travel	viaggiare
travel agency	agenzia di viaggi
traveler's check	traveler's check
travelers	viaggiatori
treasury	tesoro
tree	albero
trip	viaggio
tripod	trepiede
trouble	guaio
T-shirt	maglietta
Tuesday	martedì
tunnel	tunnel
Turkey	Turchia
turn signal	freccia
tweezers	pinzette
twins	gemelli

U

ugly	brutto[a]
umbrella	ombrello
uncle	zio
unconscious	inconscio
under	sotto
underpants	mutandine
underscore (_)	linea bassa
understand	capire
underwear	mutande
unemployed	disoccupato[a]
unfortunately	sfortunata-mente
United States	Stati Uniti
university	università
up	su

upstairs	di sopra
urethra	uretra
urgent	urgente
urinary infection	infezione urinaria
us	noi
use	usare
uterus	utero

V

vacancy (hotel)	camare libere
vacant	libero
vacation	vacanza
vagina	vagina
valid	valido
validate	timbrare, obliterare
valley	valle
Vaseline	vaselina
vegetarian (n)	vegetariano[a]
velvet	velluto
venereal disease	malattia venerea
very	molto
vest	gilè
video	video
video camera	video camera
video recorder	video registratore
view	vista
village	villaggio
vineyard	vigneto
violence	violenza
virus	virus
visit (n)	visita
visit (v)	visitare
vitamins	vitamine

voice	voce
vomit (v)	vomitare

W

waist	vita
wait	aspettare
waiter	cameriere
waiting room	sala di attesa, sala d'aspetto
waitress	cameriera
wake up	svegliarsi
walk (v)	camminare
wall, fortified	muri fortificati
wallet	portafoglio
want	volere
war	guerra
warm (adj)	caldo
wash	lavare
washer	lavatrice
watch (n)	orologio
watch (v)	guardare
water	acqua
water, drinkable	acqua potabile
water, tap	acqua del rubinetto
waterfall	cascata
waterskiing	sci acquatico
we	noi
weather	tempo
weather forecast	previsioni del tempo
website	sito Internet
wedding	matrimonio
Wednesday	mercoledì
week	settimana
weight	peso

English	Italian
welcome	benvenuto
west	ovest
wet	bagnato
what	che cosa
wheel	ruota
wheelchair-accessible	accessibile con la sedia a rotelle
when	quando
where	dove
whipped cream	panna
white	bianco
white-out	bianchetto
who	chi
why	perchè
widow	vedova
widower	vedovo
wife	moglie
wild	selvaggio[a]
wind	vento
window	finestra
windshield wipers	tergicristalli
windsurfing	windsurf
windy	ventoso
wine	vino
wine shop	negozio di vini
wing	ala
winter	inverno
wipers, windshield	tergicristalli
wish (v)	desiderare
with	con
without	senza
women	donne
wood	legno
wool	lana
word	parola
work (n)	lavoro
work (v)	lavorare
world	mondo
worse	peggio
worst	peggiore
wrap	incartare
wrist	polso
write	scrivere

X

English	Italian
X-ray	raggi x, radiografia

Y

English	Italian
year	anno
yellow	giallo
yes	si
yesterday	ieri
you (formal)	Lei
you (informal)	tu
young	giovane
youth hostel	ostello della gioventù
youths	giovani

Z

English	Italian
zero	zero
zip code	codice postale
Ziplock bag	busta de plastica sigillabile
zipper	chiusura lampo
zoo	zoo

TIPS FOR HURDLING THE LANGUAGE BARRIER

Don't Be Afraid to Communicate

Even the best phrase book won't satisfy your needs in every situation. To really hurdle the language barrier, you need to leap beyond the printed page and dive into contact with the locals. Never allow your lack of foreign-language skills to isolate you from the people and cultures you traveled halfway around the world to experience. Remember that in every country you visit, you're surrounded by expert, native-speaking tutors. Spend bus and train rides letting them teach you.

Start conversations by asking politely in the local language, "Do you speak English?" When you speak English with someone from another country, talk slowly, clearly, and with carefully chosen words. Use what the Voice of America calls "simple English." You're talking to people who are wishing it was written down, hoping to see each letter as it tumbles out of your mouth. Pronounce each letter, avoiding all contractions and slang. For bad examples, listen to other tourists.

Keep things caveman-simple. Make single nouns work as entire sentences ("Photo?"). Use internationally-understood words ("Self-service" works in Rome). Butcher the language if you must. The important thing is to make the effort. To get air mail stamps, you can flap your wings and say "tweet, tweet." If you want milk, moo and pull two imaginary udders. Risk looking like a fool.

If you're short on words, make your picnic a potluck. Pull out a map and point out your journey. Draw what you mean. Bring photos from home and introduce your family. Play cards or toss a Frisbee. Fold an origami bird for kids or dazzle 'em with sleight-of-hand magic.

Go ahead and make educated guesses. Many situations are easy-to-fake multiple choice questions. Practice. Read timetables, concert posters, and newspapers. Listen to each language on a multilingual tour. Be melodramatic. Exaggerate the local accent. Self-consciousness is the deadliest communication-killer.

Choose multilingual people to communicate with, such as students, business people, urbanites, young well-dressed people, or anyone in the tourist trade. Use a small note pad to jot down handy phrases and to help you communicate more clearly with the locals by scribbling down numbers, maps, and so on. Some travelers carry important messages written on a small card: allergic to nuts, strict vegetarian, your finest ice cream.

International Words

As our world shrinks, more and more words hop across their linguistic boundaries and become international. Savvy travelers develop a knack for choosing words most likely to be universally understood ("auto" instead of "car," "kaput" instead of "broken," "photo" not "picture"). Internationalize your pronunciation. "University," if you play around with its sound (oo-nee-vehr-see-tay), will be understood anywhere. The average American is a real flunky in this area. Be creative.

Analogy communication is effective. Anywhere in Europe, "Attila" means "crude bully." When a bulky Italian crowds in front of you, say, "*Scusi*, Ah-tee-la" and retake your place. If you like your haircut and want to compliment your Venetian barber, put your hand sensually on your hair and say "Casanova." Nickname the hairstylist "Michelangelo" or "Rambo."

Here are a few internationally understood words. Remember, cut out the Yankee accent and give each word a pan-European sound.

Amigo	Coke, Coca-Cola	Mama mia	Rambo
Attila	Communist	Mañana	Restaurant
(mean, crude)	Computer	McDonald's	Rock 'n' roll
Auto	Disco	Michelangelo	Self-service
Autobus	Disneyland	(artistic)	Sex / Sexy
("booos")	(wonderland)	Moment	Sport
Bank	Elephant	No	Stop
Beer	(big clod)	No problem	Super
Bill Gates	English	Nuclear	Taxi
Bon voyage	("Engleesh")	OK	Tea
Bye-bye	Europa	Oo la la	Telephone
Camping	Fascist	Pardon	Toilet
Casanova	Hello	Passport	Tourist
(romantic)	Hercules (strong)	Photo	US profanity
Central	Hotel	Photocopy	University
Chocolate	Information	Picnic	Vino
Ciao	Internet	Police	Yankee,
Coffee	Kaput	Post	Americano

Italian Verbs

These conjugated verbs will help you construct a caveman sentence in a pinch.

TO GO	*ANDARE*	ahn-**dah**-ray
I go	*io vado*	**ee**oh **vah**-doh
you go (formal)	*Lei va*	**leh**ee vah
you go (informal)	*tu vai*	too **vah**ee
he / she goes	*lui / lei va*	lwee / **leh**ee vah
we go	*noi andiamo*	**noh**ee ahn-dee**ah**-moh
you go (plural formal)	*voi andate*	**voh**ee ahn-**dah**-tay
they go	*loro vanno*	**loh**-roh **vah**-noh

TO BE	*ESSERE*	ehs-**say**-ray
I am	*io sono*	**ee**oh **soh**-noh
you are (formal)	*Lei è*	**leh**ee eh
you are (informal)	*tu sei*	too **seh**ee

he / she is	*lui / lei è*	lwee / **leh**ee eh
we are	*noi siamo*	**noh**ee seeah-moh
you are	*voi siete*	**voh**ee seeay-tay
(plural formal)		
they are	*loro sono*	**loh**-roh **soh**-noh
TO DO	*FARE*	**fah**-ray
I do	*io faccio*	**ee**oh **fah**-choh
you do (formal)	*Lei fa*	**leh**ee fah
you do (informal)	*tu fai*	too **fah**ee
he / she does	*lui / lei fa*	lwee / **leh**ee fah
we do	*noi facciamo*	**noh**ee fah-chee**ah**-moh
you do	*voi fate*	**voh**ee **fah**-tay
(plural formal)		
they do	*loro fanno*	**loh**-roh **fah**-noh
TO HAVE	*AVERE*	ah-**vay**-ray
I have	*io ho*	**ee**oh oh
you have (formal)	*Lei ha*	**leh**ee ah
you have (informal)	*tu hai*	too **ah**ee
he / she has	*lui / lei ha*	lwee / **leh**ee ah
we have	*noi abbiamo*	**noh**ee ah-bee**ah**-moh
you have	*voi avete*	**voh**ee ah-**vay**-tay
(plural formal)		
they have	*loro hanno*	**loh**-roh **ah**-noh
TO SEE	*VEDERE*	vay-**day**-ray
I see	*io vedo*	**ee**oh **vay**-doh
you see (formal)	*Lei vede*	**leh**ee **vay**-day
you see (informal)	*tu vedi*	too **vay**-dee
he / she sees	*lui / lei vede*	lwee / **leh**ee **vay**-day
we see	*noi vediamo*	**noh**ee vay-dee**ah**-moh
you see	*voi vedete*	**voh**ee vay-**day**-tay
(plural formal)		
they see	*loro vedono*	**loh**-roh vay-**doh**-noh

LANGUAGE TIPS

TO SPEAK	*PARLARE*	par-**lah**-ray
I speak	*io parlo*	ee oh par-**loh**
you speak (formal)	*Lei parla*	**leh**ee par-**lah**
you speak (informal)	*tu parli*	too **par**-lee
he / she speaks	*lui / lei parla*	lwee / **leh**ee **par**-lah
we speak	*noi parliamo*	**noh**ee par-leeah-moh
you speak (plural formal)	*voi parlate*	**voh**ee par-**lah**-tay
they speak	*loro parlano*	**loh**-roh par-**lah**-noh

TO LIKE	*PIACERE*	peeah-**chay**-ray
I like	*mi piace*	mee peeah-chay
you like (formal)	*Le piace*	lay peeah-chay
you like (informal)	*ti piace*	tee peeah-chay
he / she likes	*gli / le piace*	**lee**yee / lay peeah-chay
we like	*ci piace*	chee peeah-chay
you like (plural formal)	*vi piace*	vee peeah-chay
they like	*gli piace*	**lee**yee peeah-chay

TO WANT	*VOLERE*	voh-**lay**-ray
I want	*io voglio*	ee oh vohl-yoh
you want (formal)	*Lei vuole*	**leh**ee **vwoh**-lay
you want (informal)	*tu vuoi*	too **vwoh**ee
he / she wants	*lui / lei vuole*	lwee / **leh**ee **vwoh**-lay
we want	*noi vogliamo*	**noh**ee vohl-**yah**-moh
you want (plural formal)	*voi volete*	**voh**ee voh-**lay**-tay
they want	*loro vogliono*	**loh**-roh vohl-**yoh**-noh

TO MAKE	*FARE*	**fah**-ray
I make	*io faccio*	ee oh **fah**-choh
you make (formal)	*Lei fa*	**leh**ee fah
you make (informal)	*tu fai*	too **fah**ee
he / she makes	*lui / lei fa*	lwee / **leh**ee fah
we make	*noi facciamo*	**noh**ee fah-cheeah-moh
you make (plural formal)	*voi fate*	**voh**ee **fah**-tay
they make	*loro fanno*	**loh**-roh **fah**-noh

TO NEED	*AVERE*	ah-**vay**-ray
	BISOGNO DI	bee-**zohn**-yoh dee
I need	*io ho bisogno di*	**ee**oh oh bee-**zohn**-yoh dee
you need (formal)	*Lei ha bisogno di*	**leh**ee ah bee-**zohn**-yoh dee
you need (informal)	*tu hai bisogno di*	too **ah**ee bee-**zohn**-yoh dee
he / she needs	*lui / lei ha*	lwee / **leh**ee ah
	bisogno di	bee-**zohn**-yoh dee
we need	*noi abbiamo*	**noh**ee ah-bee**ah**-moh
	bisogno di	bee-**zohn**-yoh dee
you need	*voi avete*	**voh**ee ah-**vay**-tay
(plural formal)	*bisogno di*	bee-**zohn**-yoh dee
they need	*loro hanno*	**loh**-roh **ah**-noh
	bisogno di	bee-**zohn**-yoh dee

Italian Tongue Twisters

Tongue twisters are a great way to practice a language and break the ice with locals. Here are a few Italian tongue twisters (called *scioglilingue,* or "tongue melters") that are sure to challenge you—and amuse your hosts.

Trentatrè trentini arrivarono a Trento tutti e trentatrè trottorellando.	Thirty-three people from Trent arrived in Trent, all thirty-three trotting.
Chi fù quel barbaro barbiere che barberò così barbaramente a Piazza Barberini quel povero barbaro di Barbarossa?	Who was that barbarian barber in Barberini Square who shaved that poor barbarian Barbarossa?
Sopra la panca la capra canta, sotto la panca la capra crepa.	On the bench the goat sings, under the bench the goat dies.
Tigre contro tigre.	Tiger against tiger.

English Tongue Twisters

After your Italian friends have laughed at you, let them try these
tongue twisters in English.

If neither he sells seashells,
  nor she sells seashells,
  who shall sell seashells?
  Shall seashells be sold?
	Se ne lui ne lei
	  vende conchiglie
	  chi vende conchiglie?
	  Saranno vendute le conchiglie?

Peter Piper picked a peck
  of pickled peppers.
	Pietro Piper ha colto una misura di
	  due galloni di peperoni sottaceto.

Rugged rubber baby
  buggy bumpers.
	Forte paraurti di gomma
	  di carrozzelle.

The sixth sick sheik's
  sixth sheep's sick.
	La sesta pecora del sesto sciecco
	  ammalato è ammalata.

Red bug's blood and
  black bug's blood.
	Il sangue del insetto rosso
	  e il sangue del insetto nero.

Soldiers' shoulders.	Le spalle dei soldati.
Thieves seize skis.	I ladri afferano gli sci.

I'm a pleasant mother
  pheasant plucker. I pluck
  mother pheasants. I'm
  the most pleasant mother
  pheasant plucker that ever
  plucked a mother pheasant.
	Io sono uno/a spennatore/trice di
	  fagiani femmine piacevole. Io
	  spenno fagiani femmine. Sono
	  il/la più piacevole spennatore/trice
	  di fagiani femmine che abbia mai
	  spennato un fagiano femmina.

LANGUAGE TIPS

Italian Songs

Songs provide a fun way to break down the language barrier. Here's one you might recognize. Get a friendly local to help you with the words and the tune.

Volare
–Domenico Modugno, 1958

Penso che un sogno così
  non ritorni mai più,
mi dipingevo le mani e la
  faccia di blu.
Poi d'improvviso venivo
  dal vento rapito,
e incominciavo a volare
  nel cielo infinito.

I think a dream like this will
  never come again,
I painted my hands and
  my face blue.
When all of a sudden from an
  entrancing wind I came
and began to fly in the
  the infinite sky.

Volare, oh oh, cantare,
  oh oh oh oh.
Nel blu dipinto di blu,
felice di stare lassù.

Fly, sing...

In the blue painted blue,
happy to be up there.

E volavo volavo felice
  più in alto del sole ed
  ancora più su
mentre il mondo pian piano
  spariva lontano laggiù.
Una musica dolce suonava
  soltanto per me.

And I flew and I flew happily
  higher than the sun and
  higher still
while the world slowly,
  slowly disappeared.
Far down there a sweet music
  played only for me.

Volare, oh oh, cantare,
  oh oh oh oh.
Nel blu dipinto di blu,
  felice di stare lassù.

Fly, sing...

In the blue painted blue
  happy to be up there.

Ma tutti i sogni nell'alba
  svaniscon perchè

But all the dreams vanish at
  dawn because

LANGUAGE TIPS

quando tramonta la luna	the setting moon
li porta con sè.	takes them with it.
Ma io continuo a sognare	But I continue to dream
negli occhi tuoi belli	in your beautiful eyes
che sono blu come un cielo	That are blue like a sky
trapunto di stelle.	embroidered with stars.
Volare, oh oh, cantare,	Fly, sing...
oh oh oh oh.	
Nel blu degli occhi tuoi blu	In the blue of your blue eyes
felice di stare quaggiù.	happy to stay down here.
E continuo a volare felice	And I continue to fly happily
più in alto del sole ed	higher than the sun and
ancora più su	higher still
mentre il mondo pian	While the world slowly
piano scompare	slowly disappeared
negli occhi tuoi blu.	in your blue eyes.
La tua voce è una musica	Your voice is sweet music
dolce che suona per me.	that plays for me.
Volare, oh oh, cantare,	Fly, sing...
oh oh oh oh.	
Nel blu degli occhi tuoi blu	In the blue of your blue eyes
felice di stare quaggiù.	happy to stay down here.
Nel blu degli occhi tuoi blu	In the blue of your blue eyes
felice di stare quaggiù.	happy to stay down here.

Italian Gestures

Body language is an important part of communicating in Italy, especially hand gestures. Here are a few common gestures and their meanings:

Hand purse: Straighten the fingers and thumb of one hand, bringing them all together making an upward point about a foot in front of your face. Your hand can be held still or moved a little up and down at the wrist. This is a common and very Italian gesture for a query. It is used to say "What do you want?" or "What are you doing?" or "What is it?" or "What's new?" It can also be used as an insult to say "You fool."

Cheek screw: Make a fist, stick out your forefinger, and (without piercing the skin) screw it into your cheek. The cheek screw is used widely in Italy to mean good, lovely, beautiful. Many Italians also use it to mean clever.

Eyelid pull: Place your extended forefinger below the center of your eye and pull the skin downward. It means, "Be alert, that guy is clever."

Forearm jerk: Clench your right fist and jerk your forearm up as you slap your right bicep with your left palm. This is a rude phallic gesture that men throughout southern Europe often use the way many Americans "give someone the finger." This jumbo version of "flipping the bird" says "I'm superior."

Chin flick: Tilt your head back slightly and flick the back of your fingers forward in an arc from under your chin. In Italy this means "I'm not interested, you bore me," or "You bother me." In southern Italy it can mean "No."

Beckoning and waving: To beckon someone in southern Europe, you wave your palm down; to summon someone in northern Europe you bring your palm up. While most people greet each other by waving with their palm out, you'll find many Italians wave "at themselves" as infants do, with their palm towards their face. Ciao-ciao.

Numbers and Stumblers

- Europeans write a few of their numbers differently than we do. 1=1 , 4=4 , 7=7 .
- Europeans write the date in this order: day/month/year.
- Commas are decimal points and decimals are commas. A dollar and a half is 1,50 and there are 5.280 feet in a mile.
- The European "first floor" isn't the ground floor, but the first floor up.
- When counting with your fingers, start with your thumb. If you hold up only your first finger, you'll probably get two of something.

APPENDIX

LET'S TALK TELEPHONES

Making Calls within a European Country: About half of all European countries use area codes (like we do); the other half uses a direct-dial system without area codes.

To make calls within a country that uses a direct-dial system (Belgium, Czech Republic, Denmark, France, Greece, Italy, Norway, Poland, Portugal, Spain, and Switzerland), you dial the same number whether you're calling across the country or across the street.

In countries that use area codes (such as Austria, Britain, Croatia, Finland, Germany, Ireland, the Netherlands, Slovakia, Slovenia, and Sweden), you dial the local number when calling within a city, and you add the area code if calling long-distance within the country.

Making International Calls: You always start with the international access code (011 if you're calling from America or Canada, or 00 from Europe), then dial the country code of the country you're calling.

What you dial next depends on the phone system of the country you're calling. If the country uses area codes, drop the initial zero of the area code, then dial the rest of the number.

Countries that use direct-dial systems (no area codes) vary in how they're accessed internationally by phone. You always start by dialing the international access code, followed by the country code.

Then, if you're calling the Czech Republic, Denmark, Italy, Norway, Portugal, or Spain, simply dial the phone number in its entirety. But if you're calling Belgium, France, Poland, or Switzerland, drop the initial zero of the phone number.

Country Codes

After you've dialed the international access code, dial the code of the country you're calling.

Austria—43	France—33	Poland—48
Belgium—32	Germany—49	Portugal—351
Bosnia-
Herzegovina—387	Gibraltar—350	Slovakia—421
	Greece—30	Slovenia—386
Britain—44	Hungary—36	Spain—34
Canada—1	Ireland—353	Sweden—46
Croatia—385	Italy—39	Switzerland—41
Czech Rep.—420	Montenegro—382	Turkey—90
Denmark—45	Morocco—212	United States—1
Estonia—372	Netherlands—31	
Finland—358	Norway—47	

Useful Phone Numbers

Emergency: 113
 (English-speaking police help)
Ambulance: 118
Road Service: 116
Directory Assistance: 12
 (for €0.50, a message in Italian gives the number twice, very clearly)
Telephone help: 170
 (in English; free directory assistance)

Embassies and Consulates

US Embassy (Rome)
• Tel. 06-46741
• Via Vittorio Veneto 121

US Consulate in Milan
• Tel. 02-290-351
• Via Principe Amedeo 2/10

US Consulate in Florence
• Tel. 055-266-951
• Lungarno Vespucci 38

US Consulate in Naples
• Tel. 081-583-8111
• Piazza della Repubblica

Canadian Embassy (Rome)
• Tel. 06-854-443-937 (automated), 06-854-441 (emergencies)
• Via Zara 30 (consular section)

Canadian Consulate in Naples
• Tel. 081-401-338
• Via Carducci 29

Canadian Consulate in Padua
• Tel. 049-876-4833
• Riviera Ruzzante 25

Tear-Out Cheat Sheet

Keep these survival phrases in your pocket, handy to memorize or use if you're caught without your phrase book.

Good day.	Buon giorno.	bwohn **jor**-noh
Do you speak English?	Parla inglese?	**par**-lah een-**glay**-zay
Yes. / No.	Sì. / No.	see / noh
I don't understand.	Non capisco.	nohn kah-**pees**-koh
Please.	Per favore.	pehr fah-**voh**-ray
Thank you.	Grazie.	**graht**-seeay
You're welcome.	Prego.	**pray**-goh
I'm sorry.	Mi dispiace.	mee dee-spee**ah**-chay
Excuse me. (to get attention)	Mi scusi.	mee skoo-zee
Excuse me. (to pass)	Permesso.	pehr-**may**-soh
(No) problem.	(Non) c'è un problema.	(nohn) cheh oon proh-**blay**-mah
It's good.	Va bene.	vah **behn**-ay
Goodbye.	Arrivederci.	ah-ree-vay-**dehr**-chee
How much is it?	Quanto costa?	**kwahn**-toh **koh**-stah
Write it?	Me lo scrive?	may loh **skree**-vay
euro (€)	euro	ay-**oo**-roh
one / two	uno / due	**oo**-noh / **doo**-ay
three / four	tre / quattro	tray / **kwah**-troh
five / six	cinque / sei	**cheeng**-kway / **seh**ee
seven / eight	sette / otto	**seht**-tay / **oh**-toh
nine / ten	nove / dieci	**noh**-vay / dee**ay**-chee
20	venti	**vayn**-tee
30	trenta	**trayn**-tah
40	quaranta	kwah-**rahn**-tah
50	cinquanta	cheeng-**kwahn**-tah
60	sessanta	say-**sahn**-tah
70	settanta	say-**tahn**-tah
80	ottanta	oh-**tahn**-tah

90	*novanta*	noh-**vahn**-tah
100	*cento*	**chehn**-toh
I would like...	*Vorrei....*	vor-**reh**ee
We would like...	*Vorremmo...*	vor-**ray**-moh
...this.	*...questo.*	**kweh**-stoh
...more.	*...di più.*	dee pew
...a ticket.	*...un biglietto.*	oon beel-**yay**-toh
...a room.	*...una camera.*	**oo**-nah **kah**-may-rah
...the bill.	*...il conto.*	eel **kohn**-toh
Is it possible?	*È possibile?*	eh poh-**see**-bee-lay
Where is the toilet?	*Dov'è la toilette?*	doh-**veh** lah twah-**leht**-tay
men	*uomini, signori*	**woh**-mee-nee, seen-**yoh**-ree
women	*donne, signore*	**doh**-nay, seen-**yoh**-ray
entrance / exit	*entrata / uscita*	ehn-**trah**-tah / oo-**shee**-tah
no entry	*non entrare, divieto d'accesso*	nohn ehn-**trah**-ray, dee-veee**ay**-toh dahk-**sehs**-soh
open / closed	*aperto / chiuso*	ah-**pehr**-toh / keeoo-zoh
When does this open / close?	*A che ora apre / chiude?*	ah kay **oh**-rah **ah**-pray / keeoo-day
At what time?	*A che ora?*	ah kay **oh**-rah
Just a moment.	*Un momento.*	oon moh-**mayn**-toh
Now.	*Adesso.*	ah-**dehs**-soh
Soon.	*Presto.*	**prehs**-toh
Later.	*Più tardi.*	pew **tar**-dee
Today.	*Oggi.*	**oh**-jee
Tomorrow.	*Domani.*	doh-**mah**-nee
Monday	*lunedì*	loo-nay-**dee**
Tuesday	*martedì*	mar-tay-**dee**
Wednesday	*mercoledì*	mehr-koh-lay-**dee**
Thursday	*giovedì*	joh-vay-**dee**
Friday	*venerdì*	vay-nehr-**dee**
Saturday	*sabato*	**sah**-bah-toh
Sunday	*domenica*	doh-**may**-nee-kah

Making Your Hotel Reservation

Most hotel managers know basic "hotel English." Emailing or faxing are the preferred methods for reserving a room. They're clearer and more foolproof than telephoning. Photocopy and enlarge this form, or find it online at www.ricksteves.com/reservation.

One-Page Fax

To: _____ _____
              hotel   *email or fax*

From: _____ _____
                name   *email or fax*

Today's date: ____ / ____ / ____
            day *month* *year*

Dear Hotel _____

Please make this reservation for me:

Name: _____

Total # of people: _____ # of rooms: _____ # of nights: _____

Arriving: ____ / ____ / ____ Arrival time: (24-hr clock): _____
        day *month* *year*   (I will telephone if I will be late)

Departing: ____ / ____ / ____
         day *month* *year*

Room(s): Single ___ Double ___ Twin ___ Triple ___ Quad ___ Quint ___

With: Toilet ___ Shower ___ Bathtub ___ Sink only ___

Special needs: View ___ Quiet ___ Cheapest ___ Ground floor ___

Please email or fax me confirmation of my reservation, along with the type of room reserved and the price. Please also inform me of your cancellation policy. After I hear from you, I will quickly send my credit-card information as a deposit to hold the room. Thank you.

Name _____

Address _____

City _____ State ____ Zip Code _____ Country _____

Email address _____

NOTES

Start your trip at

Free information and great gear to

▶ Plan Your Trip

Browse thousands of articles and a wealth of money-saving tips for planning your dream trip. You'll find up-to-date information on Europe's best destinations, packing smart, getting around, finding rooms, staying healthy, avoiding scams and more.

▶ Eurail Passes

Find out, step-by-step, if a railpass makes sense for your trip—and how to avoid buying more than you need. Get a bunch of free extras!

▶ Graffiti Wall & Travelers' Helpline

Learn, ask, share— our online community of savvy travelers is a great resource for first-time travelers to Europe, as well as seasoned pros.

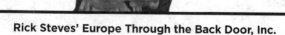

Rick Steves' Europe Through the Back Door, Inc.

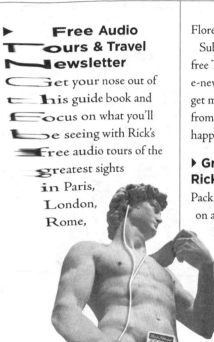

The perfect complement to your phrase book